The Life and Activities of

Sir John Hawkins

SIR JOHN HAWKINS—THE OXFORD PORTRAIT
(See p. 183)

The Life and Activities of

Sir John Hawkins

MUSICIAN, MAGISTRATE AND

FRIEND OF JOHNSON

Percy A. Scholes

M.A., D.LITT., HON. D.MUS. (OXON.)
DR. ÈS LETTRES ; F.S.A.

GEOFFREY CUMBERLEGE

OXFORD UNIVERSITY PRESS

LONDON   NEW YORK   TORONTO

1953

Oxford University Press, Amen House, London E.C. 4

GLASGOW NEW YORK TORONTO MELBOURNE WELLINGTON
BOMBAY CALCUTTA MADRAS KARACHI CAPE TOWN IBADAN

Geoffrey Cumberlege, Publisher to the University

PRINTED IN GREAT BRITAIN

ACKNOWLEDGEMENTS

To Dr. L. F. POWELL, of Oxford, I have to express deep and sincere thanks, he having kindly read this book in typescript and in proof and having enriched it by giving me a number of interesting and out-of-the-way items of information concerning various persons mentioned, such as had come his way during his prolonged Johnsonian researches. To Mr. Lawrence Haward, M.A., who also read the book in proof, I must likewise tender my gratitude, as to my secretary Mr. J. Owen Ward, B.A., for a similar service.

I have also to offer warm thanks for valuable help to Dr. Dorothy George, author of *English Social life in the Eighteenth Century*, *London Life in the Eighteenth Century*, *England in Johnson's Day*, &c.

Others to whom I am indebted for useful information are my dear friend, the late Reginald Hine, F.S.A., F.R.Hist.S., author of a number of delightful works of original historical research; Mr. F. Geoffrey Rendall, M.A., of the British Museum; Mr. J. G. Crawfurd, Secretary of the Madrigal Society; Mrs. E. G. Allingham; Mr. Gerald Finzi and Mr. William Woods, who is at present engaged in preparing an edition of Dr. Burney's Letters and in the course of his research has come across some interesting material concerning Burney's rival, Hawkins. Further I have to thank Mr. Denis Stevens, M.A., our authority on the 'Mulliner Book', the manuscript source of a number of sixteenth-century compositions which form the staple of Hawkins's appendix to his *History of Music*. This book is in the British Museum and bears the name of one of the eighteenth-century owners, John Stafford Smith, who has marked it as 'lent to Sir John Hawkins, 1774'.

After the book was in page proof and (as supposed) ready for the press, a discovery was made by Professor J. L. Clifford, of Columbia University, N.Y., who, whilst doing research work in the Bodleian Library, came across a manuscript of importance in connexion with the early life of Hawkins. Dr. L. F. Powell kindly offered to relieve me by undertaking the necessary investigation and, after some weeks of close inquiry in various directions, got together the information that is now embodied in a final Appendix to the book. I need not say that I feel deeply in the debt of these two gentlemen for their contribution to my book's completeness.   P.A.S.

CONTENTS

LIST OF ILLUSTRATIONS

INTRODUCTION

WHEN Sir John Hawkins reached middle life he was for ever hankering after, but never achieving, a record of his career. Says his daughter, Laetitia:

From the earliest years of my recollection, my father was wont to inculcate the usefulness of committing to paper, facts and circumstances; but he was generally too much employed, or too weary of employment, to do himself what he wished done. He was sometimes disposed to dictate to my elder brother; but my brother, who was himself engaged in a work of deep research, was not always at leisure; and when he *was* at leisure, my father was often taking his evening-nap. The thing wished was therefore never done; or, if attempted, it was not begun with energy enough to keep it going.

I had heard all that could be said in favour of the scheme; and made sensible of its comparative importance by the progressive accumulation of facts, I, though myself with little leisure to subtract from time which I was never allowed to call my own, began in private to do what my father recommended; but the fear that this, which was to *me* relaxation when done in secret, would, if divulged, be added to my daily labour and exacted as a task, made me do it literally, *à l'insçu de mon père,*—a singular instance, perhaps, of clandestine obedience.[1]

And so it is to Laetitia (that garrulous and rambling narrator) that we are indebted for a good deal of information about her father's career—Laetitia, helped out here and there by the memories of her two brothers, perhaps, and certainly by those of 'the oldest friend of my family', Richard Clark, successively Alderman, Sheriff, Lord Mayor, and Chamberlain of the City of London, whose profession, like that of Hawkins himself, was the law, and who was, like Hawkins (and, indeed, on his introduction), a member of the circle that surrounded the great Dr. Johnson. It is to Richard Clark that Laetitia gratefully dedicates her first volume.

Now Laetitia, as has just been hinted, was no systematic historian. She had not the very smallest idea of chronological arrangement—nor, indeed, of arrangement of any kind. Her

[1] *Anecdotes,* 4.

three volumes (one of 'Anecdotes' and two of 'Memoirs') make bewildering reading, for she just put down what came into her head at the moment it came there, gossiping along until she felt the volume was big enough and then coming to a stop. And when one has read these volumes, and analysed them, and made notes from them, and indexed them, one has not even the bones of a biography: that has to be built up by search elsewhere—in contemporary volumes of *The Gentleman's Magazine* and *The Annual Register*; in documents in the British Museum, the Public Record Office, and Somerset House; in Hawkins's own publications (though in those there is little enough about himself); and in the writings of various people who knew him.

It is an engrossing and fascinating task to re-create the story of a man's life from such scattered material, much of · which has to be fitted together, like a jig-saw puzzle. And when the Life of Hawkins is thus re-created it proves, I feel, to have been a task worth the labour.

Hawkins was not, as was his acquaintance and rival, Burney, a lovable character. 'Anything but'—to judge by the pungent verdicts left by those who knew him best. '*As to Sir John*', said Johnson, '*why really I believe him to be an honest man at the bottom; but to be sure he is penurious, and he is mean, and it must be owned that he has a degree of brutality and a tendency to savageness that cannot easily be defended.*' Malone spoke of his '*malignancy*', and so did Dyer. Reynolds called him '*mean and grovelling*'. Percy said he was '*detestable*'. His neighbour, Walpole, more generously maintained that he was '*a very honest, moral man*', and then spoilt it with a 'but' to the effect that he was '*obstinate and contentious*'. Jeremy Bentham, an early friend, lived to say, '*Sir John was a most insolent, worthless fellow*'.[1] Yet, with all this, when we come to

---

[1] The contemporary opinions of Hawkins, of which a selection is given here, can be found in Mme D'Arblay's Diary, Prior's *Malone*, Walpole's Letters and his *Journal of the Reign of George III*, Bentham's Works, vol. x, &c. Many of them are collected in Hill's *Johnsonian Miscellanies*. It is fair to remember that John Wesley, on meeting Hawkins, was favourably impressed (*Journal*, Sunday, 12 Nov. 1775).

collect the evidence we find Hawkins to have been a man of considerable public spirit and certainly a hard and conscientious worker. What he really lacked, perhaps, was a sense of humanity (of being a unit in the suffering human family) and a sense of humour—for it is rare to hear of Hawkins making a joke!

There was at least *something* good about a man whose list of familiar acquaintances was as long as his daughter shows it to have been, and of whom a Secretary of State[1] could assert that he was 'the best magistrate in the Kingdom'. Evidently John Hawkins was a man of very mixed character, but a man of marked characteristics: as the biography of such a man has been interesting to compile it may be hoped that it will be found interesting to read.

[1] See p.108.

I. *His childhood, youth, and early manhood*

JOHN HAWKINS, born on 30 March 1719, was, say some of our books of reference (following Boswell), the son of a carpenter.

Books were saying so in his daughter Laetitia's day and she resented it, being, however, careful to explain that her objection was based on no foolish snobbery (obviously a Christian could hardly admit that she looked down on the trade of carpentry, of all trades!), but merely on a commendable love of accuracy:

> Now, as to 'the carpenter's son', I am almost shocked at using lightly a term that exists in Holy Writ; and, on every account, would forbear whatever has the smallest appearance of throwing it off with contempt; but with the same unprejudiced feeling as that with which I should correct my father's having been called the son of a Scotch advocate (an origin far superior, I own, to what I can justly claim for him), I say, that his father was of a branch of business connected with building, such as I believe is now called an architect and surveyor.[1]

This 'architect and surveyor', this 'man of the trade or calling of Sir Christopher Wren', was, however, it is frankly admitted, of 'no eminence' and 'distinguished only as a good mathematician'. Possibly he was a little neglectful of his profession, for he was, it seems, 'fonder of making one in a convivial hall than of measuring its proportions or sketching its decorations'. He had 'some moral qualities to recommend him', qualities, however, of a rather embarrassing kind, for he was 'of a nature so kind as to lend money to persons in need, without interest—and worse for those who came after him—without security'.

Of 'no eminence', then, was the father—but behind him

[1] *Anecdotes*, 122.

(and not much more than a century behind) was eminence enough, for 'in the time of Sir Walter Raleigh and Queen Elizabeth knighthood for sailing round the world on a voyage of discovery was a very elevating distinction', and so was knighthood 'bestowed on the defeat of the Spanish Armada'. In these allusions Laetitia seems to have had in mind the respective exploits of Sir John Hawkins (1532–95) and his son, Sir Richard Hawkins (c. 1562–1622), and to have got herself into something of a tangle as to the occasions of the honours bestowed on them.

There is, apparently, no proof that those two great warrior-seamen of the reign of Queen Elizabeth and the 'surveyor' of the reigns of Queen Anne and the early Georges stood in the relation of ancestors and descendant, but Laetitia evidently never doubted that it was so—nor did her father (see a letter of his on p. 111 and the note thereon). She laments the first Sir John's activities in the slave trade, heraldically commemorated by 'a demi-moor *sable*, manacled', as 'the only blot on our escutcheon', and wonders 'what right the *Hankins* family have to *our* arms', saying, 'I saw them with surprise in the fine church at Tewkesbury.'[1]

Because of the first Sir John's connexion with that cruel trade gentle Laetitia, in one place, candidly calls him 'a brute of our name', but she was on one occasion in her childhood very proud to find her descent from him instantly acknowledged in a semi-official way. This was 'our willing reception into Chatham Dock-yard when the gates were closed, under the apprehension of French spies'. As she correctly says, 'Admiral Sir John Hawkins had founded "the chest", as it is called at Chatham, for the benefit of seamen', and then comes the incident:

I remember our being, on a journey to Canterbury, sent as children, with a footman to attend us, from Rochester, where Sir John and Lady Hawkins remained, to see Chatham. The gate was opened very warily; but on announcing our name it was thrown open:—the name ran from one to the other of the people who stood round, and we entered

[1] *Anecdotes,* 120 n.

with a welcome little short of huzzas—a distinction, I presume, that might be shared with us by any one of the name.[1]

So much for one parent and his alleged descent. As for the other, she was, it appears, 'Elizabeth, daughter of Thos. Gwatkin, of Townhope, co. Hereford, gentleman', and she had several children besides John.[2] And that is all we know of Hawkins's mother except that if a certain amusing story is to be believed she was not of much education, nor of very good sense. This story is to the effect that when her son was to be married, and this to a wealthy woman, she, on being congratulated on her good fortune, replied, 'Lord, Sir! good fortune, indeed! My John is a match for any lady; for to let you know, he has a dozen of as handsome shirts as any gentleman in the land!'[3]

Of Hawkins's schooling we know little or nothing. On its conclusion he entered upon some study under one Hoppus, 'author of a well-known and useful architectural work, published in 1733, entitled *Proportional Architecture, or the Five Orders regulated by equal Parts*':

But his first cousin, Mr. Thomas Gwatkin, being clerk to Mr. John Scott, of Devonshire Street, Bishopsgate, an attorney and solicitor in full practice, persuaded him to alter his resolution, and embrace the law, which he did, and was accordingly articled as a clerk to Mr. Scott.

Hawkins's daughter has left us some account of the household of which he now became a member. She tells us of Scott:

He was a bachelor, and kept but one servant, an old woman, fit (according to my father's description of her), to have kept house for the predatory band into whose power Gil Blas fell. She never drest otherwise than for the most sordid work; and I have heard my father say,

[1] *Anecdotes*, 121.
[2] Chalmers. His account is clearly based on information supplied by the family (which, perhaps, discounts slightly the 'gentleman' claim and some other statements). Where not otherwise indicated what follows in the present chapter is taken from this authority.
[3] This is given in Dr. Busby's *Concert Room and Orchestra Anecdotes* (1825), iii, 189, on the authority of 'Mr. Belcher, a surgeon of Throgmorten Street', who is stated to have been one of Hawkins's early musical friends, and to whom Hawkins's mother is stated to have made the remark quoted. As another part of Belcher's statement is incorrect it may be admitted that he cannot be implicitly relied on.

that whenever she had been obliged to make a brisk fire, to dress a mutton-chop or beef-steak, the happy tidings of a promised meal were made known in the office, by the loud crackling of the old parchment-deeds, which she tied round her, in lieu of the 'Corset à la Diane', or the 'Circassian boddice'. Of the usual *style of the table*, a judgment may be formed from the usuality, *in severe frost*, of a calf's head, cold, of which the juices were ice; and at a time, too, when ices were not a common luxury, as they have long been.[1]

An Attorney practised in the courts of Common Law, a Solicitor in the courts of Civil Law. Hawkins, in later life, was not respectful to his own branch of the legal profession, as the following passage in his *Life of Johnson* (p. 14) shows us:

In the two professions of the civil and common law, a notable difference is discernible: the former only admits such as have had the previous qualification of an university education; the latter receives all whose broken fortunes drive, or a confidence in their abilities tempts to seek a maintenance in it. Men of low extraction, domestic servants, and clerks to eminent lawyers, have become special pleaders and advocates; and, by an unrestrained abuse of the liberty of speech, have acquired popularity and wealth.

To such discomforts as those just recounted was added 'tyranny and exaction of labour more intense than even the oppressive burdens imposed on young men in offices at that time', and, says Laetitia, 'as if the joyous period of youth was to be wholly embittered, accident sometimes occurred with settled purpose':

For relief under this evil [the 'tyranny and exaction of labour'], my father had recourse to bathing; and going out one summer-evening into the then fine fields at Mile-end, he availed himself of a large pond there, and was enjoying its refreshing coolness, when a man coming by, out of the pure vulgar love of mischief, threw in to him all his clothes. The distress, as may be imagined, was great, and severely felt, in the present evil and dread of consequences; but, as I have heard him say, his spirit rose under it, and something whispered that he might not always be the victim of variegated tyranny. By his subsequent marriage

[1] *Anecdotes*, 124.

with my mother, these identical fields, then a valuable cow-farm, became his; they are now built on—are still in our family—and produce a great income![1]

Although the young fellow's nose was apparently pretty well kept to the office grindstone he was determined to lay a sound foundation for future practice on his own account; he had also intellectual interests and managed to make opportunities for their development:

His time was too fully employed in the actual dispatch of business, to permit him, without some extraordinary means, to acquire the necessary knowledge of his profession by reading and study; besides that his master is said to have been more anxious to render him a good copying-clerk, by scrupulous attention to his hand-writing, than to qualify him by instruction to conduct business. To remedy this inconvenience, therefore, he abridged himself of his rest, and rising at four in the morning, found opportunity of reading all the necessary and most eminent law-writers, and the works of the most celebrated authors. By these means, before the expiration of his clerkship, he had already rendered himself a very able lawyer, and had possessed himself of a taste for literature in general, but particularly for poetry and the polite arts; and the better to facilitate this improvement, he from time to time, furnished to the *Universal Spectator*, the *Westminster Journal*, the *Gentleman's Magazine*, and other periodical publications of the time, essays, and disquisitions on several subjects.

The first of these is believed to have been an 'Essay on Swearing', but the exact time of its appearance, and the paper in which it was inserted, are both equally unknown. It was, however, re-published some years since (without his knowledge till he saw it in print) in one of the newspapers. His next production was an 'Essay on Honesty', inserted in the *Gentleman's Magazine* for March 1739, and which occasioned a controversy, continued through the magazines for several months, between him and a Mr. Calamy, a descendant of the celebrated Dr. Edmund Calamy, then a fellow-clerk with him.'

That essay on Honesty is not badly written and as it is quite brief, it is, perhaps, worth while to drag it again into the light of day:

I was a little surprised at hearing a Gentleman whom I happened

[1] *Anecdotes*, 125.

to be in Company with not long ago, assert, that in the whole Circle of his Acquaintance (which is none of the smallest, and consists chiefly of Men in great Business) he could not pick out ten honest Men. However, a little Reflection soon convinced me of the Truth of this Assertion, and led me to consider the Nature of a Thing so much talk'd of, and so little practis'd.

In order to set this *Virtue* in a clear Light, it will be necessary for me to divide it into the *true* and the *false*.

I apprehend that *true Honesty* signifies a constant and regular *Inclination* to render to every Man his Due, and that consequently whoever is void of this Inclination, is unworthy the Appellation of an *honest Man*. It does not only consist of a mechanical Course of Dealing, a literal Conformity to the Laws and Customs of our Country, but it excludes every Species of *Fraud* and *Oppression*, however safe and profitable.

The other kind of *Honesty*, which I have distinguished by the epithet of *false*, is in some Respects like the former: with this Difference, that the one is the Result of a conscientious Principle, and the other of Necessity or Policy. A Tradesman may sell good Commodities, use lawful Weights, and pay his Debts; but perhaps it is not out of a Principle of Conscience, but to avoid the Scandal and Trouble of doing otherwise. There are many Circumstances of Fraud to which the Laws have annexed no Punishment, on account of the Impossibility of discovering the real Sentiments of Mankind, and the Principles upon which they act; but these, in the Eye of an honest Man, are as criminal as those which the Laws extend to.

I find this Virtue no where so finely illustrated as in the Story of *Tobit*, and *Esop's Fable of* Mercury *and the Carpenter*, and I am persuaded whoever reads them with Attention, will be convinc'd of the Truth of what I am advancing.

It will be needless for me to enumerate the Advantages that flow from that upright Behaviour which I am recommending, since everyone knows, that without it, or at least an Appearance of it, Trade, Commerce, Society, Friendship, &c. must inevitably fall to the Ground. I shall conclude with saying, that the candid and generous Dealing of a just Man will procure him the Love and Esteem of all that know him, while Shame and Beggary are the Portion of the Knavish and Designing.

J. H.

We have there, perhaps, little more than a schoolboy essay

(and, by the way, is its allusion to the book of *Tobit* particularly apt?). And the ensuing discussion is on a mere school debating society level: it may have interested the readers of the *Gentleman's Magazine* of two centuries ago, but has little instruction or interest for us today.

At the age of twenty-one or thereabouts, presumably, the young man would become free of his indentures and then, or soon after, he seems to have set up for himself, at first at his father's house and then in Clement's Lane, Lombard Street, where he shared a house with a young medical man called Munckley, who, to judge from Laetitia's description, must have found some of those City streets rather too narrow for his comfortable passage. 'I cannot find that his name is known,' she says, 'though his figure is, I think I may venture to say, recorded by the pencil of Hogarth in his "Warwick Lane", and may easily be discovered if the reader looks for the fattest of the comic crew. I do not think I am mistaken when I say that that blank in the well-known epigram,

> "When —— walks the street, the paviours cry,
> *God bless you, Sir*! And lay their rammers by"

may be filled up with the name Munckley.'[1] Our surmise as to the inconvenience of perambulation in that part of London is confirmed by her, for on reading farther we find that it was a Hawkins family tradition that on one occasion Munckley, 'accidently encountering a stout manservant in a narrow passage, the two "literally stuck" '.

[1] John Nichols, in his *Select Collection of Poems* (1780, iii. 162 n.), prints the epigram supplied with the name 'Tadlow' (*On Dr. Tadlow*); the same name (spelt 'Tadloe') is given by Richard Graves in *The Festoon; a Select Collection of Epigrams* (4th edn., *c.* 1767) and by Oldys in *A Collection of Epigrams* (1727; epigram 173). De Quincey, in his essay on Laetitia's *Anecdotes* (1823, see p. 230 of the present book), carries the attribution still farther back. He says, 'For about 140 years has this empty epigram, like other epigrams *to be let*, been occupied by a succession of big men; we believe that the original tenant was Dr. Ralph Bathurst' (1620–1704). The authorship of the epigram is usually attributed to the Oxonian wit and poet, the Rev. Dr. Abel Evans (1679–1737).

The print Laetitia calls *Warwick Lane* is apparently the one better known as *A Consultation of Physicians* (cf. p. 45). The Royal College of Physicians was in Warwick Lane. (The same print is sometimes seen with the satirical title *The Company of Undertakers*.)

This Munckley, it appears, beyond his physical greatness possessed no 'single claim to distinction'. He was 'a great gourmand, very fond of French wines, and a sedulous follower of great people, with whom he affected a close intimacy to a ludicrous degree'. However, it suited Hawkins's temporary circumstances to 'enter into that sort of association called living with a *chum*' ('I believe it is a college term', explains Laetitia), and the association apparently lasted for some years—for the remainder of Hawkins's bachelor life, in fact.

Up to this point we find nothing recorded as to the musical interests and proclivities of the young man. But now that he was released from the drudgery of his apprenticeship with the harsh attorney, Scott, the musical side of his nature seems to have blossomed out. We hear of many musical friendships he now formed and musical circles in which he was to be found.

The chief of these friendships was that with the already well-known and much admired young blind musician, Charles John Stanley, some of whose works are still in use by our organists.

Stanley was born in London in 1713, so that he was Hawkins's senior by six years. At the age of two, whilst carrying in his hand a china basin, he fell on a marble hearth. Both eyes were injured and henceforth he was totally blind. At seven he began to take music lessons, his first teacher being John Reading, at this time a prominent London organist. Then he came under the tuition of Handel's friend, Dr. Maurice Greene, organist of St. Paul's Cathedral and soon to become also one of the organists of the Chapel Royal.

These two sound musicians must have found the boy an apt pupil, since in 1723, aged eleven, he was successful in obtaining an organ post of his own—at All Hallows, Bread Street. Three years later (13 Aug. 1726) the following skilfully drafted appeal was to be found in the *London Journal*:

To the worthy inhabitants of the Parish of

ST. ANDREW'S HOLBOURN,

The place of Organist being vacant, your Vote and Interest are desired for

JOHN STANLEY

the Blind Youth,

who was educated under Mr. *Green*, Organist of *St. Paul's* Cathedral.

N.B. Mr. *Short*, one of the Candidates, has no less than three places, *viz.* Organist of *St. Sepulchre's*, and *St. Dunstan's*, *Stepney*, and one in the *Play-House*.

N.B. The Report of the Blind Youth's Father having a Place of Four or Five Hundred Pounds a Year under the Government is without Foundation, he having no Place of any Value whatsoever.

The Election begins on MONDAY morning next.

And after a week (20 Aug.) the result was announced in the *Weekly Journal or the British Gazetteer*:

There having been a Poll at St. Andrew's, Holbourn, for the Place of Organist of that Church in the Room of Mr. Isham, deceased; the same ended last Wednesday Night, when the Choice fell by a great Majority upon Mr. Stanley, a Youth who has had the Misfortune to be blind, but having been educated under Mr. Green, Organist of St. Paul's, and being endowed with an extraordinary Genius for Musick, is the Admiration of all that ever heard his Performances.

The talented youth was now established in a position he was to hold for the following sixty years—that is, for the remainder of his life. He celebrated this success by another, taking his B.Mus. degree at Oxford (1729) at the age of sixteen—a record so far as that university was concerned, though at Cambridge, over a century earlier, there had been a perhaps equally juvenile musical graduate, Thomas Ravenscroft, who in 1607 took his baccalaureate at about the same age.

Pluralist organists were common in the London of those days (presumably the different hours at which the various churches held their services, with some liberty to employ deputies, made this possible). An additional appointment that soon followed was at the Temple Church (1734), and this position also Stanley held throughout the remainder of his life, his skilful performances attracting, it is said, crowds of music-lovers, including other London organists (as many as fifty at a time, it is boldly asserted—but how many organists were there in London in those days, and did they all flock to the Temple?) and even the great Handel himself. Burney's *History of Music* tells us that 'Whenever there was a charity sermon or a new organ to be opened Stanley seems to have been preferred to all others'.

It was in 1742, when Stanley was twenty-eight and Hawkins twenty-three, that the two men came together, the young musician as composer of a set of six solo cantatas for which the young lawyer furnished five of the poems and a friend of his the other; and then, when these caught on, as they quickly did at Vauxhall and perhaps at the other Gardens, of another six, all of them with poems by Hawkins—eleven in all being thus provided by him.

There will, later, be a few more references to Stanley; meanwhile let us turn to Laetitia's account of her father's early relations with him—which, by the way, we need not, perhaps, take too seriously so far as it is depreciatory, inasmuch as in this it seems to be sometimes in conflict with what we find recorded by other writers:

Connected with the memory of Handel comes the recollection of Mr. Stanley, whom I have already named as an early friend and associate of my father's. To speak ingenuously, and not to involve myself in the suspicion of going into the opposite extreme of indiscriminating commendation, for fear I should be thought to censure, I must confess, that in using the term *friend*, I have rather applied it in its too common acceptation, than in its strict meaning. Music had brought the two young men together, and they were mutually assisting to each other. Mr. Stanley was, I believe,—but of this I am not sure,—newly married, when the intimacy began;—my father was a bachelor.—

I know nothing of my father's acquaintance with him earlier than their joint production of the Cantatas, of which I need not say again that my father furnished the words. I have, indeed, heard it said that they were far better than the music; and I know that my father was to have thirty guineas out of the profits—a sum, perhaps, of importance to him at that time, as it would be to many young men, even now, who spend with a peculiar relish money pleasantly earned;—but which money, if he ever did get it, he obtained with so much reluctance on the part of Mr. Stanley, that it was rendered painful to him to receive that which, perhaps, he was impatient to spend on some innocent, and, most probably, laudable gratification.

As I know of no one living who can be offended, or in any way injured, by the depreciation of Mr. Stanley's merits as a composer;—and as, on all matters of taste, the axiom is admitted, '*de gustibus non est disputandum*', I am under no obligation to conceal what I know to be a fact, that my father bestowed a very moderate degree of praise on his composition, and very little admiration on his organ-playing. He called him a good harpsichord (or, as we should now style him, *pianoforte*) player; and I think his approbation of his compositions was of a similar kind.

Nor is this wonderful; nor does it detract more from his extraordinary abilities at all in a greater degree than I am well able to repay him by telling what I believe is very little known, though more astonishing than anything that *is* known, that he was not led to the profession of music by natural taste or inclination. This I had from his sister-in-law, who told me that he began the laborious task of learning it without the assistance of sight, on the suggestion of a friend: —that he pursued it for six months, and gave up in despair; but that being persuaded to exert himself again under a better teacher, he was in a little time encouraged by success, and proceeded. Every body acquainted with the assistance given to whatever we undertake, by predilection, will see and duly estimate, the meritorious industry of one circumstanced as was Mr. Stanley, in labouring without it.[1]

What may be related of him professionally is, I suppose, to be found in a memoir of him by an author and traveller to whom the world stands deeply indebted, Mr. Coxe of Bemerton; but of this I never could obtain the sight.[2] What I have heard, from the most authentic sources, of his wonderful sagacity, almost surpassed belief. . . .

---

[1] It is, frankly, impossible to take the writer seriously in these last two paragraphs.
[2] The Coxe mentioned here is the Rev. William Coxe, historian and traveller, author of *Anecdotes of Handel and J. C. Smith* (1798).

Mr. Stanley had married a lady[1] whose passion or compassion for him had risen to the courageous undertaking of a clandestine marriage. To the arrangement of the scheme, a confidential friend was necessary: the previous intercourse was easy, as she was a scholar of her beloved; and the whole affair was conducted to a prosperous conclusion.

She was a sickly inert woman; and had not her only sister broken away from an uncomfortable home to reside with her, her fortune, though considerable, would hardly have compensated to a man whose wants were so limited by his misfortune, for the great trouble of keeping a house. But his sister-in-law, Miss Arlond,[2] was everything that an affectionate sister could be to both parties, and having powers which, though she undervalued herself, were little less than extraordinary, she met every inconvenience with a remedy or at least a palliative.

Mr. Stanley had great arithmetical quickness, and a mind capable of great tension, increased no doubt by that privation which is so often atoned for by a superabundance of other gifts. He soon after his settlement as a domestic man, showed himself an excellent whist player, when informed only of the principles of the game; but, the impossibility of knowing what were the cards he himself held, was an obstacle which his sister-in-law obviated, by marking a pack in a way not perceptible to others, and which nothing less than the acuteness of feeling he possessed, could have rendered useful to himself. Great curiosity was excited to see these cards; and to possess a pack was considered a distinction in the world of miscellaneous collectors. I have seen many, and therefore can explain what I remember to have been treated like necromancy. How the court cards were marked I really forget, but the others were simply pricked with a very fine needle, and only with the number of what are called the pips;—but the specific difference consisted in the locality of these marks, and that had been settled by Mr. Stanley himself, that is to say, that hearts should be marked in one corner, diamonds in another, and so on; there still remained the necessity of placing the cards properly, by sorting them and turning them all the right way; a card the wrong end up would have thrown him out; but one of the ladies was always at hand; and it then required only that each person should name the card they played, and the game went on as quickly as if he could have seen.

[1] 'Daughter of Captain Arlond, of the East India Company.'—L.H.
[2] In a copy of Stanley's will with which I have been furnished this name appears as '*Ann Arnold*'.

The Hawkins–Stanley Cantatas were, as we have just seen, popular at Vauxhall, for which, indeed, they were probably written. 'My father was fond of Vauxhall', says Laetitia. 'The Band was good, and he had at any time the command of the instrumental music' (by which, presumably, is meant that he was on good terms with the musical director and could call for the performance of what he wished to hear). There is a long, detailed, vigorous, and eloquent description of these Gardens in the *Gentleman's Magazine* at a somewhat later date (Aug. 1765):

These Gardens are situated near the *Thames*, on the south side, in the parish of *Lambeth*, about two miles from *London*. They are opened every day, except *Sunday*, at five o'clock in the evening from *May* till *August*, each person paying 1*s*. admittance. You enter by the great gate upon a noble gravel walk about 900 feet in length, planted on each side with very lofty trees, which form a wide vista, terminated by a landscape of the country, a beautiful lawn of meadow ground, and a grand gothic obelisk. At the corners of the obelisk are painted a number of slaves chained, and over them this inscription:

SPECTATOR

FASTIDIOSUS

SIBI MOLESTVS

To the right of this walk, and a few steps within the garden, is a square, which, from the number of trees planted in it, is called the Grove. In the middle of it is a magnificent orchestra of Gothic construction, ornamented with carvings, niches, &c., the dome of which is surmounted with a plume of feathers, the crest of the Prince of *Wales*. In fine weather, the musical entertainments are performed here. At the upper extremity of this orchestra, a very fine organ is erected, and at the foot of it are the seats and desks for the musicians, placed in a semi-circular form, leaving a vacancy at the front for the vocal performers. The concert is opened with instrumental music, at six o'clock, which having continued about half an hour, the company are entertained with a song; and in this manner several other songs are performed, with sonatas or concertos between each, till the close of the entertainment, which is generally about ten o'clock.

Then follow five columns of minute and graphic description

of the various buildings, their decorations, and their sur-
roundings, the whole constituting perhaps the fullest contemporary account now remaining to us.

Just one detail of the entertainment at Vauxhall may be
alluded to here. Those who frequented it, when tired of
perambulation in the extensive grounds or around the
orchestra, would seat themselves at tables in one of the many
pavilions, alcoves, or booths, and partake of refreshments.
The caterers were famous for their daily exhibition of careful
economy. In Colman and Thornton's *Connoisseur* there is
an account of the visit of a middle-class family which has
been summarized by Austin Dobson in his *Eighteenth Century
Vignettes* (vol. i), as follows:

Mr. Rose, a tradesman, his wife, and his two daughters, make a
turn of the place, and then sit down to supper. 'Do let us have a chick,
papa', says one of the young ladies. Papa replies that 'they are half
a crown apiece, and no bigger than a sparrow'. Thereupon he is very
properly rebuked by his wife for his stinginess. 'When one is out upon
pleasure', she says, 'I love to appear like somebody; and what signifies
a few shillings once and away, when a body is about it?' So the chick
is ordered and brought. And then ensues a dialogue between the cit and
the waiter, in which the former, from the price of the sample before
him, ironically estimates the price of an entire Vauxhall ham to be about
£24, and after being decorated by his wife with a coloured handkerchief
by way of bib, proceeds to eat, saying at every mouthful, 'There goes
twopence, there goes threepence, there goes a groat.'

Laetitia relates an anecdote reminiscent of the astonishing
skill of the carvers, acquired through long-continued daily
practice, in reducing their meat to slices of a delicate and
almost transparent tissue-paper tenuity, and as it offers one of
the rare examples of a sense of humour on her parent's part
it may be reproduced here:

I know not whether any aliments so plebeian as cold beef and ham,
are served in Vauxhall Gardens now, when, as I am told, they rival
any descriptions in the 'Arabian Nights' Entertainments', but I
remember Sir J. H.'s relishing highly the humour of a waiter who
with a most significant look pointed out the very small quantity of

these commodities allowed for money, by his caricatured anxiety to preserve a plate in his hand from the influence of a gentle evening breeze.[1]

What personal contact did Hawkins have with Handel? The following incident, related by his daughter, makes it clear that the young music-loving attorney was in touch with the old musician. It must have occurred in late 1746 or early 1747, when Hawkins was twenty-seven or twenty-eight years old:

Were I to attempt enumerating my father's musical friendships, I should copy, *a second time*, the greater part of the last volume of his 'History of Music'; I will, however, record what I have heard and known of some of those between whom and himself this powerful union subsisted. Handel had done him the honour frequently to try his new productions on his young ear; and my father calling on him one morning to pay him a visit of respect, he made him sit down, and listen to the air of 'See, the conquering Hero comes', concluding with the question, 'How do you like it?' My father answering, 'Not so well as some things I have heard of yours', he rejoined, 'Nor I neither; but, young man, you will live to see that a greater favourite with the people than my other fine things'.[2]

The following passage in Hawkins's *History* also shows a personal acquaintance with Handel. It is a reminiscence of Handel's stay in Hanover, where he found the Italian, Steffani, in charge of the music of the Elector's court, a post in which he was to succeed him:

The reception which Handel met with from Steffani was such as made a lasting impression on his mind. The following is the manner in which he related it to the author of this work:—'When I first arrived at Hanover I was a young man, under twenty; I was acquainted with the merits of Steffani, and he had heard of me. I understood somewhat of music, and,' putting forth both his broad hands, and extending his fingers, 'could play pretty well on the organ; he received me with great kindness, and took an early opportunity to introduce me to the Princess Sophia and the elector's son, giving them to understand that I was

[1] *Memoirs*, i. 307.
[2] *Anecdotes*, 195. The 'copy a second time' alludes, as we shall later see, to Hawkins's employment of his daughter as amanuensis.

what he was pleased to call a virtuoso in music; he obliged me with instructions for my conduct and behaviour during my residence at Hanover; and being called from the city to attend to matters of a public concern, he left me in possession of that favour and patronage which himself had enjoyed for a series of years'.[1]

Handel as a singer appears in the following:

In a conversation with the author of this work he once gave a proof that a fine voice is not the principal requisite in vocal performance; the discourse was on psalmody, when Mr. Handel asserted that some of the finest melodies used in the German churches were composed by Luther, particularly that which is sung to the hundredth psalm, and another, which he himself sang at the time, and thereby gave occasion to his remark.[2]

Hawkins was an enraptured admirer of Handel as organist, and expresses his feelings with eloquence:

As to his performance on the organ, the powers of speech are so limited, that it is almost a vain attempt to describe it otherwise than by its effects. A fine and delicate touch, a volant finger, and a ready delivery of passages the most difficult, are the praise of inferior artists: they were not noticed in Handel, whose excellencies were of a far superior kind; and his amazing command of the instrument, the fullness of his harmony, the grandeur and dignity of his style, the copiousness of his imagination, and the fertility of his invention were qualities that absorbed every inferior attainment.

When he gave a concerto, his method in general was to introduce it with a voluntary movement on the diapasons, which stole on the ear in a slow and solemn progression; the harmony close wrought, and as full as could be possibly expressed; the passages concatenated with stupendous art, the whole at the same time being perfectly intelligible, and carrying the appearance of great simplicity. This kind of prelude was succeeded by the concerto itself, which he executed with a degree of spirit and firmness that no one ever pretended to equal.

Such in general was the manner of his performance; but who shall describe its effects on his enraptured auditory? Silence, the truest

---

[1] *History*, ch. clxxxiv.

[2] Ibid., ch. cxcvii. A further instance of Handel's powers as a vocal interpreter follows: 'At a concert at the house of lady Rich he was prevailed on to sing a slow song, which he did in such a manner, that Farinelli, who was present, could hardly be persuaded to sing after him.'

SOME OF HAWKINS'S MUSICIAN FRIENDS

JOHN STANLEY and HANDEL. Stanley was the famous blind organist whose playing drew crowds of music-lovers to the Temple Church. As poet and composer Hawkins and he were collaborators (see pp. 10–13). Handel, as Hawkins tells us, was 'large-made, portly, and of saunter-ing gait', adding that he did him the honour *'frequently to try his new productions on my young ear'*. As to Handel's organ-playing Hawkins is detailed and eloquent (see p. 16).

JAMES BARTLEMAN and DR. COOKE. 'Bat', as the Hawkins family called the West-minster choir-boy who spent many of his boyish hours in their home, was in later life London's leading bass singer. He always gratefully maintained the friendship. Dr. Benjamin Cooke, Organist of Westminster Abbey (*'One of the worthiest and best-tempered men that ever existed'*, as Laetitia Hawkins describes him), helped Hawkins with his *History of Music* and more than once performed in the Abbey some setting of a poem of his.

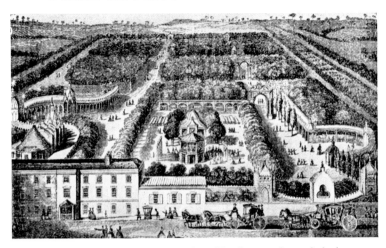

VAUXHALL GARDENS. This famous place of London entertainment had a long run—nearly two centuries (1661–1859). We read of it in Pepys and Evelyn and we are still reading of it in Dickens (*Sketches by Boz*). It and its competitor, Ranelagh, had many imitators (under the same names) not only in some other English cities, but also on the continent of Europe and in colonial America: Burney tells us in 1805, '*In every part of Europe a nominal Vauxhall has been established, nor was there a theatre on the continent thirty years ago, with scenery and ballet pantomimes, without an attempt at representing Vauxhall.*'

MRS. WEICHSEL SINGING AT VAUXHALL. Rowlandson's picture dates from a rather later period than that of the Hawkins-Stanley collaboration but well reproduces a familiar nightly scene—'At the upper extremity of the orchestra is a very fine organ and at the foot of it are the seats and desks of the musicians, placed in a semi-circular form, leaving a vacancy at the front for the vocal performers.' The repertory to which our poet and composer contributed was enormous, for from 1745 and for many years after Arne and his contemporaries were pouring out 'Vauxhall Songs' by the dozen—now nearly all utterly forgotten.

applause, succeeded the instant that he addressed himself to the instrument, and that so profound, that it checked respiration, and seemed to
controul the functions of nature, while the magic of his touch kept the
attention of his hearers awake only to those enchanting sounds to which
it gave utterance.[1]

Here is a description of Handel's personal appearance as
Hawkins, in after years, remembered it:

He was in person a large made and very portly man. His gait, which
was ever sauntering, was rather ungraceful, as it had in it somewhat
of that rocking motion, which distinguishes those whose legs are
bowed. His features were finely marked, and the general cast of his
countenance placid, bespeaking dignity attempered with benevolence,
and every quality of the heart that has a tendency to beget confidence
and insure esteem. Few of the pictures extant of him are to any tolerable
degree likenesses, except one painted abroad, from a print whereof the
engraving of him given in this work is taken: in the print of him by
Houbraken, the features are too prominent; and in the mezzotint
after Hudson there is a harshness of aspect to which his countenance
was a stranger; the most perfect resemblance of him is the statue
on his monument, and in that the true lineaments of his face are
apparent.[2]

Of Handel in his last years we are given a touching picture
that remained in the historian's memory:

For the last two or three years of his life he used to attend divine
service in his own parish church of St. George, Hanover Square,
where, during the prayers, the eyes that at this instant are employed
in a faint portrait of his excellencies, have seen him on his knees
expressing by his looks and gesticulations the utmost fervour of
devotion.

Handel's famous singer, for whom he composed the great
tenor parts in *Israel in Egypt, Messiah, Samson, Judas Macca-
beus,* and *Jephthah,* was a friend of Hawkins. Laetitia says:

Mr. Beard, the very respectable oratorio-singer, was of my father's
early acquaintance, and, having married a lady of very high rank, was

---

[1] Ibid.
[2] Ibid. The mention of the monument evidently refers to that by Roubiliac
in Westminster Abbey. The Hudson portrait is reproduced at p. 16.

his near neighbour, residing very handsomely at Hampton. His lowly appreciation of himself—only one of many virtues!—was shown when in hearing Harrison, at one of the grand commemorations of Handel, then in fine voice, sing 'Oft on a plat,' he said to my father who happened to sit next to him, '*I* never sang it half so well.'[1]

During the seventeenth and eighteenth centuries the institution of private musical clubs was very common—that is, parties of friends who met regularly to perform together. In earlier life, at any rate, Hawkins was a member of several such coteries, of which our knowledge comes chiefly from his daughter's *Anecdotes*.

Readers of Boswell will recall the many mentions of Johnson's medical adviser, DR. THOMAS LAWRENCE—more than 'medical adviser', indeed, for 'dear friend' and 'dear Dr. Lawrence' are typical expressions of Johnson in speaking or writing of him. He appears in the *Dictionary of National Biography* and there is a long obituary of him in the *Gentleman's Magazine* of March 1787, and from these we learn that he was for seven successive years President of the Royal College of Physicians; that he held a post as 'Reader in Anatomy' in the University of Oxford; that his courses of anatomical lectures in London were very popular until they were eclipsed by those of the brilliant William Hunter; and that he was the author of a number of medical treatises—all in Latin, which language he held to be the only fitting one for works of learning.

From Hawkins we find that Lawrence could boast accomplishments other than those that formed the basis of his professional success, such as skill in what he calls 'naval architecture'[2] and also in music. As regards this latter Hawkins, it seems, as a young man was associated with Dr. Lawrence

---

[1] *Anecdotes*, 13. The commemorations of Handel began in 1784.

[2] 'Able with his own hands, and a variety of tools of his own contrivance, to form a model of a ship of war of any rate; first framing it with ribs and such other timbers as are requisite in a ship of service, and afterwards covering it with planks of the thickness of a half-crown piece, and the breadth of about an inch, which he fastened to the ribs with wooden pins of a proportionable size, and in this manner of working he completed many such models, elegantly wrought and most beautiful in their forms.' Hawkins, *Johnson*, 402.

and his brother and other musical friends, professional and amateur, all of them performers:

[Dr. Lawrence] was also a lover of music, and was able to play his part in concert on the violoncello till hindered by deafness, a disorder that came upon him about the middle of his life, and at length drove him to seek a retreat from the world and its cares at Canterbury, where, about the year 1783, he died. He had a younger brother named Charles, a solicitor of great practice, who also played on the violoncello, and, having been a pupil on that instrument, of Caporale, was the best performer on it of any gentleman in England. About the year 1740, I was used to meet both the brothers at a tavern in Grace-church-street, where was a private concert, to which none but such as could join in it were admitted. Many of those who frequented it were great masters, namely Mr. Stanley, who played the first violin, the above Sig. Caporale, Vincent the hautboy player, and Balicourt, who performed on the German flute: the rest were organists and gentlemen performers.[1]

Another and still more eminent medical authority with whom the young Hawkins foregathered for musical enjoyment was DR. PERCIVALL POTT. He, too, was one of Johnson's medical advisers, for by him Johnson was, in his last years, treated for a tumour. There is but brief mention of Pott in Boswell, but a long article in the *Dictionary of National Biography* assures us that he was 'the first surgeon of his day and a scientific writer remarkable for the classic purity of his style, the scrupulous precision of his definitions, and the unerring closeness of his arguments' ('Pott's Fracture' and 'Pott's Disease', are, of course, terms that still figure in the medical vocabulary). Possibly it was Mrs. Pott who was the chief musician of the family, for Laetitia particularly mentions her in a passage in the *Anecdotes*[2] which begins:

On his emancipation [from his legal apprenticeship] my father soon made profitable and agreeable connexions. His love for music, and his prudence in indulging his taste for it, brought him into intimacy with persons of elegant pursuits and good conduct.

[1] Ibid. Dr. Lawrence died in 1783. There is a monument to him in Canterbury Cathedral.   [2] pp. 128–30.

Apparently a close association of Hawkins and the Pott family lasted throughout his life, and such an association was continued into the succeeding generation.

Still another musical household which made Hawkins welcome was that of Sir Samuel Dukinfield, who held 'weekly morning-concerts at his most comfortable and respectable mansion in Bloomsbury';[1] and still another was that of the famous letter-founder, William Caslon, whose name is today still a household word with all our printers.[2] From what Laetitia tells us[3] it is clear that the following information in Hawkins's *History of Music* is based on personal acquaintance with Caslon, as one of the musical friends who frequented his house and participated in his musical enjoyments:

Mr. Caslon meeting with encouragement suitable to his deserts, settled in Ironmonger-row, in Old-street, and being a great lover of music, had frequent concerts at his house, which were resorted to by many eminent masters: to these he used to invite his friends, and those of his old acquaintance, the companions of his youth.

He afterwards removed to a large house in Chiswell-street, and had an organ in his concert-room; after that he had stated monthly concerts, which for the convenience of his friends, and that they might walk home in safety when the performance was over, were on that Thursday in the month which was nearest the full moon, from which circumstance his guests were wont humorously to call themselves Lunatics.

The performers at Mr. Caslon's concert were Mr. Woolaston, and oftentimes Mr. Charles Froud, organist of Cripplegate church, to whom, whenever he came, Mr. Woolaston gave place, and played the second violin; Mr. William De Santhuns, who had been an organist in the country, and succeeded Mr. Prelleur as organist of Spitalfields; Mr. Samuel Jeacock, a baker at the corner of Berkeley-street in Red Lion-street, Clerkenwell, and many others who occasionally resorted thither.

The performance consisted mostly of Corelli's music, intermixed with the overtures of the old English and Italian operas, namely, Clotilda, Hydaspes, Camilla, and others, and the more modern ones of Mr. Handel.

---

[1] *Anecdotes*, 11.   [2] The present book is printed from Caslon type.
[3] Ibid. 131.

In the intervals of the performance the guests refreshed themselves at a side-board, which was amply furnished; and when it was over, sitting down to a bottle of wine, and a decanter of excellent ale, of Mr. Caslon's own brewing, they concluded the evening's entertainment with a song or two of Purcell's sung to the harpsichord, or a few catches, and about twelve retired.[1]

What part did Hawkins take in the performance of these various musical coteries or clubs? Such gatherings in the seventeenth and eighteenth centuries, as has been already mentioned, existed rather for mutual performance than for listening, and he would be expected to play his part. It seems likely that, in early life at any rate, he was something of a violinist. We know that he possessed a violin. Laetitia, after discussing her father's close association with Horace Walpole, goes on, rather amusingly, as follows:

With his brother Sir Edward, none of whose habits, manners, sentiments, or opinions, would at all have suited his, an accidental circumstance brought him into temporary contact. This circumstance was a proposed improvement in the neck of a violin, originating with Sir Edward, and which he was very willing to communicate to my father:—and well I remember the ardour with which this quackery was pursued, for arrant quackery it was, and little inferior to some speculations which have excited much ridicule.

If any amateur is curious to know in what this improvement consisted, I believe I can tell him. The neck of the violin was, strange to say! cut off and replaced by one the sides of which were plated with very thin brass;—it was the work of a watch-maker, and perhaps it was necessary to employ some one unconnected with the construction of musical instruments to undertake such a job. In the brass plates were holes made, and through them were passed, not indeed common violin-pegs, but pins of brass, with bows shaped like those to our common keys for small locks. What effect this was to produce, or what purpose it was to answer, I confess I never could find out, but as Sir Edward Walpole was the projector of this ingenious decollation, the visits to him, for he never left his house, were frequent.

My father paid the operator five guineas!—and having fortunately

<hr>

[1] *History*, ch. clxx. For further information about Caslon see Nichols, *Anecdotes*, ii. 356 et seq., and *D.N.B.*

stipulated for the return of *his own neck*, he presently begged him to let him 'enjoy his own again,' and matters were placed in *status quo*.[1]

But at a later period, at any rate, Hawkins was a violon-cellist, if we are to take seriously Peter Pindar's lines in his satirical poem *Bozzy and Piozzi* and his footnote to them (see pp. 202–4).

One of Hawkins's friends with whom the tie may have been joint musical performance (and may equally, or additionally, have been interest in law) is still to be seen in London, in part at any rate, for his skeleton is on view at University College. This was 'the since celebrated Jeremy Bentham', of whom it is probably little remembered today that he was an amateur of the violin.[2]

---

[1] *Anecdotes*, 278.
[2] Ibid. 9. *D.N.B.* records Bentham as playing the violin to the ladies' accompaniment on the harpsichord. In later life he came to think very badly of Hawkins (perhaps they had quarrelled). His frank opinion (from Bentham's *Works*, x. 87) has already been mentioned (p. x).

II. *He becomes a member of two important musical societies*

OF two valuable musical bodies Hawkins was an active member, joining them at about the period at which we have arrived—the Academy of Ancient Music and the Madrigal Society. Of the Academy he wrote and privately circulated a pamphlet account which is reproduced as an Appendix to the present book. It should be noted, however, that this appears to be strangely defective in some of its information. If the reader cares to turn to any edition of Grove's *Dictionary of Music* from the 1st (1879) to the 4th (1940) he will find an article on this institution (by the Rev. Charles Mackeson) which is clearly based on the particulars supplied by Hawkins in his *History* and his pamphlet. The date of its foundation is given as 1710, and this date has been copied into all other books of reference which mention the Academy. But from Grove's 2nd edition to the 4th the article 'Academy of Ancient Music' is closely followed by one headed 'Academy of Vocal Music' (by a sound antiquarian musicologist, the late F. G. Edwards) which clearly applies to the same body under its primitive name (the same persons being mentioned as founders), and this gives its date of foundation as 1725/6: this article is based on the Minute Book of the said Academy from its foundation to 1731, which is now in the British Museum.

At the fortnightly gatherings of this society Hawkins, that lover of old music, was assuredly 'in his element'. At what date he became a member does not appear, but when he did so he must have thought it to be fifteen years older than it actually was and must also have been ignorant of its earlier name.

The other musical body of which Hawkins was a member was the Madrigal Society, which met weekly for supper and singing. Hawkins in his *History* gives this account of it:

Mr. John Immyns, an attorney by profession, was a member of the Academy [of Ancient Music] but, meeting with misfortunes, he was occasionally a copyist to the society, and amanuensis to Dr. Pepusch; he had a strong counter-tenor voice, which, not being very flexible, served well enough for the performance of madrigals. Of this species of music he in a short time became so fond, that in the year 1741[1] he formed the plan of a little club, called the Madrigal Society; and got together a few persons who had spent their lives in the practice of psalmody; and who, with a little pains, and the help of the ordinary solmisation, which many of them were very expert in, became soon able to sing, almost at sight, a part in an English, or even an Italian madrigal.

They were mostly mechanics; some, weavers from Spitalfields, others of various trades and occupations; they met at first at the Twelve Bells, an alehouse in Bride Lane, Fleet Street, and Immyns was both their president and instructor; their subscription was five shillings and sixpence a quarter, which defrayed their expenses in books and music paper, and afforded them the refreshments of porter and tobacco.

After four or five years continuance at the Twelve Bells, the society removed to the Founder's Arms in Lothbury; and from thence, after a short stay, to the Twelve Bells again, and after that to the Queen's Arms in Newgate-street, a house that had been formerly a tavern, but was now an alehouse. In it was a room large enough for the reception of the society, who were about five-and-twenty in number, with a convenient recess for a large press that contained their library.

The meetings of the society were on Wednesday evening in every week; their performance consisted of Italian and English madrigals in three, four and five parts; and, being assisted by three or four boys from the choir of St. Paul's, they sang compositions of this kind, as also catches, rounds, and canons, though not elegantly, with a degree of correctness that did justice to the harmony, and, to vary the enter-

---

[1] As the society's books go back only to 16 July 1744 the date of its foundation cannot be checked.

tainment, Immyns would sometimes read, by way of lecture, a chapter of Zarlino translated by himself.[1]

Various books of reference speak of Hawkins as a foundation member of the Madrigal Society. This is an error, as the following information extracted from the Minute Books will show; it was supplied to the *Musical Times* in February 1904 by Mr. J. Edward Street, then the Society's Secretary:

Hawkins was *not* an original member (1741). The only entry relating to him is on September 27, 1752: 'Mr. Hawkins was proposed by Mr. Immyns.'[2] Presumably he was elected then and there, as there is no mention of his election. But thereafter his name appears regularly in the list of members, paying his monthly or quarterly subscription and an occasional contribution for special objects, e.g., new music, &c.

On July 10. 1754, occurs this entry: ' "Sweet love, when love", "This merry month of May", both presented by Mr. Hawkins.'

In 1757, I find an evening's programme (eight numbers, titles not given) 'out of Mr. Hawkins's Italian Madrigals'.

On 'May ye 2nd, 1764', the Minutes record: 'Mr. Hawkins having offered the use of his Motets of Prenestini[3] to the society for copying of them; a motion was made by Mr. Dan Richards, and was unanimously agreed to, that the same should be done, and the expense thereof be paid out of the Stock of the Society.'

At the March Quarter, 1766, Hawkins's name appears as struck out from the list of members making their quarterly payments of 6*s*. 6*d*., nor does his name appear in any subsequent list. Presumably, therefore, he retired from the Society at that date, though there is no note to that effect.

As a member of this society Hawkins was in congenial company. He was, as his *History* shows, a keen lover of our

[1] Zarlino, in charge of the music at St. Mark's, Venice, from 1565 to his death in 1590, published several theoretical works, especially important being the *Istitutioni harmoniche* (1558, with later editions and translations).

[2] The present Secretary, Mr. J. G. Crawfurd, has found an earlier entry showing that Hawkins was proposed and elected as 'a performing member' on 15 June 1748. Fifteen attendances are recorded in that year, and then he did not renew his subscription and his membership lapsed until his *second* election in 1752. His name continues to appear on the list of members until 12 March 1765 (not 1766, as stated by Mr. Street). Both elections were on the proposition of Immyns.

[3] 'Prenestini' = 'Palestrina', 'Preneste' being the ancient name of the town, Palestrina, in the Roman Campagna, where the composer was born and from which he was given the name by which he is known to us.

old madrigalian literature, and to spend a weekly evening sitting around the supper-table and singing his part was, we may be sure, bliss. To him could doubtless be applied the expression quoted by his daughter as having been said of two ladies who were in the habit of attending the performances of the Academy of Ancient Music (for 'as an audience' ladies were tolerated provided they did not obtrude their presence too markedly): 'They were not in *this* world when such music was performing.'

At the end of Hawkins's account of this Society he says: 'The Madrigal Society still subsists—but under such circumstances as render its permanency very precarious.' He need not have feared. That famous old London Society, after more than two centuries of existence, still carries on its regular happy gatherings for supper and singing.

Was Hawkins a composer? Eitner, in his standard *Quellen-Lexikon der Musiker und Musikgelehrter* (1898), says that he was, but where he acquired this information is impossible to guess. He admits that no British musical historians supply any particulars of Hawkins's activities in this direction and is, of course, unable to name any compositions.

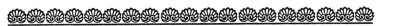

III. *He enters the Johnson circle: and is elected to the Ivy Lane Club* (1749)

WE now come to an epoch in Hawkins's life. By some means (we are not told how) he had made the acquaintance of Johnson. And so, at the age of thirty, the young attorney was invited to become a member of the club Johnson was just forming—the one known as the 'Ivy Lane Club', or 'King's Head Club'.[1]

We have accounts of the formation of this now famous coterie in Murphy's *Essay on the Life and Genius of Samuel Johnson*, in Boswell, and elsewhere, but we will take Hawkins's own account, published nearly forty years later (1787) in his *Life of Johnson*. He says of Johnson:

The great delight of his life was conversation and mental intercourse. That he might be able to indulge himself in this, he had, in the winter of 1749, formed a club that met weekly at the King's Head, a famous beef-steak house, in Ivy-lane near St. Paul's, every Tuesday evening. Thither he constantly resorted, and, with a disposition to please and be pleased, would pass those hours in a free and unrestrained interchange of sentiments, which otherwise had been spent at home in painful reflection.

The persons who composed this little society were nine in number: I will mention their names, and, as well as I am able, give a slight sketch of the several characters of such of them as cannot now be affected by either praise or blame: they were, the reverend Dr. Salter, father of the late master of the Charterhouse,—Dr. Hawksworth,— Mr. Ryland a merchant, a relation of his,—Mr. John Payne then a bookseller, but now or very lately chief accountant of the bank,— Mr. Samuel Dyer a learned young man intended for the dissenting

---

[1] Nichols, *Anecdotes*, ix. 502, gives it still another name. He calls it 'The Rambler Club'. It is possible that this name became attached to it some time after its formation (Johnson's *Rambler* began to appear in March 1750).

ministry,—Dr. William M'Ghie a Scots physician,—Dr. Edmund Barker, a young physician,—Dr. Richard Bathurst also a young physician, and myself.[1]

Then follows at great length (thirty pages) the promised 'sketch', of which Murphy has said that it was compiled, 'as it should seem, with no other view than to draw a spiteful and malevolent character of almost every one of them'— which, alas! is almost true, for Hawkins, as his life progressed, did admittedly develop those qualities which led his friend Johnson to his famous verdict, already quoted, which, while admitting his claim to the title of an honest man, charges him with 'a degree of brutality and a tendency to savageness that cannot easily be defended'. It will be better here, then, to supply a brief description of these fellow clubmen of Hawkins more akin to what he himself would have given had he retained the relative amiability which, so far as all indications go, marked his demeanour in those earlier years with which we are now concerned.

Dr. SAMUEL SALTER, a Cambridge man, was a Prebendary of Norwich and Archdeacon of Norfolk who, at the age of seventy, had retired to London, 'on account of some disagreement between him and his children', as we are told by Hawkins, who, however, is able to describe him as 'a man of general reading, but no deep scholar', who was well-bred, courteous, and affable, and enlivened conversation 'by the relation of a variety of curious facts, of which his memory was the only register'.

The well-known JOHN HAWKESWORTH (as yet not 'Doctor'), who was at this date about the same age as Hawkins, had (it is said) a few years earlier succeeded Johnson as the compiler of the parliamentary debates in the *Gentleman's Magazine*.

JOHN RYLAND (another man of about Hawkins's age) was a West India merchant, and, being a dissenter and a Whig, must have provided the founder of the club with plentiful opportunities for pungent remark.

---

[1] Hawkins, *Johnson*, 219.

JOHN PAYNE, a bookseller in Paternoster Row, was, the year after the foundation of this club, to become further associated with Johnson, as the publisher of his *The Rambler*. Concurrently he held a position in the Bank of England where he eventually rose to the high position of Chief Accountant without, however, entirely abandoning his publishing and bookselling interests.

SAMUEL DYER was a youngster of a mere twenty-four years, a classical scholar, mathematician, linguist, and philosopher. As a dissenter he had had his education not at Oxford or Cambridge but at the nonconformist academy at Northampton and at the universities of Glasgow and Leyden.

WILLIAM M'GHIE, a medical man, had qualified in his native Scotland, and was, says Hawkins, 'a learned, ingenious, and modest man, and one of those few of his country whom Johnson could endure'. Indeed, Johnson 'treated him with great civility, and may almost be said to have loved him'. (He was also a great friend of Smollett.)

Dr. EDMUND BARKER was another product of Leyden, having studied there with Hawkins's own house companion, Munckley. He had taken his doctorate in medicine two years before, and was now, at the age of twenty-eight, in practice in London. Hawkins describes him as 'an acute reasoner on the subject of ethics, and excellent classical scholar, and a deep metaphysician' and says, also, that he 'had enriched his fancy by reading the Italian poets'. He shocked our proper young attorney, however, by his slovenly appearance. He would in this, we may be sure, not worry the club's founder, but as he was in religious principles a unitarian, 'Johnson snubbed him so often that his visits to us became less and less frequent'.

Dr. RICHARD BATHURST was a Jamaican born who came to England and studied at Cambridge, where he had taken his M.B. four years before this club came into being. Johnson, says Hawkins, greatly loved him 'for the pregnancy of his parts and the elegance of his manners'. Mrs. Piozzi, in her *Anecdotes*, quotes Johnson as saying 'Bathurst was a man to my heart's content; he hated a Whig: he was a very good hater'.

When two or three years later Hawkesworth started *The Adventurer*, Johnson and Bathurst were both contributors to it.

It is gratifying to learn that the Founder's aim in establishing his little club was fully realized. Hawkins says:

> The club in Ivy Lane, composed of the persons above described, was a great relief to Johnson after the fatigue of study, and he generally came to it with both a corporal and mental appetite; for our conversations seldom began till after a supper, so very solid and substantial, as led us to think, that with him it was a dinner. By the help of this refection, and no other incentive to hilarity than lemonade, Johnson was, in a short time after our assembling, transformed into a new creature: his habitual melancholy and lassitude of spirit gave way; his countenance brightened; his mind was made to expand, and his wit to sparkle: he told excellent stories; and in his didactic style of conversation, both instructed and delighted us.[1]

As we may suppose, however, some degree of forbearance towards the founder was required of his eight fellow members, and it was a happy circumstance that the one of them who was senior to him was of a peace-loving disposition:

> It required, however, on the part of us, who considered ourselves as his disciples, some degree of compliance with his political prejudices: the greater number of our company were whigs, and I was not a tory, and we all saw the prudence of avoiding to call the then late adventurer in Scotland, or his adherents, by those names which others hesitated not to give them, or to bring to remembrance what had passed, a few years before, on Tower-hill.
>
> But the greatest of all our difficulties was, to keep alive in Johnson's mind a sense of the decorum due to the age, character, and profession of Dr. Salter, whom he took delight in contradicting, and bringing his learning, his judgment, and sometimes his veracity to the test. And here I must observe, that Johnson, though a high-churchman, and by consequence a friend to the clergy as a body of men, was, with respect to individuals, frequently, not to say wanting in civility, but to a very great degree splenetic and pertinacious. For this behaviour we could but one way account: He had been bred in an university, and must there have had in prospect those advantages, those stations in life,

[1] Hawkins, *Johnson*, 250.

or perhaps those dignities, which an academic education leads to. Missing these by his adverse fortunes, he looked on every dignitary under a bishop, for to those of that order he was more than sufficiently respectful, and, to descend lower, on every one that possessed the emoluments of his profession, as occupying a station to which himself had a better title, and, if his inferior in learning or mental endowments, treated him as little better than an usurper.

Dr. Salter was too much a man of the world to resent this behaviour: 'Study to be quiet' seemed to be his rule; and he might possibly think, that a victory over Johnson in any matter of dispute, could it have been obtained, would have been dearly purchased at the price of peace. It was nevertheless a temerarious act in him to venture into a society, of which such a man was the head.[1]

It was about eighteen months after the foundation of the club that Johnson proposed to its members that now famous nocturnal festivity in honour of Mrs. Lennox, a small book of whose poems had lately appeared (*Poems on Several Occasions, by a Young Lady*, 1747) and whose first novel was ready for the press or already in it. (How laurels fade! Who living today, unless it be some university professor of English literature in the course of his duties, has read a line of that voluminous and once celebrated authoress who could boast of the admiration not only of Johnson but of Richardson, Fielding, and Goldsmith?[2])

Hawkins did not enjoy the evening:

To return to Johnson, I have already said that he paid no regard to time or the stated hours of refection, or even rest; and of this his inattention I will here relate a notable instance.

Mrs. Lenox, a lady now well known in the literary world, had written a novel entitled, 'The life of Harriet Stuart', which in the spring of 1751[3] was ready for publication. One evening at the club, Johnson proposed to us the celebrating the birth of Mrs. Lenox's first literary child, as he called her book, by a whole night spent in festivity.

---

[1] Ibid.

[2] A third of a century later Johnson reported, 'I dined yesterday at Mrs. Garrick's with Mrs. Carter, Miss Hannah More, and Miss Fanny Burney. Three such women are not to be found: I know not where I could find a fourth, except Mrs. Lennox, who is superior to them all' (Boswell, under date 15 May 1784, iv. 275). Laetitia Hawkins held a low opinion of Mrs. Lennox. See *Memoirs*, i. 70.

[3] Actually it was published in Dec. 1750.

Upon his mentioning it to me, I told him I had never sat up a whole night in my life; but he continuing to press me, and saying, that I should find great delight in it, I, as did all the rest of the company, consented.

The place appointed was the Devil tavern, and there, about the hour of eight, Mrs. Lenox and her husband, and a lady of her acquaint-ance, now living, as also the club, and friends to the number of near twenty, assembled. Our supper was elegant, and Johnson had directed that a magnificent hot apple-pye should make a part of it, and this he would have stuck with bay-leaves, because, forsooth, Mrs. Lenox was an authoress, and had written verses; and further, he had prepared for her a crown of laurel, with which, but not till he had invoked the muses by some ceremonies of his own invention, he encircled her brows.

The night passed, as must be imagined, in pleasant conversation, and harmless mirth, intermingled at different periods with the refresh-ments of coffee and tea.

About five, Johnson's face shone with meridian splendour, though his drink had been only lemonade; but the far greater part of us had deserted the colours of Bacchus, and were with difficulty rallied to partake of a second refreshment of coffee, which was scarcely ended when the day began to dawn. This phenomenon began to put us in mind of our reckoning; but the waiters were all so overcome with sleep, that it was two hours before we could get a bill, and it was not till near eight that the creaking of the street-door gave the signal for our departure.

My mirth had been considerably abated by a severe fit of the tooth-ach, which had troubled me the greater part of the night, and which Bathurst endeavoured to alleviate by all the topical remedies and palliatives he could think of; and I well remember, at the instant of my going out of the tavern-door, the sensation of shame that affected me, occasioned not by reflection on any thing evil that had passed in the course of the night's entertainment, but on the resemblance it bore to a debauch. However, a few turns in the Temple, and a breakfast at a neighbouring coffee-house, enabled me to overcome it.[1]

---

[1] Hawkins, *Johnson*, 285. Mrs. Lennox (1720–1804) was at the period in question but at the opening of her literary career. She later published a considerable number of novels and plays, *Shakespeare Illustrated, or the Novels and Histories on which the Plays of Shakespeare are founded* (3 vols., 1753–4), and many translations from the French: see her life by Miriam R. Small (New Haven, Conn., 1925). Johnson wrote no fewer than six dedications for Mrs. Lennox: see A. T. Hazen, *Johnson's Prefaces and Dedications* (New Haven, 1937).

It may have surprised some who have often read of the Ivy Lane Club, to note in the above brief account of its membership how considerable a portion of young men it contained. Johnson himself was forty and Salter about seventy, but the others were of about Hawkins's own age or even rather less—mostly men in their twenties, indeed. Then it is interesting to note that a third of the members were medical men, and also that the strong Church of England founder of the Club had included in it a large dissenting element (for Ryland, Dyer, Barker, and Hawkesworth were all dissenters, and Hawkins himself seems to have been brought up as one and, from indications in Laetitia's *Anecdotes*, probably at this period still attended the ministrations of dissenting divines).

It will be observed, also, that the membership of the club was in no way specially eminent. Most of the members had their way to make in the world, and even Johnson's own position was still only vaguely marked; his literary work so far had been largely anonymous and of a 'hack' nature; he had eleven years before published his poem *London*, which had prompted Pope to inquire its author's name and, recognizing his obscurity, to remark, 'He will soon be déterré.' Five years earlier his life of Savage had appeared and two years earlier he had issued the plan of his Dictionary, though six years more were to pass before that great work came into the hands of the public; Garrick had just produced his play *Irene*, and it had managed to keep the stage for nine nights but was looked on as a failure.

This, then, was merely a friendly gathering of more or less congenial spirits, all men of education and character, and all capable of contributing something of value to the discussions that arose. The church, literature, law, and medicine were represented in it, and so those discussions could take a wide range. But it was not the distinguished gathering which we who know the later careers of some of its members are perhaps inclined to assume it to have been.

The Ivy Lane Club did not enjoy a very long life. Johnson, apparently, did not adopt the natural plan (as one would think it) of occasionally bringing in new blood, and six years or so saw it through. As Hawkins tells us:

About the year 1756, time had produced a change in the situation of many of Johnson's friends, who were used to meet him in Ivy Lane. Death had taken from us M'Ghie; Barker went to settle as a practising physician at Trowbridge; Dyer went abroad; Hawkesworth was busied in forming new connections; and I had lately made one that removed from me all temptations to pass my evenings from home. The consequence was, that our symposium at the King's-head broke up, and he who had first formed us into a society was left with fewer around him than were able to support it.[1]

The friendship between Johnson and Hawkins, however, continued unbroken and, as we shall later see, though they no longer had their weekly meetings at the club they met from time to time at Hawkins's house.

Music, of course, was not amongst their bonds of union. Hawkins, after dwelling upon his friend's complete insensibility to the beauties of nature, of painting, and of architecture, says:

To the delights of music, he was equally insensible: neither voice nor instrument, nor the harmony of concordant sounds, had power over his affections, or even to engage his attention. Of music in general, he has been heard to say, 'it excites in my mind no ideas, and hinders me from contemplating my own'; and of a fine singer, or instrumental performer, that 'he had the merit of a Canary-bird'. I have sometimes thought that music was positive pain to him. Upon his once hearing a celebrated performer go through a hard composition, and hearing it remarked that it was very difficult, Johnson said, 'I would it had been impossible.'

As a science of which he was ignorant he contemned it. In the early part of my life I had collected some memoirs of Abbate Steffani, Mr. Handel's predecessor at the court of Hanover, and the composer of those fine duets that go under his name, with a view to print them, as presents to some musical friends: I submitted the manuscript to Johnson's perusal, and he returned it with corrections that turned to ridicule all I had said of him and his works. Not that his hearing was so defective as to account for this insensibility, but he laboured under

1 Hawkins, Johnson, 361.

the misfortune which he has noted in the life of Barretier, and is common to more persons than in this musical age are willing to confess it, of wanting that additional sense or faculty, which renders music grateful to the human ear.[1]

These memoirs of Steffani are alluded to by Horace Walpole in a note-book preserved in the Waller Collection.[2] This gives a brief account of Hawkins, opening as follows with an anecdote relating to the period of Hawkins's life with which we are now concerned:

John Hawkins, Esq., bred a lawyer. In 1758 he published the life of Signor Agostino Steffani, some time master of the Electoral Chapel at Hanover, and afterwards Bishop of Spira: it contained but eight pages, & was printed like a music book, in order to be bound with music.[3]

That incident illustrates the ruder side of Johnson's intercourse with his friends, and so does the following one, related by Laetitia, who has just been telling her readers of the 'brutal wit' of Johnson towards certain ladies who 'made it too much of a point of honour to obtain an introduction':

My mother used to brag that he had never been uncivil to *her*:—till unfortunately at our table she asked him very gently if he would not take a little wine; and concluding by his not replying that he had not heard her, she repeated the words. He then thundered out, 'I drink no wine—why do you tease me?'

Her boasting, alas! was then all over, and she remained, in rank and distinction, just on a level with the eighteen nymphs who were so incautious as to go in a body to wait on him.[4]

---

[1] Ibid. 319 and footnote thereto.

[2] In the possession of the Waller family, at Woodcote, Warwick. See note in preface of vol. i of the Supplement to Toynbee's collection of *The Letters of Horace Walpole*, 1918.

[3] For this life of Steffani, see the Bibliography at the end of the present book. George III accepted a copy of it (*Anecdotes*, 259).   [4] Ibid. 329.

IV. *His wealthy marriage* (1753)

SOME little time before the period at which we are now arrived there were, it appears, 'very kind mediating' people who, seeing an eligible professional young man as yet unattached, wished to help him. Hawkins must in after years have recounted to his children some attempts of this kind, for Laetitia has the following tale to tell:

A very kind *mediating* lady of his acquaintance once wished to recommend to him for a wife her niece, afterwards the celebrated Mrs. Barry, the actress: he was not very likely to be drawn in; but if he had wavered, the method taken to secure him would have saved him. The young lady was a visitor in the house at the same time with himself. As a correct young man, it was to be presumed that industry and attention to religion would meet his approbation. Miss S—— was therefore at work with 'The Practice of Piety' by her, and as he was known to be fond of music, she was desired to sing; and she sung as he used to describe it, about '*mutal* love'.[1]

The pious and musical Miss S—— was evidently Miss Ann Street, daughter of 'an eminent apothecary' and perhaps this is the 'disappointment in love' which, as the *Dictionary of National Biography* tells us,[2] led the poor young thing to 'a visit to Yorkshire where . . . she seems to have acquired a taste for the stage'. So came about matrimony with an actor, a 'Mr. Dancer, who seems to have died young', then 'some scandal, followed happily by a union with the Dublin theatre manager Spranger Barry', and after his death another with one Crawford. The lady enjoyed considerable stage success, especially in tragedy, for, whatever faults may have remained in her pronunciation, she was, it appeared, capable of uttering a phrase with such dramatic force that 'it checked your breath-

[1] *Memoirs*, i. 168 n.   [2] s.v. *Barry, Mrs. Ann Spranger.*

ing, perhaps pulsation', on occasion even making 'rows of spectators start from their seats'.

The young attorney was perhaps 'well out of it', for a lady so forceful as all that might have proved to be too disturbing a factor in domestic life. But what a stickler for correct English he was! Read now the following:

Another lady was put forward by her friends in the year 1745, but unfortunately, the poor girl, in her zeal for the House of Brunswick, talked of the *veterian* corps, and he broke the meshes.[1]

Thus urged on in vain by his kind friends Hawkins seems at last to have begun to think he might do something on his own initiative. Laetitia recounts a circumstance that was, she says, a secret from her until after the death of her parents:

My father's affections were attracted towards Mrs. Stanley's sister; and, indeed, I must say his partiality did him no discredit; for, although involved of necessity in the general character of those with whom she resided, she must have been naturally much their superior in many points. She was, however, not disposed to receive his addresses, being in hope of attaching the heart of a man much older, but who was, as she found afterwards, at that time engaged to a second wife.[2]

However, in 1753, Hawkins 'pulled it off' in another quarter, and, as we shall see, he was on this occasion, as on two occasions previously, given a little push by a friend who wished him well.

One Peter Storer, of Highgate, 'brought up most strictly, and most sourly, a thorough presbyterian', but a wealthy man and 'a very honest honourable man, brought up to a superior branch of the law', seeing the approach of the decline of life, wanted at his right hand some adroit young attorney whose assistance he could occasionally use in the weighty matters of conveyancing, He had a son who was, it seems to be implied, also a lawyer, but who was sickly and so could not be of much service in this way:

Young Hawkins was named to him,—and recommended by a gentleman who loved him for a character of modest worth and his

[1] *Memoirs*, i. 168. [2] *Anecdotes*, 213.

musical talents, and had been particularly pleased with his then popular Cantatas:—the parties were brought together; and Mr. Storer often expressed regret that he had not known him sooner.[1]

But not only did Hawkins please the old gentleman; he pleased the younger also. And so this Peter Storer, junior, 'an independent Middlesex gentleman with about £2,000 a year', thought 'his younger and favourite sister, with her £10,000, would be well bestowed upon his friend'. And, as Laetitia observes, 'The rest follows of course'.

Was there love in this match? Nothing is said of it. On the face of things it looks as though the brother's and father's goodwill and the sister's ten thousand pounds were sufficient, without any incitement of another sort. And if that were so it accords pretty well with the general impression that a study of Hawkins's career leaves on one's mind—that of a steady, practical character, untinctured by romance and, without being entirely self-absorbed, yet not abounding in anything that could be called strong affection for his fellow-creatures— though, as we shall in a moment find ourselves obliged to admit, the actual sight of suffering could momentarily move him.

And now a few words as to the new Mrs. Hawkins. She was born in 1726, so that at the time of the thrilling events of the '45' she was nineteen years old:

She was at that period therefore of an age to be highly as well as deeply interested, in the event of so important a conquest. She used to describe her father, who was a zealous whig, as thoroughly dejected while matters were approaching to their crisis, and well recollected his burying two hundred guineas in his garden. She could describe all the scenery [sic] when the troops passed through to Finchley-common, and had even then before her eyes, the sumpter-mules and all the detail of the Duke of Cumberland's baggage.

Her curiosity might be great, but her terror was greater. Not being permitted to read or to hear the newspapers read, and a young man being in her father's house at the time, who had a *tendre* for her, and

[1] *Anecdotes*, 122. Chalmers names the 'gentleman who loved him'. He was a Mr. Hare, a brewer of Limehouse, a musical friend whom he had met at Stanley's gatherings.

read them to him, she listened at the door, and laid her commands on the reader to make himself distinctly heard. The newspaper to which she once thus attentively listened, stated the insurgents to have reached Dunstable;—she fainted away, and fell upon the floor. My grandfather, engrossed as he was, was startled at the noise, and the door being opened to ascertain what occasioned it, she was discovered.[1]

This vivid passage is followed by several pages of sober discussion of the characters of the Duke of Cumberland and of Sir John Cope. And then comes this interesting reminiscence:

To return to the remembrances of the memorable year, 1745. The dreadful suspense which we know to have affected the nation, before the decisive battle of Culloden, must in individuals have been succeeded by a proportionate curiosity. That it was so in my mother, was evident in her lively description of the conveyance of the 'rebel-lords', as they were called, through Highgate.

Tender-hearted as she was—and she was so, even to inconvenient excess,—either her loyalty, which was very zealous, or her sense of danger escaped, left her, I must confess, very little of the Apostle's exhortations to 'be pitiful'. I dare not say she *thought* at the moment of her indignation for what she had been made to suffer, that she with her own hand could have chopped off the heads of these aforesaid rebel-lords:—but little less indeed was the mistake of my father, who could not look at a cut finger, when he thought he could see with composure the execution of one who indeed claimed no man's pity.

This one all the nation will recognise as Lord Lovat. My father had obtained a very good situation to see the decapitation; and he could describe, up to the dreadful *making ready*. Beyond this he saw nothing, though all was clear before him: his sight became confused; his heart turned sick, and all was over before he recovered.

My mother at Highgate had nothing so dreadful to witness; she saw Lord Lovat pass, and saw him stop to take refreshment, the carriage being thrown open. Her account tallied with that of all other reporters. She bore her testimony to the strong resemblance of Hogarth's portrait to the original.[2]

The first home of the married couple was in Austin Friars, near Broad Street. It was probably here that was

[1] Ibid. 154.   [2] Ibid. 159 et seq.

held the fortnightly musical gathering of which Laetitia tells us:

> Before we, his children, knew him, he had kept up the habit of a little friendly meeting one evening every fortnight; and Mr. Savage, who was master of the boys at St. Paul's, making one in the party, this association, small as it was, could boast of some egg-shell musicians who were afterwards hatched into fame.

> My mother being extremely good-humoured to my father's tastes and pursuits, (not at all resembling the wicked misrepresentation of her in the collection alluded to,[1] where my father's endurances are compared to Purcell's) but really entering into his love for music and the arts, was very hospitable and well-bred to those amateurs, who, if they had wives, brought them, and made the evening cheerful to her.

> I have heard her sometimes say, when she heard the name of a highly-esteemed singer, 'Ah! I have boxed his ears many a time, for poking the fire between the acts': particularly I remember this of Reinhold, who seemed the greatest sinner in this way.[2]

Hawkins's establishment of a house of his own was un-fortunately followed by a serious illness. In this he was attended by his old 'chum' Dr. Munckley (see pp. 7–8), of whose unremitting attendance on the patient Laetitia in after years heard the story, recording it for our information as follows:

> He was extremely rapacious, and a very bad economist; and soon after my father's marriage, having been foiled in his attempt to borrow money of him, he endeavoured to atone to himself for this disappoint-ment, by protracting the duration of a low fever, in which he attended him, making unnecessary visits, and with his hand ever open for a fee. For this, he drew upon himself such an open censure in Batson's coffee-house, then the rallying point of the medical world, that he could hardly appear there again. It is impertinent to follow this son of Esculapius in his oblique path to fame; it will content the reader,

---

[1] The collection mentioned was in the library of Eton College but is now re-ported to be lost.

[2] Charles Frederick Reinhold (1737–1815) was a famous bass singer—in the choirs of St. Paul's Cathedral and the Chapel Royal, at Vauxhall and Marylebone, soloist in the London theatres, and at the great Westminster Abbey Handel Commemora-tions in 1784, &c. He was widely celebrated for his performance of Handel's *O ruddier than the cherry*. He was also a London organist.

if I say that dying early in life by a sudden attack of disease, his last words were, that 'it was——hard to be taken off just then when he was beginning to get into practice'.[1]

The friendship with Stanley was kept up and the young couple were the recipients of his hospitality. This, it appears, was sometimes rather too pressing. Stanley's 'detention of guests' was such a pronounced characteristic that 'unless a friend could make leisure to stay until relieved by a successor, it was advisable to forbear going into what acted very much on the principle of a mouse-trap'. Hawkins's wife, in after years, used to recall an instance of the inconvenience to which guests were liable to be exposed, but when she did so, Laetitia tells us, 'I have known my father check her for mentioning as an individual circumstance that which was the habit of a house'. This is the story:

After much pressing, and almost resolving never to be so taken in again, Sir John and Lady Hawkins [but not then 'Sir' and 'Lady'!], then young housekeepers, and without a carriage, agreed to spend a few days with Mr. and Mrs. Stanley at their villa, on condition that my father should be allowed to return to business of importance in the courts of law by a time specified:—this was solemnly promised;—but when the time came, no successor having arrived, they were entreated to help off with one more evening; and now the condition turned upon an hour instead of a day, and the promise was still more solemnly renewed.

At the hour necessary to rise, every one but those departing, was fast asleep; breakfast was ordered,—and they were assured that their chaise was bespoke, and that they would have abundance of time;— the way was shortened in idea by computation, and the horses were 'within hearing';—they came not, however, in sight. The servant who had been ordered to bespeak them, was of course next called, and of course likewise, he had had no orders;—then came the usual, 'Why I bid you tell such an one to tell such an one.'

No horses were to be had;—every public conveyance was gone by;— and it is literally fact, that the two guests were driven to the necessity of walking eight miles in a day so hot, that, accidentally meeting their family-apothecary near their own door, he ordered my mother to take

1 *Anecdotes*, 133.

instantly a spoonful of brandy. She might, it may be said, have staid behind;—true, but she neither liked the separation, nor were the trap, or the toasted cheese in it, so tempting; for the family-provision was of such cookery, that visitors had, for their best consolation, the pleasure of hearing—perhaps in the case of a raw pig—'what a nice broil it would make the day after they were gone'.[1]

[1] *Anecdotes,* 211.

V. *His new dwellings at Twickenham* (1760)
and in Hatton Garden (1763)

IN 1759, when Hawkins was forty years of age, his brother-in-law, Peter Storer the younger (who, as we have seen, was not of a robust physique), died, leaving to his younger sister, whom Hawkins had married, a considerable property and almost excluding his elder sister from any participation in his bequest. Laetitia's account of the event is as follows:

My mother had, as I have stated, an elder brother,—a man whose name still lives in sweet hereditary remembrance in that part of Middlesex where we have copyhold property. Times then afforded a single man, with an unincumbered landed property of £2000 a-year, to keep six carriage-horses, and to live with a liberality equal to this. Mr. Storer, a perfect gentleman, kept up this style, but without ever suffering the smallest accumulation of debt;—consequently he died rich.

My mother had always been his favourite sister; her lively temper and pretty person, together with the pains he had bestowed on her when hardly treated by her father because she was not a boy, had endeared her to him. She had only one sister, who had offended her brother by the ill-government of her temper and her tongue; and he having, without consulting either my father or mother, made his will, he bequeathed his elder sister only £500, leaving to my mother all the rest of his property, which almost exclusively lay within twenty miles of London. Having done this, he deposited the will with my father, telling him what it would be found, coôly giving his reason,—saying his elder sister had offended him beyond reparation, and that no pleading for her would avail.

On every point of generosity and honour my father and mother had but one mind;—they were indefatigable in their representations of the injustice of this act, and the probability of subsequent forgiveness and repentance on the part of Mr. Storer, when it might be too late:—they prevailed;—and an equal division was made, as equitable as a

pleasant
story

court of law could have decreed. We lost more than £1000 a-year by this; but our gain is inestimable:—we can ride through a manor gone from us, and see fields not our own, with exultation. It has pleased God to bless us 'in the city and in the field—in the basket and in the store'; and for this we do daily and sincerely 'give thanks unto the God of Heaven; for his mercy endureth for ever'.[1]

Several accounts put the value of the legacy that actually fell to Mrs. Hawkins at £20,000 (a considerable sum in those days): Horace Walpole[2] puts it at £30,000 but may be unconsciously adding to this legacy of Mrs. Hawkins's brother her own dowry (see p. 38).

The year after the receipt of this new legacy Hawkins retired from his attorney's practice, selling it to Richard Clark, a young man of twenty-one or so, a clever fellow whom Hawkins had brought into Johnson's company when he was no more than fifteen years of age; Laetitia says 'he was one of the oldest friends of my family' and, as we have already learnt (see p. ix), he was destined to rise to a succession of important positions in the government of the City.

Here is Clark's own account of his association with Johnson:[3]

It was Mr. Clark's good fortune, at about the age of fifteen, to have been introduced to the acquaintance of Dr. Samuel Johnson, whose friendship he enjoyed to the last year of his life. By the Doctor's invitation he attended his evening parties at the Mitre Tavern in Fleet Street, where, amongst other literary characters, were Dr. Percy, afterwards Bishop of Dromore, Dr. Goldsmith, Dr. Hawkesworth, &c.; a substantial supper was served up at eight o'clock and the company seldom departed until a late hour; and Mr. Clark remembers that at an early period of the morning he with one of the party accompanied the Doctor to his house, where he found Mrs. Williams, then blind, who was prepared to give them tea, which she made and poured out with a degree of elegance. Frequently Mr. Clark visited this great and good man at his house, and met him often at dinner parties.

[1] *Anecdotes*, 139.
[2] Walpole, Supp. ii. 116.
[3] Quoted in the long obituary in the *Gentleman's Magazine* of February 1831, which includes an extract from a manuscript by Clark.

Hawkins now bought a house at Twickenham. Being at the western extremity of the 'lovely situated and elegantly inhabited village', it was, says Laetitia, considered to be 'the last house in London'.[1] An engraving which adorns Laetitia's *Anecdotes* shows it at one end of Twickenham Common, with the house of the Marchioness of Tweeddale at the other end.

The house Hawkins had bought had been until then the property of Lady Savile, mother of the politically active Sir George Savile. Opposite this house was 'a laboratory productive of great annoyance to the neighbourhood'. Its owner, Joshua Ward, died the year after the Hawkins family came to Twickenham. This would-be M.P.[2] ('Spot Ward', as he was called, from an unfortunate facial disfigurement) was 'the celebrated inventor of those medicines that bore his name', the proprietor of 'a famous drop and pill which professed to cure every human malady'. These enjoyed an enormous sale. He was also, apparently, a manipulative healer, as such enjoying the patronage of George II, 'whose immediate displeasure and more lasting esteem he won by curing his dislocated thumb with a violent wrench'. For this service he was 'allowed an apartment in the almonry office, Whitehall, where he ministered to the poor at his majesty's expense'. Lord Chesterfield, Gibbon, and Henry Fielding[3] had been amongst his hundreds of better-class patients. He figures in Hogarth's *A Consultation of Physicians* (cf. p. 7 n.).

At the time that the Hawkins family settled in Twickenham, one of its prominent residents there, Horace Walpole, was corresponding with his friend, Sir Horace Mann, the British Minister in Florence, as to the desirability of applying

[1] *Anecdotes*, 18.

[2] He was elected as such but never sat, his name in the Return being erased by order of the House, 13 May 1717 (*Return of Members of Parliament* in Parliamentary Papers 1878, 45).

[3] For Fielding's deep gratitude and high opinion of Ward's remedies see the Introduction to the *Voyage to Lisbon*. There is in *Tom Jones* (Bk. VIII, ch. 9) an allusion to the intelligent action of the pill ('it flies at once to the particular part of the body on which you desire to operate').

Pope mentions Ward's 'drop' in the *Imitations of Horace* (Bk. II, Ep. i. 182).

Johnson had a poor opinion of Ward: he thought him the dullest man he ever knew (Boswell, iii. 389).

one of Ward's remedies for the cure of the latter's headaches, and also with George Montagu as to the 'villainy of physicians' who had caused the death of Lord Edgcumbe by preventing Ward from being called in until too late.[1]

The Ward pills, of three varieties (blue, red, and purple), all contained antimony and two of them arsenic, and were said to kill more than they cured, yet when 'in 1748 an Apothecaries Act was introduced into parliament to restrain unlicensed persons from compounding medicines, a clause was inserted specially exempting Ward, by name, from the restrictions imposed'.

There is a very copious contemporary literature (*pro* and *con*) concerning Ward, in the shape of books, pamphlets, and communications to journals, much of which has been consulted in the preparation of the present note on him. His obituary in the *Annual Register* of 1761 is entirely laudatory; it says that 'many who have been pronounced dead have been restored to life' (piously adding, '*sub Deo*'), but elsewhere a very different tale is told. For instance the *Grub Street Journal* of November 1734[2] relates the sad case of 'a Gentleman of a strong habit of body, but having Symptoms of a Scurvy' who took one or two doses of Ward's drops and pills, and whose 'Constitution was so shattered by the Violence of the Operation that his Jaw became Paralytic, Eruptions broke out in his Body, the Tendons of his Insteps and Hands swell'd, and he at last fell into a Fever', from which, happily, he 'was recover'd by safer remedies' (for authentication readers are told, 'This Person is to be heard of at the Printer's of the *Grub Street Journal*, in *Chancery Lane*'). It also saddens us by the case of a Servant (name and address given) who, 'having Hysteric Fits, took two pills without their operating at all', and on the third, the next Day, 'fell to screaming and crying out of an intolerable Pain in the Stomach and Guts, declaring the *Pill* had killed her and died the Day following'. And then

---

[1] Walpole, iv. 344, 363; v. 52 (Jan. and Mar. 1760 and Apr. 1761).
[2] Reprinted in the *Gentleman's Magazine* in the same month, p. 616; reply by Ward in *The Daily Advertiser* of December of that year, similarly reprinted.

there was poor 'Hester Staps, a Waiter of the Bagnio, Charing Cross, who unfortunately, being troubled with scorbutic Pimples, which broke out Spring and Fall, would needs take *Ward's Panacea*', which 'threw out all over her Body a most violent Leprosy, of which she miserably wasted and soon died'. And so on—many similar distressing cases being put on public record.

And yet people believed in Ward. His thousands of paying patients brought him in an enormous income, from which he gave generously to charities,[1] and his confidence in national gratitude was such that in his Will he directed that he should be buried in front of the altar of Westminster Abbey, or 'as near the Altar as might be'. The nearest he got to such permanent public recognition, however, was the placing of a statue by Carlini in the great hall (later in the vestibule) of the Royal Society of Arts, in John Adam Street, Adelphi, where it is still to be seen.[2]

In R. S. Cobbett's *Memorials of Twickenham* is a description of Hawkins's house as it was over a century later (1872). It tells us of a club of which no other information seems to be available, and also of a concert room:

> Turning towards the old village, the house called Twickenham House, near the railway bridge, on the S. side of the road, now occupied by Dr. Hugh M. Diamond, is celebrated as having been the residence of Sir John Hawkins, Knt.
>
> There is a building in the garden of Twickenham House which was built for the meetings of the club to which Hawkins belonged. The circular room with a dome roof, now used as a drawing room, was originally his concert room. There is a very curious fence in the grounds formed of sword-blades which tradition affirms to have been collected after the battle from the field of Culloden.

The house and its appurtenances are no longer to be seen.

'Twickenham had lost its title of *classic* when my father bought his house there in 1760', says Laetitia, 'but it was still

[1] See for instances the *Gentleman's Magazine*, Dec. 1759 and June 1760.
[2] See John Thomas Smith's *Nollekens and his Times*. Also Sir Henry Trueman Wood's *History of the Royal Society of Arts*, 519.

the abode of many distinguished persons'. Amongst these was
conspicuous 'a most venerable personage', Sir Samuel Prime,
who dwelt in the house that had once been that of the painter
Kneller—nowadays known as 'Kneller Hall' and as the home
of the British Army's School of Music. Sir Samuel, 'a profound lawyer', a 'nisi prius Counsel', was, says Laetitia, 'much
too awful for my intimate observation', after which remark she
shows evidence of an observation very intimate indeed. Sir
Samuel's person recalled days of long ago—in fact those of
Queen Anne:

> He wore a most voluminous wig, which yet, by the lightness of its
> curls, or I might almost say ringlets, seemed no heavier than the same
> quantity of smoke; it was, I suppose, though a little powdered, of the
> palest flaxen colour, corresponding with his really blooming com-
> plexion: his whole scale was large, but without any tendency to
> corpulency, his features were commanding, and his voice probably was
> pitched to Westminster Hall; it was exceedingly distinct, grave, and
> sonorous; his enunciation slow; and be began every sentence in address-
> ing my father, with a 'Sir', as profound as if he had addressed the House
> of Commons, by claiming the attention of their Speaker.
>
> Sir Samuel's dress, I may truly say, I want words to describe; for
> I really know not the terms that will describe it. His suit, including
> stockings, I recollect to have been all of one hue in summer, and that
> the lightest that could be called colour. In winter we saw him less
> frequently; but he was then clad in a brown, that might be called
> snuff-colour. He had been, I suppose, a beau of his own time; for the
> nicety of the disposition of his cravat and ruffles, the exactitude with
> which his stockings preserved their place in the obsolete form of roll-
> ups, and the *tout ensemble*, seemed rather the labour of a sculptor than
> the adroitness of a valet.
>
> Everything he wore or used—his stiff-topped gloves of the gauntlet
> form, his carpets, nay, even his lady's lap-dogs, were all perfumed to
> a degree that would be insupportable to the better taste of the present
> age; and which, had he gone to Rome, would have excluded him from
> its polite society.[1]

Whether Laetitia was born at the time of the removal to
Twickenham seems doubtful (she never tells us the date of her

---

[1] *Anecdotes,* 49 et seq.

LONDON AS HAWKINS KNEW IT

WHITEHALL. As seen from near Charing Cross. On thel eft of the picture is the Banqueting House completed by Inigo Jones in 1622, and still existing, and at the end, bestriding the street near where Downing Street now enters it, is the Holbein Gate (removed in 1758).

HYDE PARK CORNER. Showing 'Allen's Apple Stall', at the right of the gate, with the inn known as 'The Hercules Pillars'. The drawing dates from 1756.

TWICKENHAM COMMON. The Hawkins home is seen in the distance on the left. The nearer house, at the right, is that of the Marchioness of Tweeddale—as to whose friendship with the Hawkins family see pp. 50–53.

STRAWBERRY HILL. Horace Walpole's '*bauble villa*', as Laetitia Hawkins calls it. Here Hawkins and his wife and family were '*licensed visitors without form*' (see pp. 52 et seq.).

(*left*) HORACE WALPOLE
(*above*) GARRICK AND HIS WIFE

birth but must have been born just about that time); what she relates belongs evidently to a period some years later. She begs her readers to imagine 'in what species of undertaking they could suppose two such grave gentlemen' as Sir Samuel Prime and her father to have engaged together, and then, not waiting for the agitated guessing to mature, kindly tells them —and one wonders how many of them have felt able to accept her account literally (Can we ourselves do so?):

Not to tease beyond bounds, be it known that these two sages became, by purchase, part owners of an East India ship!—and as if to make certain that feature of the adventure to which it was the more difficult to give credence, the ship was named 'the Prime'. I remember even my own astonishment, not indeed at the coalition, but at the purpose of it. A great deal of business was transacted before its sailing, but this, though of course it added to my labour of writing, afforded me no speculation. I learnt something from it, as I did from everything;— in particular, I was *au faite* [*sic*] in the distinctions of ship-broker, ship-owner, ship's husband, and ship's captain. I knew that my father, having no East Indian connexions, sent no letters by the Prime; and I knew that my mother, being far removed in honourable feelings from coveting that which is to be obtained only by an infraction of the law, expressed no wish for baubles or decorations. What Sir Samuel Prime could wish for, I could not have imagined: time showed.

But I would not have it supposed that this episode in a grave character was entirely an unprofitable excrescence. No; we had occasionally our proportion of those pieces of ship-beef, which, in culinary phrase, 'Will not take the salt'. Nearer to our table than the cart which brought them, in a promiscuous and unsightly heap, to the house-door, I never saw them; and whether the servants—a description of persons tolerably versed in catering for themselves,—ever admitted them nearer to their table than the larder, I should question; at least if I might judge by the usual style of Lady Hawkins's house-keeping, and the little likeness these donations bore to it in their rough state.

At length, home came 'the goodly argosie', and the Prime East Indiaman was announced amongst the arrivals in the ports. Then ensued a festival, and on the 19th December, a dainty season for a water-frolic, did Sir John Hawkins and his lady sally forth, to meet, at Blackwall, Sir Samuel and Lady Prime, and a large party of friends;—

all to proceed to dine on board this galleon of treasures. Had I known what I then for the first time knew, 'that *my dear mamma* was to be drawn up the sides of a ship from a boat', I should have been most nervously anxious; but at the return, I heard with great delight, what she related as comic, her spinning round like an apple on a string before the fire, in consequence of her very little weight.

But still, what was or had been Sir Samuel Prime's commission? It was duly executed, and proved to have been four drops of Otto or Atta of Roses, at one guinea a drop!

The affair concluded by a grand *démêlé*. The Captain was taken to task for flogging young Master Sheldrake, Lady P.'s housekeeper's son; the ship's husband proved a rogue; the broker put the ship up to auction; *we* had no more beef—Sir Samuel no more perfume.[1]

Youthful portraits of Lady Prime showed her to have been what was called 'a prodigiously fine woman', and even her 'remains' were 'on a grand scale'. Moreover Lady Prime, though she 'did not live in an educated age' had 'observed well', so that time spent in her company never dragged. She had, it appears, a speciality which Hawkins shared (rather unexpectedly, surely in such a city-bred man). She 'would have astonished any gardener by her accurate knowledge of fruit and its cultivation':

She never made a display even of this knowledge; but on a point-blank question from my father, who had a similar taste, I heard her confess that she believed she knew every pear that grew in England;— and, which is more surprising than her knowledge, she would at more than seventy years of age, I believe, sup on them in the coldest evenings without suffering![2]

As for the Marchioness of Tweeddale already mentioned (one of the Hawkins' nearest neighbours), her speciality as a child, at any rate, had been anti-Jacobitism.

She had been brought up by an Aunt, Lady Worsley, 'one of the most zealous' of the anti-Hanoverians:

The Marchioness herself told my father, that on her aunt's upbraiding her when a child, with not attending prayers, she answered 'that she heard her ladyship did not pray for the King'.—'Not pray for the

[1] *Anecdotes*, 52.   [2] Ibid. 60.

King?' said Lady Worsley, 'who says this? I will have you and those who sent you, know that I *do* pray for the King;—but I do not think it necessary to tell God Almighty *who is King*'.[1]

The Marchioness was a widow and some charged her with having 'worried her gouty lord out of his life by her tender solicitudes':

But I am sure if she did so, it was with a perfectly good intention, for his memory still remained very dear to her; and the rooms which he used in the town-house, which was in Upper Grosvenor-street, never had the day-light let in to them; nor had she ever been at Court, though a royal message of condescending inquiry had often given her a hint to pay her duty there.[2]

This kind lady, when the two Hawkins boys, Sidney and Henry, grew big enough to be sent to the Charterhouse, expended some of her 'solicitude' on them, for she 'most kindly and earnestly opposed the plan', urging that they should be educated under her son's private tutor, 'rather than that they should be exposed to the hardships of a public school':

My mother declining the favour, though I am sure she could not have departed from due respect in her manner of doing so, the Marchioness with some asperity replied, 'well, I thought you loved your children!' Lady H. replied, 'I do, and therefore I part with them.'[3]

Her solicitude extended also to the Hawkins's daughter. She took it into her fanciful head that the little Laetitia 'would grow up awry', and 'to satisfy this doubt, and convince her, if possible, that she was wrong, she was suffered from time to time', says Laetitia, 'to undress me'. The Marchioness's daughters took an interest in this procedure, and when the poor child was 'sent to the nursery to be made decent again', pursued her there and made her unload her pockets (a pocket being then the ambition of every girl who was anxious to appear womanly), whereupon the 'amassed treasures were turned over, and, half in earnest and half in playfulness, a selection of them was made'. This was doubtless, 'amongst those of their own high rank, jocular', but to poor little Miss

[1] *Anecdotes*, 63.   [2] Ibid. 64.   [3] Ibid. 66.

Hawkins, who felt her inferiority, 'grievous': consequently she 'was not fond of them'.

One of the closest Twickenham friends of the Hawkins family was Horace Walpole. We see the man before us in Laetitia's vivid description of his person and dress, as follows:

His figure was as has been told, and every one knows, not merely tall, but more properly *long* and slender to excess; his complexion and particularly his hands, of a most unhealthy paleness. I speak of him before the year 1772. His eyes were remarkably bright and penetrating, very dark and lively:—his voice was not strong, but his tones were extremely pleasant, and if I may so say, highly gentlemanly. I do not remember his common gait; he always entered a room in that style of affected delicacy, which fashion had then made almost natural; *chapeau bras* between his hands as if he wished to compress it, or under his arm —knees bent, and feet on tip-toe, as if afraid of a wet floor.

His dress in visiting was most usually, in summer when I most saw him, a lavender suit, the waistcoat embroidered with a little silver or of white silk worked in the tambour, partridge silk stockings, and gold buckles, ruffles and frill generally lace. I remember when a child, thinking him very much under-dressed, if at any time except in mourning, he wore hemmed cambric. In summer no powder, but his wig combed straight, and showing his very smooth pale forehead, and queued behind:—in winter powder.[1]

The Hawkins family were much attached to Walpole but did not admire his famous villa, 'Strawberry Hill'. 'I liked the man', says Laetitia, and 'knew him as well as a child knows a parent's friend, and his recollection is so pleasant to me that I cannot reconcile myself to the contemptuous manner in which his memory has been treated, or believe the general assertion that he was unworthy'. But, says she:

His bauble villa was made out of three tenements: but I reckon him so amply punished by his crazy bargain, and the enormous folly into which it led him, in patching up a house anything but habitable, that I will not bear hard upon him. I wonder he was not, long before his death, sickened of a thing so childish, and so little able to face injury; for his external decorations frequently provoked the wanton malice of the lower classes, who almost as certainly as new pinnacles were put

[1] *Anecdotes*, 105.

to a pretty Gothic entrance, broke them off; which, to do him justice, he bore with great patience, almost confessing that he merited the punishment by the indulgence of his taste. Madame du Deffand, in one of her well-edited letters, says to him, that 'she presumes he is building for posterity;' when, as the editor very humorously remarks, 'his Lordship outlived three sets of his battlements'.

That Horace Walpole was an atheist, I deny, on the testimony of his own expressions. To speak out, and to leave nothing to be misunderstood, he believed, I am confident, in a God; and he had an awful sense of his power, and relied on his mercy. I am afraid that beyond this, I must not go in pledging myself for him. . . .

It would be fair, when we bitterly condemn the principles of those not of the present generation, to ask ourselves what would have been their denomination in the religious world, had they had the benefits we enjoy—had they, as we have, heard in their docile years revealed religion inculcated, as we may say, from the throne—had they seen a Bible put into the hand of every individual, and the triumph of Great Britain over her infidel enemies, in a manner that cannot leave our Saviour's care of his church a doubt. . . .

On a sad catastrophe in his own family, he wrote to my father immediately, a letter which I wish I possessed, conjuring him to keep my brothers out of dissipated society, and not at all in the style of one who looked on deviations from right as of little importance.[1]

The family were 'licensed visitors without form at Strawberry Hill', and once, as Hawkins and his wife were going round it with its owner, Mrs. Hawkins was 'struck with surprise at seeing two small pictures that had been her brother's'. 'Mr. Walpole pressed her to accept them; she gratefully declined the favour, but burst into tears on recollecting where she had been accustomed to see them. Nothing more was said; but the pictures were not in sight when she next visited the collection'.

Mr. Walpole always gave my father the Strawberry-hill books as they came out, and amongst the rest the 'Fugitive Pieces', but, wherefore I know not, the pretty volume was given with an injunction not to lend it. Lest he might through forgetfulness transgress, my father

---

[1] Ibid. 87. All the passages quoted here come from that page and the following ones.

wrote this engagement in the first leaf of the book, signing it with his
initials. But even this proved insufficient to guard him from erring:—
his friend came into the library, took down the book and asked him
for the loan of it. The promise was broken, and the book lent.

It was returned, and it coming to my care to be replaced, I had
a natural curiosity to see the contents, and accidentally opening on the
fly-leaf, I was struck with astonishment at seeing not only the pro-
hibition, of which I was not at all aware, but an underwritten memo-
randum, written and signed by the friend for whose gratification the
fault had been committed, that, on such a day, Sir J.H. had lent him
that book. I showed it instantly to my father:—he was wounded
by the unkindness, but confessed that he merited the punishment,
though not from the hand that inflicted it. So sensible was he of
this, that in corresponding with him who had been so unkind, he
never named it.

Close to Walpole's 'Strawberry Hill' was 'Little Straw-
berry Hill', the house which he had allotted to the actress
Kitty Clive ('at least as perfect in low comedy', he says, as
Garrick in tragedy,[1] and he avers that Garrick, of whose
Drury Lane company she was a star member, 'hated Mrs.
Clive till she quitted the stage, and then cried her up to the
skies to depress Mrs. Abington'[2]).

Mrs. Clive had been famous not only as actress but as
vocalist. Handel had chosen her as the Dalilah in the first
performance of his *Samson* in 1742.

Walpole several times uses a solar metaphor or simile to
describe his neighbour's face—'Mrs. Clive looks like the
sun rising out of the ocean', or (quoting Lady Townshend)
Mrs. Clive's face 'rose on Strawberry Hill and made it
sultry', or 'Strawberry Hill is in perfection . . . the orange
trees are loaded with blossom, the gallery all sun and gold,
Mrs. Clive all sun and vermillion'.[3]

Many of the Johnson circle admired Mrs. Clive. Johnson
himself said, 'Mrs. Clive was the best player I ever saw', and
'What Clive did best, she did better than Garrick . . . she was
a better romp than any I ever saw in nature', and 'Clive, Sir,

---

[1] Walpole, vi. 204.   [2] Ibid. x. 371.   [3] Ibid. vii. 27, 429; x. 69.

is a good thing to sit by; she always understands what you say' (balanced by her own remark on Johnson, 'I love to sit by Dr. Johnson; he always entertains me').[1]

To a conversationalist like that one could forgive errors in her written communications—'vexation and fretting in the theater are the foundation of all Billious complaints I speak by expeariance. I have been fretted by managers till my gaul has overflowed like the river Nile'.[2]

Laetitia has a little to tell us of 'Mrs. Clive, the comic actress, who, I believe, by her agreeable or rather diverting society, pays rent for what is called little Strawberry Hill'. She was not entirely sympathetic to the lady. She praises 'her bounty to her indigent relations', and her 'perfect abstinence from spirituous liquors', but blames her for an occasional roughness in manner and speech:

Mrs. Clive visited my father and mother, but on my mother's running out of the house one evening, when she had called accidentally, to prevent her alighting from her carriage, as the small-pox had made its appearance amongst us and she knew Mrs. Clive not to have had it,—utterly insensible to the politeness of her attention at a moment of such anxiety, she roughly replied, 'it was not you I wanted to see; it was your husband; send him out'.

And I remember a reply of the same hue, which she made to two very decent respectful men, then in office as surveyors of the roads in the parish, on my father's sending them to her, as being the acting magistrate of the place, to demand some payment which she had refused:—it was in the laconic terms, 'By the living G—— I will not pay it.' I suppose this might destroy entirely all intercourse with our house, for she was of course compelled to break her oath. A strange expression to use of one of my own sex, but I have no choice.

I suppose it was to show 'what some actresses *can* do—what some *will* do',—that she worked for the Holbein chamber at Strawberry-hill, the carpet with blue tulips and yellow foliage.[3]

When Kitty Clive died, nearly a quarter of a century after the Hawkins family became her neighbours, Walpole put up

[1] Boswell, iv. 7, 243; v. 126.
[2] Forster, *Life and Times of Oliver Goldsmith*, Bk. III, ch. xvi.
[3] *Anecdotes*, 84.

an urn in the shrubbery of Little Strawberry Hill with these
lines on it:

> Ye smiles and jests, still hover round;
> This is mirth's consecrated ground.
> Here lived the laughter-loving dame,
> A matchless actress, Clive her name.
> The comic muse with her retired,
> And shed a tear when she expired.[1]

Another of Hawkins's neighbours was the satirical poet,
Paul Whitehead, who had 'purchased a cottage upon Twickenham Common, and from a design and under the inspection
of his friend Isaac Ware, at a small expence improved it into
an elegant dwelling'. Of this man, 'by nature a friendly and
kind-hearted man', Hawkins tells a good deal in his *Life of
Johnson*.[2]

Whitehead, of course, had been, in earlier years, one of the
notorious 'monks of Medmenham Abbey', and in other ways
there was a good deal to his discredit. 'In his conversation
there was little to praise; it was desultory, vociferous, and
profane; he had contracted a habit of swearing in his younger
years, which he retained to the latest.'

At Twickenham he never frequented divine service; and when
pressed by one of his friends there to shew himself at church, excused
himself by saying he was not settled. He was visited by very few of the
inhabitants of the village; but his house was open to all his London
friends, among whom were Mr. Hogarth, Isaac Ware the architect,
George Lambert and Hayman the painters, and Mr. Havard the
player, men who had spent all their lives in and about Covent-garden,
and looked upon it as the school of manners, and an epitome of the
world.[3]

However, Hawkins found him to be by nature a friendly and
kind-hearted man and one who 'manifested the goodness of
his nature in the exercise of kind offices, in healing breaches,
and composing differences between his poor neighbours'—and

---

[1] *D.N.B.* s.v. *Clive, Catharine.*
[2] 329–38. According to Boswell, Johnson 'undervalued' and 'slighted' Whitehead.
[3] Hawkins, *Johnson*, 335.

that is something! He had bought his cottage with the profits of his place of Deputy-Treasurer of the Chamber and in dying left a legacy to the superior under whom he had served:

> In a grateful sense of his obligations to lord Le Despenser, he directed, that after his decease, his heart, inclosed in a vessel for the purpose, should be presented to him, which being done, his lordship caused it to be deposited in his church of West Wycomb. It is reported that lord Le Despenser had afterwards the vessel with the heart deposited in the golden ball of the spire of the above-mentioned church.[1]

A certain astronomer whose many erudite works are still remembered (and sometimes consulted) was another friend and neighbour of the Hawkins family and from him Laetitia imbibed her earliest cosmological conceptions:

> Our vicar, at the time I mention, was Mr. George Costard, whose name is always preceded by the epithet 'learned'. He was a feeble, ailing, emaciated man, who had all the appearance of having sacrificed his health to his studies. His library, whither I was occasionally sent on an errand, strongly resembled, to my unformed judgment, the back-ground of Hogarth's design for that part of Hudibras which describes the knight's visit to Sidrophel. It was he who first gave me a hint that the world was at all approaching in form to round, and who undertook the unavailing task of persuading me to believe that it was not ten times bigger than the sun.[2]

One suspects that Costard had been spending his income on his hobby, for when he died at Twickenham in 1782 he left so little that it was necessary to raise a public subscription to pay for his funeral.[3]

At Hampton, about two miles from the Hawkins dwelling, was that of Garrick and his wife. They had had a house there since soon after their marriage thirteen years before, and six years later had bought the villa with which their name is still associated. It was on the common on one side and by the

---

[1] Ibid. 338. Baron Le Despenser (as Sir Francis Dashwood) was the founder of the 'Monks of Medmenham'. The church he rebuilt can be seen in the distance by road passengers from London to Oxford. The gilded ball holds niches for funerary urns, now mostly empty. Whitehead's heart was carried off by some curious collector in 1839.

[2] *Anecdotes*, 80.   [3] *Monthly Review*, 1787.

river on the other, and a part of the grounds, separated by a road from the other part and reached by a tunnel, had been embellished by the building of 'that little bit of affectation, more fitted to Drury Lane than to the little country villa— the Shakespeare Temple, with its famous Roubiliac statue of the bard, and a great collection of Shakespeare curiosities'.[1]

Laetitia tells us that 'Garrick was our neighbourly neighbour'.[2] The Hawkins and the Garricks seem to have been much together and in Hawkins's *Life of Johnson* and Laetitia's books there are a number of anecdotes illustrating this intimacy. In the former we read:

Living at Twickenham, at about two miles distance from his house at Hampton, I made him, as I frequently did when in the country, an afternoon visit. It was in the month of August, and I found him and Mrs. Garrick in the garden, eating figs. He complained that the wasps, which that year were very numerous, had left him very few; and talking farther about those noxious insects, told me he had heard, that a person near Uxbridge, having swallowed one of them in a draught of liquor, had died of the sting. I told him it was true; for that at a turnpike-meeting at Uxbridge I had dined with the apothecary that had attended him, and he had assured me of the fact.—'I believe it,' said Mr. Garrick, 'and have been persuading this lady', pointing to Mrs. Garrick, 'to do so; but I cannot convince her, and yet, she can believe the story of St. Ursula and the eleven thousand virgins!'—Mrs. Garrick, it is no secret, is of the Romish persuasion.[3]

Mrs. Garrick's credulity about those virgins seems to have been a good deal on her husband's mind; Laetitia, also, tells a story in which it comes in:

In a paddock, we had an oblong piece of water supplied by a sluice. Keeping poultry, this was very convenient for ducks; now and then there were also a few geese in this paddock. On a sudden, a prodigious consternation was perceived among the ducks; they were with great difficulty persuaded to take to the water, and when there, shuddered, grew wet, and were drowned. They were supposed diseased; others were bought at other places, but in vain; none of *our* ducks could swim.

---

[1] Fitzgerald, *Life of Garrick* (1899 edn.), 197.   [2] *Anecdotes*, 10.
[3] Hawkins, *Johnson*, 431.

Men of learning, and especially those of Twickenham's medical fraternity, were invited to explain the phenomenon, but admitted themselves completely baffled.

It was told of course to Mr. and Mrs. Garrick. Mrs. Garrick would not give credit to it. I believe she thought it some juggle in which the gardener had a concern. Garrick himself was not incredulous, and after a discussion he turned to my father, with his jocose impetuosity, and said, 'there's my wife who will not believe the story of these ducks, and yet she believes in the eleven thousand virgins.'[1]

Laetitia, years after, described Garrick's appearance as she remembered it:

I see him now in a dark blue coat, the button-holes bound with gold, a small cocked-hat laced with gold, his waistcoat very open, and his countenance never at rest, and, indeed, seldom his person; for in the relaxation of the country, he gave way to all his natural volatility, and with my father perfectly at ease, sometimes sitting on a table, and then, if he saw my brothers at a distance on the lawn, shooting off like an arrow out of a bow in a spirited chase of them round the garden.[2]

The little girl, however, felt a certain fear of Garrick who 'had a frown and spoke impetuously'.

We get some tales of Garrick's casual ways in whatever concerned business. Says Hawkins—'In all that related to the theatre he was very acute; but in business of other kinds a novice.' He tells how Garrick appealed to him for legal advice in the matter of some property which he wished to buy and had been promised but which, by a ruse, was being sold over his head to another person, so that he was 'in danger of being troubled with an ill neighbour'. It so happened that Hawkins had just been reading the life of Lord-keeper Guilford (1637–85) and had come across a case of a similar fraud in which Guilford had given a sane verdict:

Upon hearing Mr. Garrick's story, I searched farther, and found the case in law language in Vernon's Chancery Reports, and giving him a note of it, told him he might file a bill in chancery, and, on the authority of that determination, hope for relief.

[1] *Anecdotes*, 24.   [2] Ibid. 21.

About six months after, I being in town, a message came to me in the evening from Mr. Garrick, signifying, that his cause was to come on the next morning, and requesting me to furnish him with a note of a case that I had formerly mentioned to him as resembling his own.

Astonished at his remissness, and knowing that no time was to be lost, I immediately borrowed the book I had referred him to, and giving it my servant [*sic*], went with it to Drury-lane theatre, where, upon enquiry, I was informed, that he was busily employed in exhibiting an imitation of a spectacle then recent, the procession of the coronation of his present Majesty, in an afterpiece to the play for that night.

I waited in an outer room till all was over, when in entered Mr. and Mrs. Garrick, and, after giving him time to recover from his fatigue, I told him what I had been doing to help him in his distress, and produced the book; but his thoughts were so wholly taken up by the pageant he was come from, which seemed still to be passing before his eyes, that he could scarcely attend to me, but asked Mrs. Garrick twenty questions about it, how it went off, and whether she did not think the applause of the audience great. He then turned to me, took from me the book, and said he should lay it before his counsel.

The book was returned in a few days, but I heard nothing of the decree of the court till some months after, when meeting with his brother George, in the court of requests, I asked him how the cause had gone:—'Oh,' said he, 'with us:—the first purchase is decreed fraudulent, and the defendant is condemned in costs.'[1]

Another example of Garrick's appealing to Hawkins in trouble and then showing his indifference is the one of 'a wicked report that he and Mrs. Garrick lived so ill together as to be about to separate and that the proximate cause was his infidelity to her':

He complained of the injustice done him and the danger incurred by it of giving uneasiness to Mrs. Garrick. . . . This serious part of his complaint over, he dashed off in imagination to the various representations of this supposed fact that would probably be made by each inhabitant of Twickenham:—it was a most perfect piece of acting as to every imitable particular, even to the click of encouragement,— impossible to be written,—with which one gentleman, inclined to be

[1] Hawkins, *Johnson*, 429.

the hasty bearer of news about a village, would set off his horse again when he had disburdened his mind.[1]

Laetitia remembered when, as a very little girl, she had been walking on the common with her father and meeting Garrick, 'riding on his pretty pony', she had been moved to compassion by his 'lamenting the misery of being summoned to town in hot weather to play before the King of Denmark':

I thought him sincere and his case pitiable, till my father assured me that he was in reality very well pleased, and that what he groaned at was an honour paid to his talents.[2]

When Johnson's edition of Shakespeare appeared, four years after the Hawkins family settled in Twickenham, Garrick consulted his friend Hawkins about 'an insinuation in the preface that his friends had been backward in furnishing him with assistance':

Few there were who saw this passage, and knew that Mr. Garrick had the earliest editions of all Shakespeare's plays, but construed this into a reproach on him; in that sense he understood it, and it gave him great offence. To clear himself of the imputation of a conduct so unfriendly, he protested to me, that his collection had ever been accessible to Johnson, and that himself had signified, that any or all the books in it were at his service; and, farther to convince me, he, at the next visit I made him, called in his man Charles, and bade him relate to me his instructions respecting the use of his library, or the loan of books to Johnson. 'Sir,' said the man, 'I was told to let Mr. Johnson have whatever books he wanted; but he never applied for any.'[3]

Not long after Hawkins had acquired his country house at Twickenham he acquired also a new town house in Hatton Garden. Laetitia tells us:

Hatton Garden was then an esteemed situation for the gentry; no shops were permitted but at the lower end, and few parts of the town could vie with it. We lived in a part of it which afforded us, beside a wide street in front, and a sharp descent within a few yards, an opening behind overlooking a good garden, and, without the intervention

---

[1] *Anecdotes*, 27.   [2] Ibid. 21.   [3] Hawkins, *Johnson*, 444.

even of a chimney, a view of the fields, where Pentonville was afterwards built; but this situation, like all others in succession, is ruined
by trades and low associations.[1]

Shortly after taking up residence here he and his
neighbours were alarmed by a proposal which would have
placed Hatton Garden within the rules of the Fleet Prison.
Hawkins became active in opposition to this. His friend,
Horace Walpole, has recorded:

> In 1769 [should be 1764] he drew up the case of the parishioners of
> Hatton Garden against the agreement between the Bishop of Ely and
> the City for removing Fleet Street Prison to Ely House. This case
> induced the House of Commons to reject the bill; on which the parish
> gave Mr. Hawkins a large silver cup & Bishop Warburton wrote the
> inscription for it.[2]

The very polemic Warburton, a year or two before appointed to the See of Gloucester, would be likely to take an
interest in such a good fight. Possessing a London house he
was probably *au fait* with the affair. As the son of a town clerk
and himself an attorney (for he had served his five years
apprenticeship and is said to have been for a short time in
practice for himself), he would be able to appreciate Hawkins's handling of the business.

Warburton, however, had not always enjoyed Hawkins's
complete approval. Soon after the setting up in the Twickenham and Hatton Garden houses Hawkins had written to
Horace Walpole thanking him for 'the curious and most
acceptable present, the Anecdotes' (i.e. the first two volumes
of his *Anecdotes of Painting*, printed at his private press
at Strawberry Hill), and he alluded to the fact that 'the
Bp. of Gloucester has taken Fire at a Passage in it which to
several of his Friends he has declared he looks on as a *malignant unprovoked Attack on him*', so that 'with a Spirit as resolute
as that which animated *Becket* he has vowed revenge' (which

---

[1] *Memoirs*, i. 315.
[2] Notebook of Walpole, preserved in the Waller Collection; reproduced in
Walpole, Supp. ii, 116.

revenge he intended to take in his edition of Pope then in the press):

As much as I admire the Bp's Learning & Parts I never had the least Opinion of his Judgment and to sum up his Character I think that with all the Haughtiness of a *Scaliger* or a *Bentley* towards his Adversaries, he has shewn himself capable of such Meanness & Servility in his Dedication of his & Pope's Shakespeare to Mrs *Allen*, a plain well meaning Woman and nothing more, as no honest Man could practice. By Honesty I mean Sincerity & Integrity the want of which, in most of the Concerns of Life no Degree of Parts or Knowledge will atone for.[1]

Amongst the inhabitants of Hatton Garden was Hawkins's old friend Stanley (see p. 8) and we may suppose that this contributed to the keeping up of the friendship.

[1] Walpole, Supp. iii, 174. The 'Mrs. Allen' mentioned was the wife of the ingenious and munificent Ralph Allen, of Bath, a close friend of both Pope and Warburton. Warburton married Allen's niece and heir.

VI. *His activities as angler and angling authority and as magistrate*

HAWKINS, it appears, was an ardent angler and Twickenham, of course, afforded him the opportunity for the prosecution of his hobby:

He now indulged his taste for music and literature, and imbibing that which is every-where to be met with on the banks of the Thames, he became an enthusiastic lover of fly-fishing, and valued himself on throwing a line fourteen yards long, baited with a fly of his own making.[1]

The year he settled in this riverside house he published an edition of Walton's classic work on the subject. It had appeared in 1653, 1655, 1661, 1668, and 1676 (all these during Walton's lifetime). Then there had been no edition until that of the Rev. Moses Browne, which had been undertaken at Johnson's suggestion. Browne was vicar of Olney. Hawkins, hearing of his intention of producing an edition of Walton, wrote to him, offering material he had collected.[2] He received no reply and, hearing of Browne's intention of 'filing off the rust' (i.e. modernizing the style), wrote again and said that if that was so he himself should bring out an edition preserving the authentic text. That must have been some years before the period at which we have now arrived, as Browne's edition first appeared in 1750, then being reprinted in 1752 and 1759–60. Hawkins's edition appeared in 1760, and possibly that is the reason that Browne's made no further appearances. Hawkins's Twickenham friend, Horace Walpole, in June 1760 wrote to Sir David Dalrymple as follows:

There is a little book coming out, that will amuse you. It is a new

[1] *Anecdotes*, 140.
[2] Chalmers. See also references to Browne in Nichols, *Anecdotes*, ii. 436, and v. 36, 41, 43.

edition of Isaac Walton's *Complete Angler*, full of anecdotes and historic notes. It is published by Mr. Hawkins, a very worthy gentleman in my neighbourhood, but who, I could wish, did not think angling so very *innocent* an amusement. We cannot live without destroying animals, but shall we torture them for our sport—sport in their destruction? I met a rough officer at his house t'other day, who said he knew such a person was turning Methodist; for in the middle of conversation, he rose, and opened the window to let out a moth. I told him I did not know that the Methodists had any principle so good, and that I, who am certainly not on the point of becoming one, always did so too. One of the bravest and best men I ever knew, Sir Charles Wager, I have often heard declare he never killed a fly willingly. It is a comfortable reflection to me, that all the victories of last year have been gained since the suppression of the Bear Garden and prize-fighting; as it is plain, and nothing else would have made it so, that our valour did not singly and solely depend upon these two Universities.[1]

Here is a legal case in which Hawkins the angler and editor of our standard book on angling may be supposed to have been able to apply specialized knowledge. We hear of it in a footnote to one of his editions of Walton:

About the year 1770, upon the trial of an indictment before me at Hicks's Hall, a basket was produced in evidence, containing flounders that had been taken with unlawful nets in the river Thames, so small that scarce any one of them would cover a half-crown piece. The indictment was, for an affray, and an assault on a person authorized to sieze unstatutable nets; and the sentence of the offender, a year's imprisonment in Newgate.[2]

[1] Walpole, iv. 399. What, one wonders, did the compassionate Walpole think of the pious Walton's device, when using a frog as bait for pike, for keeping the poor creature 'long alive'?

Put your hook into his mouth, which you may easily do from the middle of April till August; and then the frog's mouth grows up, and he continues so for at least six months without eating, but is sustained none but He whose name is Wonderful knows how: I say, put your hook, I mean the arming-wire, through his mouth, and out at his gills; and then with a fine needle and silk sew the upper part of his leg, with only one stitch, to the arming-wire of your hook; or tie the frog's leg, above the upper joint, to the armed-wire; and, in so doing, use him as though you loved him, that is, harm him as little as you may possible, that he may live the longer (*Compleat Angler*, ed. Hawkins, Pt. I, ch. viii).

[2] Hawkins, *Angler*, Pt. I, ch. ii.

F

However ardent an angler Hawkins might be he once met a brother angler who excelled him. He tells us that 'Fishing for Barbel is, at best, but a dull recreation', for 'they are a sullen fish, and bite but slowly', and then goes on:

Living some years ago in a village on the banks of the Thames, I was used, in the summer months, to be much in a boat on the river. It chanced that, at Shepperton, where I had been for a few days, I frequently passed an elderly gentleman in his boat, who appeared to be fishing, at different stations for Barbel. After a few salutations had passed between us, and we were become a little acquainted, I took occasion to enquire of him what diversion he had met with.

'Sir,' says he, 'I have had but bad luck to-day, for I fish for Barbel, and you know they are not to be caught like Gudgeons.'

'It is very true,' answered I; 'but what you want in tale, I suppose you make up in weight.'

'Why, Sir,' says he, 'that is just as it happens: it is true I like the sport, and love to catch fish, but my great delight is in *going after them*. I'll tell you what, Sir,' continued he; 'I am a man in years, and have used the sea all my life (he had been an India captain), but I mean to go no more; and have bought that little house which you see there (pointing to it), for the sake of fishing. I get into this boat (which he was then mopping) on a Monday morning, and fish on till Saturday night, for Barbel, as I told you, for that is my delight; and this I have done for a month together, and in all that while have not had one bite.'[1]

There is one matter in which Walton had been remiss and which impelled his editor to supply a want in his book—the making of rods of all kinds, which subject supplies him with material for one of his prodigiously long footnotes. It even seems as though this worthy magistrate-angler had a tender spot for the poaching-angler, for he includes suggestions for making a 'bag-rod which the angler may easily conceal and which does not proclaim to all the world where he is going'.[2]

It is pleasing to know that whatever Horace Walpole and other kindly people might think of Hawkins's encouragement of the practice of angling, one of Hawkins's own children, his younger son, Henry, although 'entertaining a decided aver-

sion to the sport', being employed by his father in editorial
work, was rewarded by advantage to his moral nature:

> There are passages in the work itself which no heart awake to the
> beauty of virtue, can read without at least wishing to be virtuous; nor
> could I transcribe my father's commentary on these, without improve-
> ment in various points of moral prudence and religious attention.[1]

The new edition of Walton became popular and was reprinted
during Hawkins's lifetime and frequently later (1775–84–
92–97, 1808–15–26–36–93). Laetitia, when old enough,
became her father's habitual amanuensis. Of this book she
says:

> It was this passion for angling which led him to bestow his time
> and attention on the small volume, 'Izaak Walton's Complete Angler'.
> What might be its popularity before he published his enlarged edition
> of it, with notes, I know not: I can only say, that it has been, ever
> since I can remember, a general favourite; and that while my father
> lived, it, from time to time, added to my toil by the demand of a new
> edition. This, I confess, was greatly sweetened by the natural charm of
> the work itself, even to one not only acquainted with the subject, but
> entertaining a decided aversion to the sport.

In 1761 Hawkins became a Middlesex magistrate. As such
he was entitled to certain fees from some of those who required
his services. At first he remitted them, but later, finding that
in doing this he had encouraged litigation, he accepted them,
handing each year's proceeds to the clergyman of the parish
for relief of the poor.

Another honour was about this time, we are told, offered to
Hawkins:

> He was now solicited by the editors of Shakespeare to contribute
> his acute observations to their labours. He was of consideration sufficient
> to be offered the degree of Doctor of Laws by the University of Oxford,
> and was one of the select few in the world of 'belles lettres', to whom
> a copy of the grand quarto edition of Sir Thomas Hanmer's Shake-
> speare, printed at the University press, was presented.[2]

---

[1] *Anecdotes*, 141.
[2] Ibid. 143. Hanmer (Speaker of the House of Commons, 1714–15) had

If any doctorate was offered it was certainly not the Doctor of Laws (LL.D.; a degree always unknown to Oxford) but the Doctor of Civil Law (D.C.L.).[1] But, on receiving the offer of an honorary degree, was Hawkins the kind of man to refuse it? We find him later (see p. 111) exerting himself to obtain the prefix 'Sir' to his name and at this earlier period he would surely not have disdained the prefix 'Dr.'[2]

Another somewhat unexpected statement of Laetitia's is to the effect that 'The Royal Society had expressed a wish to add him to their number': as usual no date is given, but the implication is that it was about the same period as the alleged offer of a doctorate by the University of Oxford. She tells us (surely very oddly!) that 'his answer was that being no mathematician, he thought himself unworthy the distinction', and she goes on to express surprise 'that his father should not have communicated to him this species of knowledge':

I must confess that which added much to my labour, that a viler

published his edition of Shakespeare, in 6 volumes, in 1743–4. It is condemned by Horace Walpole in a letter to Horace Mann, of 14 Jan. 1745:

'Sir Thomas Hanmer has at last published his Shakespeare: he has made several alterations, but they will be the less talked of, as he has not marked in the text, margin, or notes, where or why he has made any change; but everybody must be obliged to collate it with other editions. One most curiously absurd alteration I have been told. In *Othello*, it is said of Cassio, "a Florentine, one almost damned in a fair *wife*". It happens that there is no other mention in the play of Casssio's wife. Sir Thomas has altered it—how do you think?—no, I should be sorry if you could think how—"almost damned in a fair *phiz*!"—what a tragic word! and what sense!'

There were reprints (presumably revisions) in 1744, 1745, 1747, 1748, 1750–1, 1760, and then the one to which Hawkins contributed in 1770–1. This last was edited by Thomas Hawkins—later the author of *The Origin of the English Drama*: whether he was a relative of Sir John Hawkins is not known to the present writer; presumably had he been so Laetitia would have mentioned it.

The preface of that last edition mentioned above makes acknowledgements to Percy and to Dr. Thomas Warton, and then to:

'John Hawkins esquire of Twickenham; to whom was submitted the inspection of the additional glossary: which the editor begs leave thus publicly to acknowledge.'

[1] In Sept. 1760 the *Gentleman's Magazine* reports the conferring by Oxford of the LL.D. on the great Clive; this description of the law degree is common.

[2] In Chalmers, Oxford's alleged offer of a degree is allotted to a considerably later date—that of the publication of the *History of Music*—'The University of Oxford, in consequence of its publication, made him a voluntary offer of the degree of doctor of laws, which he had reasons for declining, and afterwards paid him the compliment of requesting his picture'. (As to the picture see p. 183.)

arithmetician is seldom to be found:—for convenience, he made me a tolerably good one. I know not that the study of mathematics would have aided him; for Mr. Munckley, who was deep in the latter, was so ill-practised in the former, that he used to call Lady Hawkins his multiplication-table.[1]

In 1764 there was a proposal to remove Newgate Prison. Hawkins, whilst not necessarily opposing this, took strong exception to the suggestion that the cost should be borne 'by the County and City in the proportion of two to one'. On behalf of his fellow County Magistrates and citizens he prepared a document cogently setting forth the grounds of the objection—*The Case of the County of Middlesex with respect to the Gaol of Newgate*. It opens as follows:

The gaol of Newgate is, and for upwards of 600 years hath been, a common prison and place of security for felons and other offenders; and, so far as it tends to secure and bring to punishment those who, by acts of rapine and violence, endanger the persons and properties of mankind, it seems to be of public use and benefit; notwithstanding which, the citizens of London, and several tradesmen inhabiting near the said gaol, have of late laboured to represent it as a most dangerous nuisance.[2]

The reasons given for this allegation of the prison being a nuisance are that it was 'ill-constructed, close, and incommodious, and unfit for the reception of prisoners', that at the opening of every session a great number of prisoners were crowded into it, and that 'the prisoners have frequently been visited with a malignant disease called the gaol-distemper, whereby the health of all persons resorting to the sessions house must be endangered'. This was not at all an exaggeration, as many contemporary accounts show us.[3]

The county, he says, has never heretofore been charged with any expense concerning Newgate. It is true that, just

---

[1] *Anecdotes*, 144. The 'Mr. Munckley' who is mentioned here was Nicholas Munckley, brother of Hawkins's former house-mate (see pp. 7–8): his mathematical capacity appears to have been of a curiously limited order.

[2] *Memoirs*, i. 318.

[3] See Besant, *London in the Eighteenth Century*, 538 et seq., for a convenient collection of some of these. They are appalling!

occasionally, the Middlesex magistrates had found it necessary to commit prisoners for felonies to Newgate, rather than
to other gaols, but 'the exceptions are hardly worth opposing
to the general rule'. And 'at the County Sessions, at Hicks's
Hall, eight times a year, are tried double the number of
prisoners tried at the Old Bailey and whilst awaiting trial
incarcerated in Newgate...'. And so on!

That disease is rampant in the gaol is not denied and a
horrible instance is given—an outbreak fourteen years earlier
in which 'two of the King's Judges and the Mayor of London
lost their lives'.

This misfortune did indeed awaken the attention of the city, and
led the magistrates into a survey of the prison in which the seeds of
this infection had long been treasured up. The consequence of this
survey was a discovery of a vast quantity of filth, which had been many
years accumulating in the several apartments of the prison, of such
various kinds, as left very little room to doubt of the causes of that
contagion, to which the above calamity was owing.

Upon this the city set about a work, which it would have been
happy if they had thought of sooner: viz. the cleansing the prison; the
filth was collected together and, for very obvious reasons, the night
was chosen as the properest time for its removal to some distance from
the town; and to one or other of the adjacent fields, it was carried by
cartloads, and buried, and, through the Providence of God, since that
time, no such misfortune has happened. Thus, however plausibly the
citizens may argue from the supposed danger of infection, from a
distemper to which the gaol of Newgate is said to be subject, it seems
that that danger may be averted by methods less expensive, than a total
demolition of the fabric.[1]

Hawkins then goes on to declare that a source of revenue
has existed which, had it been kept for such purposes as this
rebuilding, would have abundantly covered the cost. The
city received sums as fines from persons nominated as
Sheriffs but refusing to serve. This gave the Lord Mayor a
'power, not possessed by the King himself', of 'raising money
on the subject, whenever, and to what amount he pleases'.
The inhabitants of the county, on whose behalf Hawkins is

[1] *Memoirs,* i. 324.

speaking, do not endorse this system, but it is pointed out that during the past ninety years the money received in this way has amounted to nearly £148,750 and that this would amply suffice for all needs of repair and rebuilding. 'The citizens might have reasoned in this way: money has been raised by sheriff's fines; the strength of the prison is the sheriff's security; let therefore the person who serves the office avail himself of the default of him who has declined it; and let the money so raised be a fund for the maintenance of that prison, without which no man could serve it at all.'

Many similar statements and arguments follow, building up to an unanswerable case, and as Laetitia tells us, 'It had its proper effect'.

It may be remarked, in passing, that Hawkins, who in much of his later writing showed himself to be a literary rambler, in this document goes straight to the mark. His drafting of it is, indeed, admirable.

The prison was burnt down during the Gordon Riots sixteen years later and in its rebuilding improvements were no doubt introduced.

Twickenham, it seems, with all its charms as a place of residence lacked one—that of security. In that it was not alone. 'In spite of repressive measures, until the end of the eighteenth century the conditions alike of London and the provinces were deplorable. Robbery and violence were rampant everywhere, highwaymen infested the roads, footpads lurked in the streets, whilst, but too often, both watchmen and innkeepers were accessories to the commission of crime.'[1] Laetitia, half-a-century or more later, when her father was dead, alludes pointedly to the cruel unconcern with which 'the legislature leave such a village as Twickenham in an utterly lawless state': she says that in that otherwise delightful retreat, crime was still rampant, and does not hesitate to declare that even Sabbath-breaking went on unchecked![2]

[1] *Encyclopaedia Britannica*, 14th edn., s.v. 'Police'.
[2] Cf. Mark Twain, who somewhere sagely warns us against even small sins. He says that an unthinking man may begin with a simple murder, go on from that to burglary and, if not checked in his downward course, end up by breaking the

Two or three miles off we *may* chance to find redress for *great* grievances; but for general and daily police it is vain to seek. So near the metropolis, we need looking after. Distinguished by rank, wealth, and the highest tone of society, we need to be guarded while we are off guard; and offering, as we do, little short of premiums to beggars, we take exercise in peril almost of our lives. Surely every village should have its magistrate:—and surely there ought to be some authority to prevent or punish the uniform breach of a commandment in employing gardeners and carpenters in the subordinate classes, to trim up flower-beds, and do small repairs, before church time on Sundays.[1]

The Hawkins establishment suffered from the unfaithful-ness of its own servants:

It would be beneath the reader's attention, were I to relate what I now myself began to notice as discouragements. To say nothing of the universality of the pilfering system—of the disappointment of seeing fruit on the trees planted by the hand of the owner, just ready for presents or the entertainment of friends, and, when called for, hearing 'they had all drapt off',—which was borne till the vehicle into which they had drapt, was detected in the coach-yard by sunrise; to find the fish-pond ready dragged when carp were wanted;—and, on inquiry for the gardener, hearing that he was gone drunk to Kingston-fair to sell his master's saddle-horse for his own profit.

All these things are common; but a singular nuisance to us poor souls![2]

Horace Walpole, in 1778, complained of the dangers of Twickenham:

Poor Mrs. Clive [see p. 54] has been robbed again in her own lane, as she was last year, and has got the jaundice, she thinks, with the fright. I don't make a visit without a blunderbuss, so one might as well be invaded by the French.[3]

A deplorable outrage was the following (which, however, as we shall see, was properly resented).

Sabbath. But Mark Twain probably stole this idea from De Quincey's *Murder considered as one of the Fine Arts*—'If once a man indulges himself in murder, very soon he comes to think little of robbing, and from robbing he comes next to drinking and Sabbath-breaking, and from that to incivility and procrastination'. (De Quincey's essay appeared in 1827, i.e. three years later than Laetitia's book so that it is at any rate possible that he got the idea from her).

[1] *Memoirs*, i. 18.   [2] *Anecdotes*, 142.   [3] Walpole, x. 267.

Hawkins and his wife were on the road from London to Twickenham when their lives were seriously endangered by the brutality of a stage-coachman, who wantonly drove his heavy-laden vehicle against their chariot, and with so much violence, as to bend the wheel-iron, and wrench the handle from the door.

On their coachman's remonstrating, he was silenced by the grossest abuse, and blinded by two cuts across the face with the whipcord. The by-standers most willingly encouraged a disposition to punish such an unprovoked outrage: they informed my father of the man's name, and to what place the coach belonged; and some could add that the driver was a nuisance on the road.

Hawkins determined that, 'at any trouble and expense, he would make an example of such a public culprit', and 'went the shortest way to do so'.

But the man got intelligence of his danger, and first kept out of sight, hiring a man to drive for him, and then changed his situation, and was no more seen on that road.

But my father knew mankind well enough to surmise that, the sense of danger once abated, he would revisit his old haunts. He therefore kept Lord Mansfield's tipstaves on the watch at the White-horse Cellar, and one of them had the satisfaction of seeing him enter the kitchen, where he was soon recognised by those of his own stamp. Each told what had occurred since they last met; and he had to account for his temporary invisibility, which he did by an exulting description of his heroic deed, particularly dwelling on the vengeance he had taken on the coachman.

He had now furnished evidence in abundance—he was beckoned out, and handcuffed; and at the next quarter sessions tried, Sir J.H. appearing only as prosecutor: his sentence was six months' imprisonment in Newgate.[1]

It is surprising to learn that not only was the culprit thus suitably punished, but Hawkins's coachman was subjected to 'a small fine'—presumably being adjudged to have contributed in some small measure, by his manner of driving, to the initial exasperation of his bellicose colleague.

[1] *Memoirs,* i. 22.

There are those nowadays whose sentimentality inclines them to sympathy with every sufferer, however well-merited may be his suffering, and the late eighteenth century was no less prone to this ill-applied compassion than the twentieth.

As soon as the sentence was carried into effect, my father was attacked on all sides with letters and petitions; and probably by some of those who had volunteered their evidence. It was strongly urged that the time of his imprisonment would preclude him from the gains of Christmas; but nothing speeding, he, as a *dernier ressort*, sent my father a brace of patridges!

The false compassion of the present day may blame this as vindictive, but Sir J.H. had the thanks of many for persevering in an act of justice.[1]

[1] *Memoirs*, i. 23.

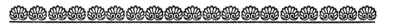

VII. *He becomes a member of Johnson's 'Literary Club'* (1763)

In 1756 (or thereabouts) the Ivy Lane Club had quietly faded out of existence and about seven years later (in 1763, Hawkins says) Johnson, prompted by Reynolds, brought into being another club, meeting at the Turk's Head, Gerard Street. Johnson had now reached a height of distinction far beyond that which he enjoyed when the earlier club was founded. *The Rambler* had appeared in 1750, the Dictionary in 1755, *The Idler* in 1758–60, *Rasselas* in 1759. In 1755 had come the M.A. from Oxford and in 1762 the government pension. And all the time Johnson had been coming into touch with more and more men of literary, artistic, political, and social interests and pursuits, whose company was very congenial to him. Hawkins records:

Johnson had now considerably extended the circle of his acquaintance, and added to the number of his friends sundry persons of distinguished eminence: among them were, Sir Joshua Reynolds, Mr. Edmund Burke, Mr. Beauclerk, and Mr. Langton. With these he passed much of his time, and was desirous of being still closer connected. How much he delighted in convivial meetings, how he loved conversation, and how sensibly he felt the attractions of a tavern, has already been mentioned; and it was but a natural consequence of these dispositions that he should wish for frequent opportunities of indulging them in a way that would free him from domestic restraints, from the observance of hours, and a conformity to the regimen of families.

A tavern was the place for these enjoyments, and a weekly club was instituted for his gratification and the mutual entertainment and delight of its several members. The first movers in this association were Johnson and Sir Joshua Reynolds: the number of persons included in it was nine: the place of meeting was the Turk's-head in Gerrard-street: the day Monday in every week, and the hour of assembling seven in the evening. To this association I had the honour of being invited. The members were,

Johnson,	Mr. Topham Beauclerk,
Sir Joshua Reynolds,	Mr. Bennet Langton,
Mr. Edmund Burke,	Mr. Anthony Chamier, and
Christ. Nugent, M.D.,	Myself.[1]
Oliver Goldsmith, M.B.	

The original intention, as we have just seen, was to limit the membership of the club to nine, but later the number was increased. 'The hours which Johnson spent in this society', says Hawkins, 'seemed to be the happiest in his life':

He would often applaud his own sagacity in the selection of it, and was so constant at our meetings as never to absent himself. It is true, he came late, but then he stayed late, for, as has been already said of him, he little regarded hours. Our evening toast was the motto of Padre Paolo, 'Esto perpetua'. A lady, distinguished by her beauty, and taste for literature, invited us two successive years to a dinner at her house. Curiosity was her motive, and possibly a desire of intermingling with our conversation the charms of her own. She affected to consider us as a set of literary men, and perhaps gave the first occasion for distinguishing the society by the name of the Literary Club, an appellation which it never assumed to itself.[2]

A short account may here be given of those fellow clubmen of Hawkins and of his associations with them.

Laetitia says that she does not know when Hawkins became acquainted with REYNOLDS, but that he used to visit their house before he lived in Leicester Fields, which would push the date back some years before the Club began to bring the two regularly into one another's company. It rather surprises one, by the way, to find her stating in this connexion that her father 'always lived in great intimacy with artists' and that he was 'very fond of being with them while they worked'.

[1] Hawkins, *Johnson*, 414.

[2] Hannah More (*Memoirs*, 1783) tells us that the bluestocking Mrs. Vesey, whose husband had now been elected to the club, also, at a later period, entertained the members. She had 'a select society which meets at her house every other Tuesday, on the day on which the Turk's Head Club dine together. In the evening they all meet at Mrs. Vesey's, with the addition of such other company as it is difficult to find elsewhere' (see also Boswell, iii. 425).

She remembered being, as a child of ten or eleven, 'drest in pink satin and muslin' for a party in the Leicester Fields house, to which, on the invitation of Reynolds's sister (known as 'Mrs. Reynolds', likewise a painter), her mother took her, and says that 'after tea we juniors accompanied the younger of Sir Joshua's nieces, the then Misses Palmer', into his painting room, where she stole, for the service of her aunt, 'all the colours she could scrape from his esel' (footnoting the last word to convince the world of an etymological theory of hers which demanded a revision of the usual spelling), and she recalls a conversation between Reynolds and her father in which the painter admitted his error in the use of a certain unlasting material[1] and another conversation in which, walking in St. James's Park, he 'spoke feelingly of his happiness in being able to 'get his bread' by doing that which, 'of all things, he best loved to do'.

That, despite the intimacy, Reynolds did not wholly admire Hawkins's character, we have already been plainly told (see p. xii).

BURKE was, from his conversational powers, a most valuable member of such a gathering as we are considering. Johnson said, 'Burke is the only man whose common conversation corresponds with the general fame he has in the world.' Of the relations between Burke and Hawkins something will be said a page or two later. (We do not hear of Burke frequenting the house of Hawkins: in that of Hawkins's rival, the genial Burney, he was sometimes to be seen.)

Dr. NUGENT (Burke's father-in-law) had some years before attracted notice by his researches into the nature and cure of hydrophobia. He had had a fashionable practice in Bath, and had removed to London only about the time that this club was founded and had apparently at once been seized on as a desirable member. As a Roman Catholic he could not, on certain days, eat the same dinner as the other club members

---

[1] This 'unlasting material' was, as Laetitia explains, the colour carmine. The present-day complaint is as to Reynolds's use of bitumen, which has in time broken the surface of some of his pictures into deep crevasses.

and evidently Johnson sometimes joined him, since Mrs.
Piozzi, in her *Anecdotes of the Late Samuel Johnson*, recalls
Johnson's 'painful sensations' at the sight of an omelette, soon
after Nugent's death, and his exclamation, 'Ah, my poor dear
friend! I shall never eat omelette with thee again!—quite in an
agony.'

Nugent seems to have been one of the most loved members
of the club. Hawkins, in his *Life of Johnson*, speaks of him as
'an ingenious, sensible, and learned man, of easy conversation,
and elegant manners'.

Of GOLDSMITH something is said elsewhere in this book
(p. 118).

TOPHAM BEAUCLERK (though not only gay but dissipated and immoral) nevertheless enjoyed the admiration
of the serious and respectable Hawkins, who says of
him:

> Travel, and a long residence at Rome and at Venice, had given the
> last polish to his manners, and stored his mind with entertaining infor-
> mation. In painting and sculpture, his taste and judgement were accurate,
> in classic literature, exquisite; and in the knowledge of history, and
> the study of antiquities, he had few equals. His conversation was of the
> most excellent kind; learned, witty, polite, and, where the subject
> required it, serious; and over all his behaviour there beamed such a
> sunshine of chearfulness and good humour, as communicated itself
> to all around him.[1]

And when, on Beauclerk's death, the remark was made to
Johnson, 'Our Club has had a great loss since we last met',
the rejoinder was, 'A loss that perhaps the whole nation could
not repair', whilst on another occasion Johnson remarked
that, 'Beauclerk's talents were those which he had felt himself more disposed to envy, than those of any whom he had
known.'[2]

Of the charms of LANGTON, a frequent visitor at the Hawkins's house, there is abundant description in Laetitia

---

[1] Hawkins, *Johnson*, 422.

[2] Boswell, iii, 424. Boswell says that Beauclerk was 'too polite to offend Johnson
by sallies of infidelity or licentiousness' (i. 249).

Hawkins's *Anecdotes* and her *Memoirs*. She quotes her brother Henry as saying:

His amiable qualities, indeed, are sufficiently known to the world, and, no doubt, are highly appreciated.... He had a high relish for classical learning, and had read much; and having great powers of memory, he could quote with very great effect. His recollections of 'Hudibras', and his humorous quotations from it, were in the highest degree amusing.

He was superabundant in anecdote of all kinds, and could with equal facility enliven general conversation with stories of the greatest humour, or conversation of a graver cast, with narratives of weight and importance.

His talk was never frivolous;—something profitable might always be got from it; and a young man who might spend an hour in Mr. Langton's company, could scarcely fail to have his love for attainments increased, and his ardour in the pursuit of them stimulated, by contemplating the stores of instruction and amusement which the mind may acquire by the due cultivation of its powers.[1]

Laetitia herself says of Langton:

What nourishment he might take in his family, I know not, but from a dinner-party, he might have risen fasting, and unconscious of it, such was the perpetual flow of his conversation, and so incessant were the claims made on him.[2]

Hawkins has this to tell us of the remaining member of this distinguished little group:

MR. ANTHONY CHAMIER was descended from a French Protestant family, that has produced one or more very eminent divines, and were refugees in this country at the end of the last century. He was bred to the profession of a stock-broker; but, having had a liberal education, his deportment and manner of transacting business distinguished him

---

[1] *Anecdotes*, 318.

[2] *Memoirs*, i. 278 (see also 144, 234, 271, 276, 281, 300). There is an admirable chapter on Langton in Hill's *Dr. Johnson, his Friends and Critics*, and much about him in the *Diary and Letters of Madame D'Arblay*, for Langton was as great a favourite with the family of Burney as with that of Burney's rival. Boswell, however, does not always speak well of him, and his treatment of him in the *Life of Johnson* is far from kind, his foibles and bad housekeeping coming in for constant criticism under very thin disguise. He is described anonymously as 'one of our friends', 'a gentleman of our acquaintance', 'a worthy friend', &c., more than a score of times: even his learning is laughed at ('a very learned man whose learning did not lie straight'). Langton, on the whole, seems to have borne this somewhat malicious treatment with good humour.

greatly from most others of that calling. He had acquired a knowledge of the modern languages, particularly of the Spanish, in the study whereof he took great delight.

His connections, at his setting out in the world, were of the best kind, for very early in his life, he was employed by those liberal-minded brothers, the Van Necks, whose riches, and general muni-ficence, have ranked them in the same class of wealthy men with the Fuggers of Augsburg, a company of money-dealers, who, in their time, held the balance of the Antwerp exchange, and by their transac-tions at that mart, influenced the politics of all the courts of Europe.

By his dealings in the funds, and, it was supposed, with the advantage of intelligence which, previous to the conclusion of the peace before the last, he had obtained, he acquired such a fortune as enabled him, though young, to quit business, and become, what indeed he seemed by nature intended for, a gentleman.[1]

Some years after the formation of the Club Chamier became a Member of Parliament and after a time he held office—first as Deputy-Secretary at War and then as Under-Secretary of State.

Mrs. Thrale speaks of Johnson's delight in the club meet-ings as follows (at a later date when the membership had been somewhat enlarged):

Mr. Johnson had ever since I knew him an enthusiastick fondness for Poetry, indeed for all sorts of Literature; and had a respect for a Club he belonged to, that was little less than ridiculous; our Club, Madam said he, is a Society which can scarcely be matched in the World—we have Reynolds for Painting, Goldsmith for Poetry, Percy for Antiquities, Nugent for Physick; Chamier for Trade, Politics and all Money Concerns; Mr. Burke for Oratory, Mr. Beauclerk for Polite Literature, Dyer for Modern History & Travels, Chambers for the Law, Langton for Ecclesiastical History & indeed all Branches of Learning, Sir John Hawkins for Judicature & ancient Musick.[2]

One reason for restricting the membership to a small number of men, all having something in common, has been thus explained:

It was intended, according to Malone (*Account of Reynolds*, lxxxiii),

---

[1] Hawkins, *Johnson*, 422.
[2] *Thraliana*, ed. Balderston, Dec. 1777 (i. 187–8).

REYNOLDS and JOHNSON. Hawkins 'always lived in great intimacy with artists' and he and his daughter used to visit Reynolds and his sister in their Leicester Square house (see p. 76). Johnson and Reynolds were the 'first movers' in the institution of the 'Literary Club' (see p. 75).

GOLDSMITH and BURKE. Hawkins was little appreciative of Goldsmith, whom he pityingly described as 'This idiot in the affairs of the world!' As for Burke, the club's most accomplished conversationalist, Hawkins's rudeness to him gave offence to his fellow members and led to his own resignation.

that the club should consist of such men as that, if only two of them chanced to meet, they should be able to entertain each other sufficiently, without wishing for more company with whom to pass an evening. 'This,' writes Percy to Boswell (Nichols's *Illustrations*, vii. 311), 'I have heard Johnson mention as the principal or avowed reason for the small number of members to which for many years it was limited.'[1]

As has been mentioned, this principle was gradually departed from; the club was enlarged to twenty members, and in 1777 Johnson wrote to Boswell as follows:

It is proposed to augment our club from twenty to thirty, of which I am glad; for as we have several in it whom I do not much like to consort with, I am for reducing it to a mere miscellaneous collection of conspicuous men, without any determinate character.[2]

According to Hawkins, Johnson's behaviour at this club (which, it may be remembered, had at the earlier one been sometimes overbearing) was now exemplary:

At these our meetings, Johnson, as indeed he did every where, led the conversation, yet was he far from arrogating to himself that superiority, which, some years before, he was disposed to contend for. He had seen enough of the world to know, that respect was not to be extorted, and began now to be satisfied with that degree of eminence to which his writings had exalted him. This change in his behaviour was remarked by those who were best acquainted with his character, and it rendered him an easy and delightful companion.[3]

Hawkins has something to tell us of a frustrated ambition of one of his Twickenham neighbours:

The institution of this society was in the winter of 1763, at which time Mr. Garrick was abroad with his wife, who, for the recovery of her health, was sent to the baths at Padua. Upon his return, he was informed of our association, and trusted, that the least intimation of a desire to come among us, would procure him a ready admission, but in this he was mistaken. Johnson consulted me upon it, and when I could find no objection to receiving him, exclaimed:—'He will disturb us by his buffoonery';—and afterwards so managed matters, that he was never formally proposed, nor, by consequence, ever admitted. . . .

---

[1] Forster, *Goldsmith*, Bk. III, ch. 8.   [2] Boswell, iii. 106.
[3] Hawkins, *Johnson*, 424.

Garrick took his rejection very patiently, and shewed his resentment of it no otherwise, than by enquiring of me from time to time how we went on at the club. He would often stop at my gate, in his way to and from Hampton, with messages from Johnson relating to his Shakespeare, then in the press, and ask such questions as these:—'Were you at the club on Monday night?'—'What did you talk of?'—'Was Johnson there?'—'I suppose he said something of Davy—that Davy was a clever fellow in his way, full of convivial pleasantry; but no poet, no writer, ha?'—I was vexed at these enquiries, and told him, that this perpetual solicitude about what was said of him, was unnecessary, and could only tend to disturb him; that he might well be content with that share of the public favour which he enjoyed, that he had nothing to do but to possess it in quietness, and that too great an anxiety to obtain applause would provoke envy, and tend to intercept, if not totally deprive him of it.

Johnson's objection to the admission of Garrick may seem to be cynical, and to have arisen from jealousy or resentment, but it admits of palliation: the truth is, that Garrick was no disquisitor; his reading had been confined, and he could contribute but little to the pleasures of sober and instructive conversation. Even his knowledge of the world was derived through the medium of the dramatic writers, who, all men know, are not guides to be trusted.[1]

According to Boswell, however, Garrick's election was merely delayed. He contradicts Hawkins as follows:

In justice both to Mr. Garrick and Dr. Johnson, I think it necessary to rectify this mis-statement. The truth is, that not very long after the institution of our club, Sir Joshua Reynolds was speaking of it to Garrick. 'I like it much, (said he,) I think I shall be of you.'

When Sir Joshua mentioned this to Dr. Johnson, he was much displeased with the actor's conceit. *'He'll be of us,* (said Johnson) how does he know we will *permit* him? The first Duke in England has no right to hold such language.' However, when Garrick was regularly proposed some time afterwards, Johnson, though he had taken a momentary offence at his arrogance, warmly and kindly supported him, and he was accordingly elected, was a most agreeable member, and continued to attend our meetings to the time of his death.[2]

A prominent member of the London clergy, a Chaplain to the

---

[1] Hawkins, *Johnson,* 425–8.   [2] Boswell, 480.

King afterwards hanged for forgery, also wished to be a member: of him Hawkins gives us one of his candid accounts:

Besides Mr. Garrick, there were others that were desirous of becoming members of this our club, the fame whereof had spread abroad, and induced many, who hoped to acquire a reputation for literature, to wish for an admission among us. That unfortunate divine, as he was called, Dr. William Dodd, was one of the number, and made a secret effort for this purpose.

This person, at that time, dwelt with his wife in an obscure corner of Hounslow heath, near a village called Worton; but kept, in a back lane near him, a girl who went by the name of Kennedy. His pretensions to learning, and especially to classical erudition, were very great; and he had in his house a few young gentlemen, who, at very expensive rates, were committed to his care, as to an academy, for instruction. A brother of his wife's rented some land of me, and of him I learned from time to time many particulars respecting his character and manner of living, which latter, as he represented it, was ever such as his visible income would no way account for. He said that he was the most importunate suitor for preferment ever known; and that himself had been the bearer of letters and messages to great men, soliciting promotion to vacant livings, and had hardly escaped kicking down stairs.

Dodd's wish to be received into our society was conveyed to us only by a whisper, and that being the case, all opposition to his admission became unnecessary.[1]

Hawkins himself had now, apparently, developed some of those qualities that were in time to make him so generally unpopular, and, indeed, but for Johnson's friendship this would probably have stood in the way of his election. Fanny Burney, in her Diary, reporting a conversation in 1778 at the Thrales' house at Streatham, says:

The next name that was started was that of Sir John Hawkins; and Mrs. Thrale said, 'Why, now, Dr. Johnson, he is another of those whom you suffer nobody to abuse but yourself: Garrick is one too; for, if any other person speaks against him, you brow-beat him in a minute.'

[1] Hawkins, *Johnson*, 434. Many more important men than Dodd had applied for admission to the Club and been actually blackballed, e.g. (to name only a few) Gibbon, Bishop Shipley, Malone, Lord Palmerston (all of whom were subsequently admitted), Dr. Parr, Lord Camden, Bishop Porteus, Dr. Lort, Samuel Rogers, Hoppner, and Kemble (see Boswell and *Annals of the Club*, 1914, p. 133).

'Why madam', answered he, 'they don't know when to abuse him, and when to praise him; I will allow no man to speak ill of David that he does not deserve; and as to Sir John, why really I believe him to be an honest man at the bottom; but to be sure he is penurious, and he is mean, and it must be owned he has a degree of brutality, and a tendency to savageness, that cannot easily be defended. . . . He said that Sir John and he once belonged to the same club, but that as he eat no supper, after the first night of his admission he desired to be excused paying his share.

'And was he excused?'

'O yes; for no man is angry at another for being inferior to himself. We all scorned him, and admitted his plea. For my part, I was such a fool as to pay my share for wine, though I never tasted any. But Sir John was a most *unclubable* man.'[1]

Hawkins eventually retired from the club. His own account of his secession and the accounts of others do not quite tally. He says:

As I was the only seceder from this society, my withdrawing myself from it seems to require an apology. We seldom got together till nine: the enquiry into the contents of the larder, and preparing supper, took up till ten; and by the time that the table was cleared, it was nearly eleven, at which hour my servants were ordered to come for me; and, as I could not enjoy the pleasure of these meetings without disturbing the oeconomy of my family, and foresaw the impossibility of preventing the subversion of our society by the admission of exceptionable persons, I chose to forego it.[2]

That explanation, one may suggest, hardly rings quite true. There may be truth in it (or at any rate in the first half of it) but is it the whole truth? Boswell was no friend of Hawkins (see pp. 194–5, &c.) and we may always have our grain of salt at hand for anything he may say about him, yet he can hardly have invented the following:

Sir John Hawkins represents himself as a 'seceder' from this society, and assigns the reason of his '*withdrawing*' himself from it, that its late hours were inconsistent with his domestick arrangements. In this

---

[1] In Austin Dobson's edition of the Diary, i. 58.

[2] Hawkins, *Johnson*, first edition, 425. The offensive sentence at the end of this quotation was omitted in the second edition.

he is not accurate; for the fact was, that he one evening attacked Mr. Burke, in so rude a manner, that all the company testified their displeasure; and at their next meeting his reception was such, that he never came again.[1]

Moreover Laetitia, doubtless with this passage in mind, also candidly alludes to some trouble with Burke:

The club at the Turk's Head Tavern, in Gerrard Street, was, in my earliest recollection, a source of great pleasure to my father; and I am sure he regarded his own secession as a painful, but perhaps it might be a fancied, necessity. It has been invidiously commented on, and even I must own that the reason he has assigned is short of satisfactory. In my own mind I am convinced, however he might persuade himself, that he was disgusted with the overbearing deportment of Burke, and his monopoly of the conversation, which made all the other members, excepting his antagonist, Johnson, merely his auditors. My father used often to quote that passage in one of the quaint productions of Herbert, the author of 'The Country Parson',—

———— 'A civil guest
Will no more talk all, than eat all the feast.'

He was not himself impatient of listening; and it was his rule, and one which he expected others to observe, never unnecessarily to interrupt a speaker; but, that Burke's practice was not as forbearing, I have heard Mr. Langton complain very seriously.

'The Burkes', as the men of that family were called, were not then what they were afterwards considered, nor what the head of them deserved to be considered for his splendid talents; they were, as my father termed them, 'Irish adventurers', and came into this country with no good auguries, nor any very decided principles of action. They had to talk their way in the world that was to furnish their means of living; and it could not be expected that they would lay down their tools to witness the prowess of those who had less stimulating motives. But this intolerance did not recommend them to favour; and, perhaps, part of that which the luminary of their house obtained in the club, was owing to the amusement afforded by the conflict of eloquence, when Johnson was excited into argument.[2]

[1] Boswell, i. 479. It is stated that Reynolds supplied this information. Malone states 'Sir John Hawkins. . . sent to Coventry withdrew' (Malone MS. 36, fol. 9, in the Bodleian).

[2] *Memoirs*, i. 98 et seq.

When in 1792 Boswell revised his *Johnson*, he reported as follows on the then state of the club:

This club has been gradually increased to its present number, thirty-five. After about ten years, instead of supping weekly, it was resolved to dine together once a fortnight during the meeting of Parliament. Their original tavern having been converted into a private house, they moved first to Prince's in Sackville-street, then to Le Telier's in Dover-street, and now meet at Parsloe's, St. James's-street.

Between the time of its formation, and the time at which this work is passing through the press (June 1792) the following persons, now dead, were members of it: Mr. Dunning (afterwards Lord Ashburton), Mr. Samuel Dyer, Mr. Garrick, Dr. Shipley Bishop of St. Asaph, Mr. Vesey, Mr. Thomas Warton and Dr. Adam Smith. The present members are, Mr. Burke, Mr. Langton, Lord Charlemont, Sir Robert Chambers, Dr. Percy Bishop of Dromore, Dr. Barnard Bishop of Killaloe, Dr. Marlay Bishop of Clonfert, Mr. Fox, Dr. George Fordyce, Sir William Scott, Sir Joseph Banks, Sir Charles Bunbury, Mr. Windham of Norfolk, Mr. Sheridan, Mr. Gibbon, Sir William Jones, Mr. Colman, Mr. Steevens, Dr. Burney, Dr. Joseph Warton, Mr. Malone, Lord Ossory, Lord Spencer, Lord Lucan, Lord Palmerston, Lord Eliot, Lord Macartney, Mr. Richard Burke, junior, Sir William Hamilton, Dr. Warren, Mr. Courtenay, Dr. Hinchliffe Bishop of Peterborough, the Duke of Leeds, Dr. Douglas Bishop of Salisbury, and the writer of this account.

A century later Sir Walter Besant stated:

The club still exists and I believe, for I have not seen the list of members, has a roll of members distinguished in arms as well as letters. But the club no longer possesses any influence in literature, nor is any distinction conferred by membership. . . . The chair is taken by the members in turn, the only permanent official being the treasurer.[1]

---

[1] *London in the Eighteenth Century* (1902).

The Club now numbers forty members. It meets monthly at the Cannon Street Hotel. As already mentioned (p. 83 n.), an informative history of it was privately issued in 1914.

VIII. *His chairmanship of Quarter Sessions* (1765)

THE year after Hawkins's successful opposition to that unfair proposal concerning the Fleet Prison his grateful fellow magistrates elected him Chairman of the Middlesex Quarter Sessions and he held this position for over fifteen years. The Sessions House was Hicks's Hall, 'a mean old building, situated in St. John's Street, Clerkenwell, and named from Sir Baptist Hicks, who built it on crown land, about the year 1610 [actually 1612] for the purpose to which it was applied'.[1]

Crime in those days, as we have already realized, was rampant. If we turn the pages of *The Annual Register* for this year in which Hawkins was appointed to his high office we find that at the Summer Circuits alone, all over the country, no fewer than fifty persons were sentenced to death. But the Lent Circuit had been far worse, for at that one hundred and three had been capitally convicted, including a boy of seventeen, and 'Mary Norwood, for poisoning her husband' (she who was burnt to death at Ivelchester on 11 May!)[2]

A hanging was in those days, of course, a popular entertainment. Laetitia tells this story:

A lady of my acquaintance was at a milliner's, nearly opposite Marlborough House, when a very handsome coach, pale blue, with silver initials, and servants in blue and silver, drove up. A young lady, in the height of morning-fashion, and betraying herself only by the expensiveness of her dress, and what *then* were thought the manners of her profession, alighted gaily, and coming into the show-room, which was, excepting the form of the windows, a public shop, desired to

---

[1] *Memoirs*, i. 222. The Hall might be 'a mean old building' but it enjoyed this distinction—that from it the distances from London on England's Great North Road were measured.

[2] *Annual Register*, 1765, 81, 121. *The Gentleman's Magazine* of March that year records the Old Bailey trial of 'a lad of 14' for stealing, and his receiving the death sentence.

see some dress hats for the morning; none exactly suiting her, she ordered one, with an injunction, that it should be got ready immediately. 'For', said she, 'one of our young ladies has a brother who is to be hanged to-morrow morning, and we are all going to see him go.'[1]

'The commission of the peace for the most important county in England naturally included men of just ability' but a few years later it came to include also some who 'had picked up a little knowledge . . . and thought themselves lawyers', and the presence of these the Chairman (who 'did all in his power to keep the commission, as he termed it, *pure*') found to be 'extremely vexatious', so that his daughter regrets that he did not, 'on the first failure of a justifiable remonstration, resign his situation'.

It used to be said of one of them, whose name was David, and who had been a bricklayer at the east end of the town, where by prescription, these *justices* were of the lowest order, that he never wrote more of his baptismal name than the two first letters, having a doubt in his mind as to one of the subsequent ones. I myself heard this personage say, that he had 'breakfasted on such a day with government, and that his daughter was going to send to government's daughter a present of a pair of turtle-doves'. Lest any question should arise as to the identity of government, I must inform the reader, that in this acceptation of the term it means the secretary to the prime minister.

There was, however, a species of amiability about this worshipper of the ruling powers. He was soft in his manners; and if my father was at all less informed than was requisite to understand him, he would patiently explain. For instance:—talking one day of 'the generals', he saw that he was not perfectly clear; he therefore spoke more diffusely, and said, 'There are two generals, the soliciting general and the returning general'. Sir J.H. thanked him for the trouble he had taken; they were now on equal terms, and could get on.[2]

An anecdote of another of Hawkins's colleagues may be given here. She says:

There was on the bench at the time when my father was Chairman of the Quarter Sessions, a very lordly sort of man, an apothecary in the east quarter of the town, who took upon him very improperly a kind

---

[1] *Memoirs*, ii. 21.　　　　　　　　　　[2] Ibid. i. 19–20.

of moderatorship, if I may make such a word, and having himself very little command of his temper, would advise Sir John to keep his—an unnecessary counsel; for my father was not at all prone to anger. Some coal-heavers who had committed terrible excesses amounting to riot, were to be tried, and Mr. P. warning my father as usual on such an occasion, my father jocularly said, 'Well then! since you cannot trust *me*, admonish them yourself.'

Proud of the deputation, he began, 'You fellows there, that stand with halters round your necks'—he paused, as if to give time for effect. 'Well,' said my father in a low voice, 'I think *I* should hardly have said more; but pray go on.' He could not, and my father then spoke in his deliberate coolness.[1]

We have a picture of a magistrate by a novelist who was himself one in the following, from Henry Fielding's *Amelia*:

Mr. Thrasher, the justice before whom the prisoners above-mentioned were now brought, had some few imperfections in his magistratical capacity. I own, I have been sometimes inclined to think that this office of a justice of the peace requires some knowledge of the law: for this simple reason; because in every case which comes before him, he is to judge and act according to law. Again, as these laws are contained in a great variety of books; the statutes which relate to the office of a justice of the peace, making of themselves at least two large volumes in folio; and that part of his jurisdiction which is founded on the common law being dispersed in above a hundred volumes, I cannot conceive how this knowledge should be acquired without reading; and yet certain it is, Mr. Thrasher never read one syllable of the matter.

It must have been galling to Hawkins, with his legal training and experience, to have associated with him such sorry amateurs in jurisprudence as some of his colleagues seem to have been. Laetitia insists that he himself enjoyed a very high reputation in matters of law and proudly quotes her lawyer brother Henry as follows:

On the authority of one of the first men of the age (Mr. Serjeant Hill), I am justified in stating Sir J.H. to have been an excellent lawyer; and Mr. Justice Gould, one of the most experienced Judges in Westminster Hall, has been known to stop him, to ask his opinion on a law-question.[2]

---

[1] *Anecdotes*, 101.   [2] Ibid. 127.

The colleague on the bench on whom Hawkins came to rely, 'in any need of a *locum tenens*' as Chairman of the Sessions, seems to have been a man of mixed qualities. He was a 'Colonel Brettell' (the military title being a relic of 'his situation in the Middlesex militia on its earliest establishment'). He had been 'a *gay man*, as it was then termed, and a *free liver*', yet was nevertheless 'one of the best', having 'great good sense and an extensive knowledge of the world, most honourable in all his dealings, most liberal wherever his great and accumulating wealth could be useful', and notable for 'very fine features and waving silver locks which gave him *credit wherever he appeared*'.[1] This notability, however, had habits of the most excessive parsimony and occupied 'a town house to the last degree dirty' and 'a villa on one of the most beautiful eminences north of London which was in a condition that would have deterred many from sleeping in it, even in a moderate breeze'.

Next to Colonel Brettell, the 'other associate upon whom my father could rely', says Laetitia, 'was the well-known Saunders Welch, who would now be called a police-magistrate, and was at the head of an office in which certain magistrates sat in rotation'. At this office Welch was a colleague of Sir John Fielding (cf. p. 100 n.). Presumably collaboration was sometimes called for between the Middlesex and London magistrates, and it is in this sense that we are to understand Laetitia's remark as to Welch being 'associated' with her father.

Welch was a remarkable man who had begun life in a workhouse, had then been apprenticed to a trunk-maker in St. Paul's Churchyard, and had graduated as a tradesman on his own account, keeping a grocer's shop near the British Museum. He did well in trade, apparently, and also inheriting some property in Buckingham became High Constable of Westminster. We must imagine the one-time workhouse child 'dressed in black, with a large nine-story George the Second's wig, highly-powdered, with long flowing curls over

[1] *Memoirs*, i. 43.

his shoulders, a high three-cornered hat, and his black bâton tipped with silver at either end, riding a white horse to Tyburn with the malefactors'.[1]

Laetitia describes Welch as 'in person, mind, and manners, most perfectly a gentleman', and describes him entering her parents' drawing room before dinner, at a period when 'the dinner dress required the bag, the sword, and *chapeau bras*, and the clothes were frequently decorated with gold or silver'.[2] Johnson had a very high respect for Welch: Boswell tells us that in his 'eager and unceasing curiosity to know human life in all its variety he attended Mr. Welch to his office for a whole winter to hear the examination of the culprits', and quotes him as saying:

Saunders Welch, the Justice, who was once High Constable of Holborn, and had the best opportunities of knowing the state of the poor, told me, that I under-rated the number, when I computed that twenty a week, that is, above a thousand a year, died of hunger; not absolutely of immediate hunger; but of the wasting and other diseases which are the consequence of hunger.

All readers of Boswell will remember the long and beautiful letter which, in 1778, Johnson sent to Welch ('one of my best and dearest friends'), then in Italy for his health.

Welch, who was a big-built and strong man, had a high reputation for personal courage. J. T. Smith and Laetitia Hawkins both tell stories of his going unattended to quell riotous assemblies. We hear, too, of his arresting a notorious miscreant by catching him asleep:

After hiring the tallest hackney-coach he could select, he mounted the box with the coachman, and when he was close against the house, he ascended the roof of the coach, threw up the sash of a first-floor window, entered the room, and actually dragged the fellow from his bed out at the window by his hair, naked as he was, upon the roof of the coach; and in that way carried the terror of the green lanes down New-street, and up St. Martin's-lane, amidst the huzzas of an immense throng which followed him to Litchfield-street.[3]

[1] J. T. Smith, *Nollekens and his Times*, ed. Whitten, i. 102.   [2] *Memoirs*, i. 46.
[3] Ibid. It is difficult to accept quite literally the phrase 'dragged . . . by his hair'!

One of Welch's daughters was the wife of the sculptor, Nollekens (becoming, as we shall see, as miserly as her husband). It is this relationship which explains Nollekens's remark to J. T. Smith, then his young apprentice, when he took him to see 'Sixteen-string Jack' hanged—'Tom, now, my little man, if my father-in-law, Mr. Justice Welch, had still been high-constable, we could have walked by the cart all the way to Tyburn'.

Smith has an amusing passage concerning the Hawkins family and the Nollekens:

One day, when some friends were expected to dine with Mrs. Nollekens, poor Bronze [the household drudge], labouring under a severe sore-throat, stretching her flannelled neck up to her mistress, hoarsely announced '*all the Hawkinses*' to be in the dining-parlour! Mrs. Nollekens, in a half-stifled whisper, cried, 'Nolly! it is truly vexatious that we are always served so when we dress a joint: you won't be so silly as to ask them to dinner?'

NOLLEKENS. 'I ask them! let 'em get their meals at home; I'll not encourage the sort of thing; or, if they please, they can go to Mathias's, they'll find the cold leg of lamb we left yesterday.'

MRS. NOLLEKENS. 'No wonder, I am sure, they are considered so disagreeable by Captain Grose, Hampstead Steevens [i.e. George Steevens], Murphy, Nichols, and Boswell.'

At this moment who should come in but Mr. John Taylor. . . . He looked around and wondered what all the fuss could be about.—'Why don't you go to your dinner, my good friend?' said he; 'I am sure it must be ready, for I smell the gravy.' Nollekens, to whom he had spoken, desired him to keep his nonsense to himself.

TAYLOR. 'Well, well, well, I own, I ought to have nothing to do with family affairs.'

The dispute had lasted so long that perhaps the *Hawkinses* had over-heard it, for they had silently let themselves out without even ringing the bell.

In another passage we are told how Mrs. Nollekens was shocked by her young maid giving a trifle of her own money, on a bitterly cold day, to two miserable men almost dying for want of nourishment:

What good will your wages do you, child, if you give alms so often to such people? Doctor Johnson has done all our servants more injury by that constant practice of his, of giving charity, as it is called, than he is aware of—and I shall take an opportunity of telling him so when I next see him at Sir John Hawkins's; and I know Sir John and all his family will be on my side, for they are far from being extravagant people.

After this digression we return to Mrs. Nollekens's father, the worthy Mr. Welch. When he died his will was found to include the bequest of five guineas each to Johnson and Hawkins. The five guineas were, of course, for a ring, and Boswell records that Johnson 'received the bequest with tenderness, as a kind memorial'.

Hawkins was the author of the mural monument to Welch in St. George's, Bloomsbury, with its poetical tribute:

> As long as Themis with impartial hand
> Her blessings shall disperse throughout this land;
> Or lenient statutes, or vindictive law,
> Protect the good, or hold the bad in awe;
> Or Mercy, blending Grace with Justice, shed
> Her milder beams on the delinquent head;
> While Probity and Truth shall be rever'd
> And legal power as much belov'd as fear'd;
> So long shall fame to each succeeding day
> Thy virtues witness and thy worth display.

Scattered in the writings of Hawkins and his daughter, and in various records of the time, are accounts of some rather curious cases that appeared before Hawkins and his colleagues. Some of them seem to be worth reproducing for the light they throw on the life of the times. Here is one concerning something which happened in 'a house of lewd resort' which went under another designation. Hawkins himself tells the story:

I once, while I was chairman of the Middlesex sessions, tried an indictment for a riot committed in one of these coffee-houses, and in the course of the evidence discovered, that it was kept by a woman, who appeared before me as a witness in the assumed dress of a quaker, and was the reputed wife of a sea-faring man, who, being abroad, had left her to pursue this lawless occupation. I was greatly puzzled to reconcile in my mind, such a solecism in manners as the profession of purity with the practice of lewdness, as also to account for her retaining the garb of a sect, who are known to discountenance vice and immorality, and even to expel from their society all persons of scandalous lives. I reproved her for her course of life, and exhorted her to quit it, but could not perceive that my words made any impression on her.[1]

And here is an incident recollected by Hawkins's daughter: it concerns a bold offender and hardened recidivist:

A lady known too well, by the probably borrowed name of Kitty Frederick, was to appear to answer to a complaint of one of those manufacturers of finery who are the most subject to such ephemeral customers. She had, in the shop phrase of the time, 'run up a bill': it would now be called 'opening an account'; and was considered as having obtained goods under false pretences.

The lady was then under the protection of Lord M[arch], afterwards entitled, with infinitely appropriate wit, 'the Star of Piccadilly'. His chariot bore her to the *arena*: one of the footmen behind it was said to be her father! Her appearance was in no way remarkable; it was genteel, without any assiduity; and she was, though not of the first beauty, pretty enough to recommend whatever guise she assumed. She sate unmoved while all the formalities were gone through; and then, when called on by the court to state her defence, she said in a tone which needed repetition to make her excuse audible, that she was 'not of age'. This it was impossible to disprove; she therefore retreated to her carriage, preserving in all its integrity the *nonchalance* with which she had entered a court of justice on a most disgraceful accusation, from which she could not clear herself. Perhaps like the eels of the proverbial story, she was 'used to it'. . . .

The next time I had the *honour* of meeting her, was in Vauxhall Gardens, where she was hanging on the arm of a new protector, the then Imperial ambassador. In the course of a long and gay evening, she became extremely elevated, to such a degree indeed, as to call to the by-standers, whose notice her freaks had attracted, to ask what *those people* wanted. She was very expensively drest: the ambassador gave distinguished liveries to all her servants.

[1] Hawkins, *Johnson*, 73. A Rotherham reader of the *Gentleman's Magazine* (May 1787) expresses an indignant protest against what he takes to be Hawkins's assumption that the woman was an actual Quaker.

Again I met her, and before my father, but not as a principal; she was only one of the many gudgeons whom the sweep-net of the police had surprised in a house of ill fame near St. Giles's, at a merry moment, when she was on full swing, going down a dance, which was identically sworn to as 'The Trip to Highgate'. At this time, I suppose, she was *independent*. Her dress was composed of the remains of 'style'. She escaped again.

In her next situation I only *heard* of her: she was then playing at battledore and shuttlecork with a gay young man in the King's Bench prison.[1]

It is rather amusing to find that Mrs. Charlotte Lennox, whose entertainment by Hawkins and his fellow members of the Ivy Lane Club, at Johnson's instigation, has been reported earlier (p. 31), once came before one of her entertainers in his magisterial capacity.

I remember waiting at Hicks's-hall till a trial came on before my father and the other justices;—a trial in which it must be confessed she had *some* concern; for it was an indictment preferred by her maid against her, for beating her! It came out that a battle had taken place between 'the Female Quixotte', and her solitary domestic. How the legal question was decided, I have, I regret to say, forgotten:—it gave me an opportunity of seeing the illustrious lady, and at a safe distance.[2]

And here is another amusing case reported by Laetitia. It covers 'the complaint of a man who sold milk, against a servant-maid who would not rise of a morning as early as he required':

The girl, when called on for her defence, did not attempt to deny the charge, but she archly replied, that she rose early enough to heat a quantity of water, which she named, for her master to put into the milk which he carried about to his customers.[3]

Despite the harsh sentences often imposed (and often duly carried out) Hawkins was sometimes worried by an undue tendency to clemency. He writes seriously on the subject:

We live in an age in which humanity is the fashion. If the reports of

---

[1] *Memoirs*, ii. 13 et seq. ('Shuttlecork' is the original spelling of what we now call 'shuttlecock'. The body of the thing is, of course, for lightness made of cork.)

[2] *Anecdotes*, 331.   [3] *Memoirs*, ii. 12.

the gaol-committee in 1726 are, in all particulars, to be depended on, and do not exaggerate the facts therein stated, there was a time when, as well prisoners for debt, as for offences, were cruelly treated by those who had the custody of them; but, at this day, the temper of the times is under a contrary bias, for, not only in actual confinement, are prisoners treated with greater lenity than till of late years was ever known, but, in the courts of justice, the regard shewn to offenders falls little short of respect. In prosecutions at the suit of the crown, the indulgence of prisoners is nearly as great as it ought to be, were that true which the law does but hardly presume, viz. that every offender that is brought to a legal trial, is innocent, till his guilt be proved. Those whose duty it is to conduct the evidence, fearing the censure that others have incurred by a contrary treatment of prisoners, are restrained from enforcing it; and as it is an exercise of compassion that costs nothing, and is sure to gain the applause of vulgar hearers, everyone interests himself on the side of the prisoner, and hopes, by his zeal in his behalf, to be distinguished as a man of more than ordinary humanity.[1]

At the time when Hawkins wrote all that (in 'an age in which humanity is the fashion') there were over one hundred and sixty capital offences on the statute book:

Theft from the person of an article one shilling in value, theft from a shop of an article five shillings in value, sending threatening letters, illegally cutting down trees, cutting hopbinds or breaking down the banks of a fish-pond—all these, and many more equally trivial, were nominally punishable by death, though in practice the penalty was frequently commuted to transportation for life.

The laws relating to offences committed by women were still of ferocious cruelty. The statute ordaining that women should be burnt alive at the public stake for high or petty treason was not repealed until 1790. In 1777 a girl of fourteen was sentenced to be burnt alive for whitewashing farthings to make them look like sixpences, and a reprieve only arrived when the cart was ready to take her to the stake. . . . A case is reported of a young married woman of nineteen, whose husband had been carried off by the pressgang, leaving her and her child without any means of support. Rendered desperate by hunger, she entered a shop and took up a piece of linen that lay on the counter; but, perceiving that her action was observed, she laid it down again.

1 Hawkins, *Johnson*, 521.

CRIME AND PUNISHMENT, I

THE SESSIONS HOUSE, CLERKENWELL. This superseded the early-17th-century Hicks's Hall, where for some years Hawkins and his colleagues administered 'justice'. It was in 1779 that from that rather dingy old Court House to the fine new one there walked in dignified procession a 'train of Justices of the County of Middlesex closed by Sir John Hawkins' (see p. 103).

MR. JUSTICE WELCH and JOSEPH NOLLEKENS, R.A. Beginning life as a work-house boy, Welch rose, by probity, diligence, and ability, to be High Constable of Westminster. As a Stipendiary Magistrate he enjoyed the high regard of Johnson, who for a whole winter frequented his court 'to hear the examination of the culprits'. For a remarkable anecdote of his courage see p. 9. Nollekens, son-in-law of Welch and acquaintance of the Hawkins family, was famous as a sculptor, and notorious as a miser. He shared in the public pleasures of the day by attending malefactors to the gallows (see p. 92).

PRISONERS AT THE OLD BAILEY. Newgate Prison was burnt down during the Gordon Riots (see pp. 149 et seq.), and then rebuilt. Many executions took place here. One morning in 1785 twenty men suffered together: of this a newspaper report tells us that '*The unhappy criminals kissed each other in the quadrangle and then marched in solemnity, two-and-two, singing a funeral hymn*'.

AN EXECUTION AT TYBURN. Tyburn, at the junction of Edgware Road, Oxford Street, and Bayswater Road, was a place of execution from the late 12th century to the period when Hawkins served as one of the administrators of 'justice'. Throughout this long period it was one of the Londoners' most popular places of entertainment, for here collected huge crowds to see criminals 'turned off'—many of whom we should now consider to be mere petty offenders. (*The Annual Register* on 16 Feb. 1775 records, 'Yesterday four convicts were executed at Tyburn . . . one for robbing a farmer of sixpence'.)

For this terrible crime she was condemned to death, and was hanged, we are told, with her infant at her breast![1]

It must be remembered that none of the criminals just mentioned had the advantage of being defended by counsel, nor were they furnished with a copy of the indictment or a list of the witnesses who were to appear against them. Years later when these injustices were discussed in the House of Commons one of the arguments brought forward against the employment of counsel was that it would be a heavy expense to prisoners![2]

Hawkins continues, 'The chances of eluding conviction, or if not that, of punishment are so many that they deter many injured persons from the prosecution of great criminals.' He says he has often employed his thoughts upon this question so will 'endeavour at an enumeration':

The chances are these:

1. That the offender is not discovered, or if discovered not apprehended.
2. That the person injured is not both able and willing to prosecute him.
3. That the evidence is not sufficient for the finding of the bill, or if it be,
4. That the indictment is so framed as that the offender cannot be convicted on it; or,
5. That the witnesses to support it may die, or be prevailed upon to abscond, or to soften their testimony; or,
6. They may be entangled or made to contradict themselves, or each other, in a cross examination, by the prisoner's council; or,
7. A mild judge; or,
8. An ignorant or perverse jury:
9. A recommendation to mercy; or,
10. Appeals to the public by statements of his case in pamphlets, or newspaper paragraphs, which the Newgate solicitors know very well how to get drawn.

[1] 'George Paston', *Side Lights on the Georgian Period*, 122.
[2] And despite what Hawkins says as to the treatment of prisoners, the condition of the gaols (after all Howard's efforts) was often abominable (see J. L. and B. Hammond in *Johnson's England*, ed. Turberville, i. 300 et seq.).

11. Practices with a jury to obtain a declaration, that some of them were dissatisfied with the verdict.

12. A motion in arrest of judgement.

13. A writ of error grounded on some defect or mistake on the face of the record.

14. An escape;

And lastly, Interest to procure a pardon.[1]

As regards that 'lastly, Interest to procure a pardon', there are in various documents in the Public Record Office details of cases of it in which Hawkins and his colleagues had been concerned and in which such interest was brought to bear. In 1768 there is that of Henry Ludlow, a boy of eleven and a half brought up in the Foundling Hospital, whose Governors had apprenticed him to a London pawnbroker.[2] The boy, who whilst in the Hospital had sometimes been found pilfering, promptly robbed his new master of a silver spoon. Within two days of his arrest he had appeared before the Middlesex Justices and been sentenced to seven years transportation. But three weeks after that their Chairman, Hawkins, received a letter from Lord Shelburne, Secretary of State for the Southern Department, asking whether the boy, on whose behalf the Governors had now put in a plea, might not be considered a 'proper object of his Majesty's Mercy for a Free Pardon'.

Hawkins replied that the Governors' account of the circumstances of the case was 'partial and fallacious', to which the Governors replied in a tart minute, of which a copy was forwarded by Lord Shelburne's office to Hawkins. They, moreover, promised that if the pardon were granted they would provide for the boy, and stated that they had, indeed, already secured an opening for him 'in the seafaring way'. As the object in sentencing the child to transportation had been to remove him from certain associations with persons 'who had corrupted him', this seemed reasonable enough;

[1] Hawkins, *Johnson*, 521 et seq.
[2] This case will be found in the Record Office under the designations 'S.P. 44/90, f. 18 and f. 211'; 'S.P. Dom. 37/6, f. 216'; and '44, 90, f. 35'.

Hawkins did not dissent and in due course there came a royal communication as follows:

GEORGE R.

To our Trusty and Well-beloved the Chairman and Justices at Hicks's Hall, the Sheriffs of London and all others whom it may concern. Whereas Henry Ludlow, aged about 11 years and eight months, a Child of the Foundling Hospital, Apprentice to John Brice of Islington, Watch Maker, was tried at the Sessions at Hicks's Hall, on the 26th Feb^ry last, for Felony, in stealing a Silver Tea Spoon of his Master, the said John Brice, and was sentenced to be transported for the Term of Seven Years, and is now under the said Sentence in the Gaol of Newgate; And, Whereas We have thought fit, upon Consideration of his Youth, to grant him Our Pardon for the said Crime, upon Condition that the Said Henry Ludlow be discharged from his Said Apprenticeship, and delivered into the Custody of the Person who shall be appointed by the Committee of the Foundling Hospital, to take Care to provide him a Master to serve at Sea until he shall attain the Age of Twenty-one Years. And for so doing This shall be your Warrant.

Given at Our Court at St. James's the 8th day of April, 1768, in the Eighth Year of Our Reign.

In another case[1] we find one Roger Rooker, sentenced to a fine of £50 for an assault, but on whose behalf a number of persons had signed a petition. As to this Hawkins gave his opinion in what is surely a reasonable way:

My Lord,

Roger Rooker was tried before me for an assault on a woman against whose husband he falsely pretended he had a warrant; he had neither witnesses, nor Council at the trial and the evidence against him was not contradicted.

He was obstinate and refused making the least satisfaction. The fine of £50 was set on him on a suggestion that he was in circumstances to pay it. It should seem by the numerous subscription to his petition and by his having lain so long in prison that that suggestion was not true.

[1] S.P. Dom. 37/6, f. 125/7; 126, 37/6, 126. The last of these documents is in Hawkins's own handwriting.

This is the whole of his case; what is proper to be done I refer to your Lordship's wisdom.

> I am with all due respect
> Y^r Lordship's most obed^t
> humble Servant
> John Hawkins

There is, however, a case in which Hawkins was obstructive and had to be 'told off'.[1] Hawkins, as we shall see, was extremely jealous of Sir John Fielding, Chairman of the Westminster Quarter Sessions (which, like those of Middlesex, sat at Hicks's Hall).[2] Hawkins and his colleagues had sentenced a certain Elizabeth Humphrey to six months imprisonment for assaulting one William Turner. Fielding and his colleagues represented that 'the said Turner had been convicted before them of a violent assault upon the said Elizabeth, which appears to have given occasion to the said malicious prosecution against her'.

'George R' duly signed a pardon, which was transmitted to Hawkins. Mrs. Humphrey's attorney then went to the gaol but could not secure an immediate release—on the pretence that 'Mr. Hawkins says he must have the approbation of the rest of the Justices'. This brought down upon the usually so loyal Hawkins a concise rebuke as follows:

Sir,

I have the Earl of Rochford's Directions to acquaint you that his Lordship was extremely surprised to be informed that you should presume to make any delay, and to expect the Approbation of your Brother Justices, for the discharge of Eliz. Humphreys, after His Ma$^{ty's}$ Command that she should be forth with discharged from her Imprisonment, and that His Lordship expects that due Obedience be immediately paid to His Majesty's Warrant.

> I am etc.
> R. Sutton.

[1] S.P. 44/90, f. 76.
[2] Sir John Fielding was half-brother of Henry Fielding, the novelist, who was from 1748 a stipendiary magistrate, with offices in Bow Street and from the following year Chairman of the Westminster Quarter Sessions. In the first of these positions John Fielding served as assistant to Henry and on Henry's death, in 1754, he succeeded him as Chairman of Sessions. The 'Bow Street runners' brought into existence

The number of pardons that were in those days granted strikes one as somewhat great—showing that the severity and injustice of the law were recognized. In 1772 there were submitted to Hawkins, for reconsideration and report to Lord Shelburne, over thirty cases of the previous three-and-a-half years. In nearly all these cases a pardon was recommended.

An odd case in which Hawkins and some of his colleagues took different views is the following:

Messrs. Kelly, Lindsay, Carter, Hill, Durell, and another, six Westminster schoolboys, were tried for an assault on a man in Dean's-yard, Westminster, in January last, when they beat and wounded him in a most shocking manner, and after that Kelly, with a drawn knife in his hand, said, 'If you don't kneel down and ask pardon, I will rip you up', which the man was compelled to do to save his life.

Hill and Durell pleaded not guilty; the rest pleaded guilty. Hill was acquitted for want of evidence, and Durell found guilty, but fined only 1s. on a doubt of his being a principal among these polite young ruffians. The facts being fully proved, the other four were sentenced to a month's imprisonment in Bridewell, and £100 fine to be paid among them: but if they would in court ask the prosecutor's pardon on their knees, as they had compelled him to ask theirs, the court would take off the imprisonment; they absolutely refused asking pardon on their knees. The sentence stood thus for about an hour, when the father of Carter, one of the four, applied to the court, and told them that his son was elected to Christ-college, Oxford, and must go there in a few days, or lose the benefit of that election. On this the court took off his imprisonment.

This being done, some of the magistrates moved, that the rest might have their imprisonment taken off also. This was strongly opposed by the chairman, Sir John Hawkins, and several other justices, but on a division it was carried to take off the imprisonment nine against seven.

They then were directed to make the prosecutor satisfaction, and he said, as he had before offered to take £50, besides his costs, he would take it then. The friends of the boys paid the prosecutor in court £50 and Mr. Denton, his attorney, £20 for the costs, who, to his honour,

by these two constituted the first rudiments of a competent police force. Both the brothers were able and active men promoting social reforms. Sir John was blind (probably from birth) but was said to be able to recognize by their voices over three thousand criminals. He was knighted in 1761.

carried on the prosecution with a spirit due to the atrocious barbarity of the petty classical bravoes.[1]

Another case of undue sympathy with a wrongdoer was the following: Laetitia tells it. Her father had 'tried a man for an assault on a sheriff's officer'. She says:

I do not know whether the offence would not *now* be deemed *capital*, as it consisted in stabbing the man near the stomach. The culprit was, either by profession or trade, of the lower order of medical men: he was cutting sassafras with a knife, and made this use of it to defend his own person.

My father saw the offence from two points of view, as an atrocious resistance to authority, and as connected with a most dangerous principle of conduct. The man was found guilty, and sentenced to two years imprisonment in Newgate. He petitioned the Crown, and my father had the usual letter from the Secretary of State, commanding him to report on the case: he did so, but was very much surprised to find that, contrary to all usage, it was wished that he would reconsider his opinion; and above all, when he had done so, and only strengthened his report by argument, to hear that the remission of the sentence was to be looked for.[2]

Sometimes Hawkins's own friends troubled his spirit with appeals for clemency:

Sir J.H. had recently tried two men for stealing dead bodies, and Mr. Langton was unfortunately induced, by the solicitation of Dr. Hunter, to intercede for the remission or mitigation of their punishment. It was extremely embarrassing to my father, and it required some address to stand firm, and yet not to wound the gentle spirit of his friend Langton, of whom I must say that he, in this instance, took the contrary side of the question from that which he might have been supposed to take;—but he acted under a powerful influence, and he could not be accused by his client of having been tepid in the cause.

At the moment of his departure, Dr. Percy, then Dean of Carlisle, came in, and my father mentioned to him the very awkward situation in which he had been placed. The Dean was astonished at Mr. Langton's suffering himself to be employed in such an embassy; and I remember his referring to natural feeling, adding, 'Why, one would keep a troop of horse over the grave of a friend, if there were any

___

[1] *Annual Register*, 1779, 213.   [2] *Memoirs*, i. 27.

danger of such an outrage.' His countenance, always lively, was at the moment lighted up with tenderness and indignation.[1]

Like Sir John Fielding and some other magistrates Hawkins objected to the performance of *The Beggar's Opera*. His daughter tells us, 'My father, in pure care for the morals of the town, prevailed on the managers of the theatres to desist from exhibiting that vulgar caricature.'[2]

In the *History of Music* (soon to be described) Hawkins holds forth on this subject at some length. He says that 'the public were little aware of the injury they were doing to society by giving countenance to an entertainment which has been productive of more mischief to this country than any would believe at the time'. Amongst other ways in which its bad influence is exerted, he says, is that of representing the libertine Macheath as a hero, as one moreover who attains to some degree of wealth and so, in the end, is able 'to escape with impunity'.[3]

However, Hawkins was an enemy of the theatre *as such*—'Although of plays it is said that they teach morality, and of the stage that it is the mirror of human life, these assertions are mere declamations, and have no foundation in truth or experience: on the contrary, a playhouse, and the regions about it, are the very hotbeds of vice: how else comes it to pass that no sooner is a playhouse opened in any part of the kingdom, than it becomes surrounded by a halo of brothels?'[4]

Two little facts may be mentioned in closing. One is rather amusing: 'The oppressive Scott' had now, in his capacity of attorney, to appear submissively before his old apprentice in his capacity of Chairman of Sessions; and the other is that in 1779 Hawkins and others went in procession from the dingy

---

[1] *Anecdotes*, 315.   [2] Ibid. 100.
[3] Cf. Peake, *Memoirs of the Colmans*, i. 317. Also Forster, *Life of Goldsmith*, Bk. III, ch. 4. See likewise *A Letter to Sir John Fielding occasioned by his extraordinary request to Mr. Garrick for the suppression of 'The Beggar's Opera'*: this appeared in 1773. Johnson did not altogether agree with Hawkins as to the harm done by this opera; Boswell did (see Boswell, ii. 367).
[4] Hawkins, *Johnson*, 75.

old Hicks's Hall, in St. John's Street, to a fine new one not far away:

> 20th August. This day the Duke of Northumberland, preceded by the Rev. Mr. Sellon, with many of the commissioners for pavements, and inhabitants of Clerkenwell; the artificers and workmen, with the several ensigns of their respective employments, and followed by a train of justices of the county of Middlesex, closed by Sir John Hawkins, chairman, went from Hick's-hall to Clerkenwell-green.[1]

In 1763 the public-spirited Hawkins (it will by now be admitted that he deserves that epithet) had published a pamphlet compendiously entitled: *Some Observations on the State of the Highways, and on the Laws for amending and keeping them in Repair; with an Account of a Bill for comprehending the whole Law relative to this Subject, in one Statute, with such Alterations of the Laws now in force, and additions to them, as are supposed to be necessary.*

This pamphlet was summarized in a seven-column editorial article in the *Gentleman's Magazine* in May of that year. It treated of the upkeep of such roads as were under the control and care not of the various commissioners of turnpikes but of the justices of the peace of the various districts, who had been empowered by a statute of Philip and Mary to call on occupants of plough land to send 'four days in each year one wain or cart, with oxen, horses, or other cattle, or two men, or to forfeit for each draught making default 10s', and on 'House-holders, Cottagers, and able Labourers', to 'work on such days in mending the highway, or to forfeit for every day 12d'.

The statute had been somewhat modified by successive further statutes in the reigns of Elizabeth, Charles II, William and Mary, and George I, but an unfair incidence of the burden on individuals of varying classes and circumstances still remained. As one instance it may be mentioned that certain 'noblemen of the first rank' who were continually wearing the highway with horses and carriages were 'legally

[1] *Annual Register,* 1779, 222.

chargeable with no more than the poor peasant, whose only use of the public highway is walking over it to and from his daily labour'.

These poor people, from a sense of the hardship they suffer by so unequal a law, either perform the labour required by it imperfectly or not at all; and the justice, who by his office is required to fine them for neglect, performs this duty with as much reluctance as they perform theirs, and for the same reason. The poor, therefore, frequently elude the duty, trusting to the chances that the law will never be executed against them, or, if it is, that the penalty will be commuted: but the rich not being compellable to make good what is thus, by natural equity, tho' illegally, remitted to the poor, the highways are constantly out of repair.

Moreover, the value of money had in the course of time greatly changed, so that the fines imposed were no longer adequate and the statute was thus 'pregnant with a motive for disobedience'. Then:

The surveyor, before he can apply their forfeitures, must receive them; before they can be received, the offenders must be brought to justice; but before this can be done, the wet weather will set in, and there is an end of road-work for that year. The surveyor is then busied in making up his accounts against *January* sessions, or perhaps in defending actions, founded on some irregularity in the form of his proceedings, to recover the penalties of defaulters; and when *January* comes, he pays the balance to the new surveyor, who has the same difficulties to encounter as his predecessor.

Then follows a detail of many further defects in the operation of the statute, the whole set out in an extremely practical spirit and a very clear manner.

In some places, instead of the labour statutably required, a rate had been imposed, which was an improvement but subject to abuse owing to the method of assessment and, moreover, strictly speaking, illegal. Says the *Gentleman's Magazine*:

Upon the whole, Mr. Hawkins is of opinion, that the highways might be kept in as good a condition as the turnpike roads, with half the present labour and expence; that the labour and expence necessary for this purpose might be procured in such a manner as neither to injure the rich, nor leave any cause of complaint to the poor; and that an act for these purposes might be so framed as to be easy in its execution.

Then follows a closely-worked-out scheme, under nineteen heads, for amending the system in such a way as both to be fair to the various classes of person and to result in an altogether improved state of the public roads. The *Magazine* does not pay an empty compliment when it closes with these words: 'This pamphlet is written with great knowledge of the subject, and contains much good sentiment, and many judicious observations.'

As has been mentioned Hawkins's proposals concerned merely the roads not administered by Turnpike Trusts. A few years later (1768 or 1769), however, reforms in the Turnpike Trusts also came under consideration. These Trusts, by their very number[1] over-sectionalizing the country, must have led to inefficiency, and no doubt consolidation was exceedingly needful.

Hawkins's activity in this latter matter brought him the offer of still another honour—which, again, he refused. His daughter says:

My father got great credit with the government for framing an act of parliament, consolidating those respecting the turnpike-trusts. It led him into an intercourse with the ministry, at the head of which was the Duke of Grafton. His Grace foreseeing that his administration would be unsparingly attacked, advised with him as to the conduct to be adopted. Sir J. gave it as his firm opinion, that written attacks required to be repelled by writing.

After some conferences on the subject, the Duke pressed him to accept a seat in parliament. Every inducement was held out: he should be guaranteed against all injury to his family, and should have every support from government. I trust it is just cause of respect to his memory, that though the use into which his argumentative powers would have been brought was consentaneous with the energy of his mind, and though under such favour he might have done much for his children, he was not to be prevailed on, in this instance, nor ever to lend his pen to ministerial interests.[2]

[1] Even sixty years later, there remained 1,100 of them.　　　　[2] *Memoirs*, ii. 3.

IX. *How he became 'Sir John'* (1772)

IN 1771 the Twickenham house was given up and the family
henceforth resided throughout the year in London. The
following year, aged fifty-three, Hawkins was knighted. How
this came about is explained by Boswell[1] as follows:

> He was . . . for several years Chairman of the Middlesex Justices,
> and upon occasion of presenting an address to the King, accepted the
> offer of Knighthood.

Our books of reference, from Chalmers's *Biographical Dictionary* of 1817 downwards, tell a different tale. Here, for
instance, is what we find in the *Dictionary of National Biography*:

> His services in suppressing the election riots at Brentford in 1768
> and the Moorfield Riots in 1769 recommended him to the King, by
> whom he was knighted, 23 Oct. 1772.

It is true that the period of Hawkins's Chairmanship of the
Middlesex justices, especially that part of the period when
there was so much public excitement over the thrice-repeated
refusal of the House of Commons to accept the election for
Middlesex of Wilkes, was one of frequent rioting and that he
was called upon to act in its suppression. His daughter represents his conduct on such occasions as heroic:

> In all the tumults occasioned by Spitalfields weavers and Wapping
> coal-heavers, in all the riots occasioned by the *patriotism* of Johnny
> Wilkes, or the want of management in those who should have known
> their own powers, my father, without making himself a party man,
> performed the duty of a firm, undaunted magistrate. In the last of
> these calls upon him, my mother's solicitude made her come to
> Twickenham, during the Brentford election, but she never said a word
> or expressed a fear that could hinder him in the discharge of his duty.[2]

---

[1] Boswell, i. 191 n.   [2] *Memoirs*, ii. 6.

This example of his 'firm' spirit is given:

For this spirit he had occasion, in the season of what are called Wilkes's riots, and in the insurrections of the Sailors and Weavers in London. In one of the latter calls on the county-magistracy, he was under the necessity of holding a conference with the malcontents in Moorfields, at a time when the extensive space so called, was the repository for the stones of the old pavement of London. Their weapons were thus at hand; and my father presented himself, perfectly aware of this advantage against him. He had a good person, at that time rather commanding, and a voice well toned to gain attention; and he had uttered but a few words, when the ringleader of the sailors proposed hearing what the gentleman had to say, and the rest, making a fence of their bludgeons, became rather his guard than his assailants.

When I speak of these situations, I do not mean to state that he stood a solitary individual; he had the peace-officers around him, and perhaps some of his 'brethren', as they were then worthy to be styled.[1]

If these statements are correct then, perhaps, there was some justification for the eulogy of Lord Rochford, one of the Secretaries of State, who, Laetitia says, in presenting her father to the King on the occasion of the conferment of the honour, 'described him as "the best magistrate in the kingdom"'.[2] But are the statements correct? Dr. Dorothy George has discussed the matter in an interesting article, entitled *Sir John Hawkins as a Justice of the Peace*,[3] in which she says that 'some amusing contrasts arise when family legend is compared with the actual facts as they are recorded in the State Papers'. Investigations support her statement that Hawkins's jealousy of Sir John Fielding played a part in the affair. There are several letters of Hawkins to Lord Rochford, as Secretary of State, in which this jealousy creeps in, and also several of Fielding to Lord Suffolk showing his recognition of the existence of this jealousy. In these latter Fielding shows his reluctance to communicate direct with Hawkins but asks that Lord Suffolk shall do so, as for instance in a letter of 1773 proposing the offering of 'a handsome reward' of £50 for information as to subversive handbills and meetings of 'the

---

[1] *Memoirs*, i. 16.   [2] *Anecdotes*, 126.
[3] *National Review*, Nov. 1926.

weavers of Spitalfield and the coal-heavers of Wapping, Shad-well, and that neighbourhood'. As to this proposal Fielding says that if it were to go from himself 'it would not be taken up perhaps in the spirit it ought to be', adding that 'there should be no time lost—'tis a pity it had not gone to-day, as it is the County day; they [i.e. the Middlesex Justices] break up at five'.[1] Evidently Lord Suffolk acted immediately on Field-ing's suggestion and it looks as though Hawkins suspected the presence of Fielding's hand in the business, for the follow-ing day there is a letter from Hawkins to Lord Suffolk in which he duly throws his cold water on the handbill-and-reward project:

Sir John Hawkins presents his respects to Lord Suffolk. He is now engaged in attending the business of the Session, but after all the information that he has been able to procure by means of the High Constable of the Tower division and others employed by him for the purpose, he cannot find that there is any reason to apprehend an insurrection of the weavers. He nevertheless thinks that an intimation to them and others, pointing out the legal consequences of riotous and tumultuous assemblies may be expedient at this time, and wishes for an Opportunity of submitting his opinion on this Subject to his Lord-ship's Judgement whenever he shall think proper.

Hicks's Hall
23 April 1773.[2]

Those letters just quoted belong to the year 1773, the year after Hawkins got his knighthood. How came it to be given? Alas! not spontaneously but as the result of a pressing request on the part of Hawkins himself, prompted by his desire to stand on level ground with his hated London colleague. On 13 October 1772 Hawkins had written to Lord Rochford as follows:

My Lord,

That your lordship may be thoroughly acquainted with the nature of my application, be pleased to understand that the justices for the

---

[1] S.P. Dom. 37/10, nos. 89 and 93, 22 Apr. 1773.
[2] Ibid., no. 18. Other letters of the period, bearing on the subject, are also to be found in the Record Office.

County of Middx. find it necessary to rebuild their prisons and mean to exert their utmost endeavours to substitute actual hard labour as a punishment, instead of transportation and in this they are unanimous.

The scite of the present prisons with the ground adjacent to them will admit of their being enlarged to almost double their present extent and the majority of the justices, which includes in it the most ancient and experienced of them, are for rebuilding upon the old spot.

About six justices who all came in with the last commission are for covering an immense tract of ground to the amount of some acres with the prisons and session house at an expence of at least £50000 a year for ever.

The friends of this latter Scheme are but very few and it is imagined that a proposal has been made to Sir John Fielding that if he with his friends support it, he shall in requital be voted into the chair in February next, that being the time of the half-yearly election.

This much is certain that it has been with great confidence declared that I, who have ever opposed unnecessary burthening the county, am to be removed to make way for Sir John Fielding.

An event of this kind cannot be brought about but by surprize and would never be acquiesced in: but by these very means did Sir John Fielding get to be chairman at Westminster.

I was unanimously chosen by the justices in 1765, without the least solicitation on my part, I have repeatedly recd their thanks and been requested to continue my care of the public, the thanks also of the government have frequently been sent to me. I interfere not with Sir John Fielding, he is in possession of great emoluments which I desire not to intercept; I hope for protection in my office from that government which I profess to be a friend to, and wish to have it said to Sir John Fielding from the highest authority that any attempts of Sir John Fielding to render the seat of Mr. Hawkins uneasy or precarious, will be properly resented.

If Sir John Fielding should deny that any such design has been entertained Proof is at hand that Mr. Justice Sherwood declared last week that it was canvass'd in Bow Street by certain justices in his presence, who said they should be able to carry their point.

I have the honour to be with great truth and respect

Yr Lordships greatly oblig'd and most

devoted servt

John Hawkins.[1]

1 S.P. Dom. 37/9, f. 271.

And that letter was followed by another six days later (19 October 1772):

My Lord,

The application which I have the honor to make to your Lordship is grounded on the following reasons.

In the year 1765 having retired into the country and being then in the commission of the peace, upon Master Lane's quitting the office of Chairman of the sessions for the county of Middlesex, without the least solicitation on my part, I was unanimously chosen to succeed him.

In the course of my office I have constantly inculcated the principles of loyalty and a due submission to those in authority; and being of the profession of the Law, I have been able to inforce my exhortations by arrangements founded on legal decisions, as will appear by a printed charge of mine enclosed and which I delivered and published at the request of my brethren at a very critical juncture.

I have a considerable real estate in the Counties of Middlesex, Essex, and Suffolk.

I am a descendant from Sir John Hawkins, an admiral who bore a considerable part in the defeat of the Spanish Armada in 1588, and for that service was knighted by Lord Charles Howard, the Lord High Admiral, on board his own ship.[1]

Sir John Fielding, who is chairman of a jurisdiction subordinate to that of the County of Middlesex, viz. the City and Liberty of Westminster, has received the Honour of Knighthood, and the Justices of the County would look on it as a sanction to their choice, if I, their chairman, might receive at his Majesty's hands, the same mark of his royal favor.

Whether that constant and invariable attention to the duties of my office, and the sacrifice I make of my time and studies to the service of the public and the interests of Government are a ground for me to expect such an honorable testimony in my favour as that above mentioned, is not for me to say; the consideration thereof is submitted to that one personage whose pleasure it is as much my will as it is my duty, to obey.   I have the honor to be with great respect

Y^r Lordships much obliged and

Hatton Garden   most obed^t servant

Oct. 19th 1772.[2]   John Hawkins

[1] There is no evidence to support Hawkins's statement of his descent. Miss Mary S. Hawkins wrote a history of the family (*Plymouth Armada Heroes: the Hawkins Family*, Plymouth 1888) and compiled an elaborate genealogical table, and the Sir John Hawkins with whom the present book is concerned does not appear in either.

[2] S.P. Dom. 37/9, f. 278.

That, then, is how Hawkins came to be knighted—and let it be added that his request was not altogether unreasonable, for it is true that he had taken his public responsibilities very seriously and repeatedly shown his public spirit. But as to the family tradition that his behaviour in times of riot was exemplary—well, we shall get a hint as to that some pages farther on.

X. *He publishes his 'History of Music'* (1776)

On 3 December 1776 Horace Walpole wrote to his close friend and constant correspondent, the Countess of Upper Ossory:

> I have been three days at Strawberry, and have not seen a creature but Sir John Hawkins's five volumes, the last two of which, thumping as they are, I literally did read in two days. They are old books to all intents and purposes, very old books; and what is new is like old books, too, that is, full of minute facts that delight antiquaries: nay, if there had never been such things as parts and taste, this work would please everybody. The first volume is extremely worth looking *at*, for the curious facsimiles of old music and old instruments, and so is the second. The third is very heavy; the two last will amuse you, I think, exceedingly, at least they do me.[1]

And six days later he wrote to his friend the Rev. William Cole, the Cambridge antiquary:

> As you have time and patience, too, I recommend to you to peruse Sir John Hawkins's new *History of Music*. It is true, there are five huge volumes in quarto, and perhaps you may not care for the expense, but surely you can borrow them in the University, and though you may, no more than I, delight in the scientific part, there is so much about cathedral service, and choirs, and other old matters, that I am sure you will be amused with a great deal, particularly the two last volumes, and the facsimiles of old music in the first. I doubt it is a work that will not sell rapidly, but it must have a place in all great libraries.[2]

[1] Walpole, ix. 445.
[2] Ibid. 447. Cole took Walpole's advice. Writing to him on 18 May 1777 he says, 'I lately read over, on your recommendation, the four first volumes of Sir John Hawkins's *History of Music*, which are in our University Library. In the course of my reading I made a few observations which I put down, and am tempted to have them put into the *Gentleman's Magazine* but will not do so except you approve of the paper, which I have sent to Mr. Lort with this letter in a packet, and beg the favour of your looking at them. . . I know you are acquainted with Sir John, who, I suppose will not be offended at them. If you think he would, I will

I

Walpole must have felt a personal interest in this work since it was he who, long before, had proposed to Hawkins that he should undertake it.[1] For sixteen years his friend had been busy with the task that had been set him; they must often have discussed its progress and at last it was before the public.

This was the first history of music that had ever been completed in the country.[2] Another friend of Walpole, Dr. Charles Burney, had four months earlier published the first volume of a huge work of the same kind, but his last volume was not destined to appear for another thirteen years. The two authors must have known that they were engaged in a race to publish England's first history of music: in one sense Burney won it and in another Hawkins.

Walpole had not only suggested Hawkins's great task but had also given a little help towards its accomplishment. Nearly sixteen years earlier, when the preliminary clearing of the ground was just beginning, we find him writing to his friend Sir Horace Mann, British Envoy at Florence:

'Behold a new commission, but, I trust, not a troublesome one. A friend of mine, one Mr. Hawkins, is writing the *History of Music:* the sooner you could send us the following books the better; if by any English traveller, we should be glad.

   1. *Tutte le Opere di Giuseppe Zarlino.* Venezia, 1589; 2 vols. folio.
   2. *History of Music,* in Italian, by Gio. Andr. Angelini Bontempi, 1695; folio.
   3. *Dialogo della Musica antica e moderna, di Vincenzo Galilei.* Folio, 1602, or 1541, in Firenze.

---

suppress them.' Walpole, at whose house Cole had met Hawkins, approved and the Observations were printed in the Magazine for May, 1777 (xlvii. 219–21). See Walpole's *Corr. with Cole,* ed. W. S. Lewis and A. Dayle Wallace, 1937, ii. 45–6. Should any modern edition of Hawkins's *History* ever be undertaken these corrections ought to be taken into account.   [1] *Anecdotes,* 101, 143.

   [2] A small exception may be made to this statement. There had been published in London in 1731, a tiny work entitled *A Brief History of Musick; wherein is Related the Several Changes, Additions, and Improvements, from its Origin to this present Time. Collected from Aristoxenus, Plutarch, Boetius, Bontempi, Zarlini, Tho: Salmon, and many others.* This little treatise consists of merely twenty-four pages of an extremely theoretical character. It appears to have been followed by a collection of about one hundred and forty tunes, in sections allotted to Voice, Flute, German Flute, Hautboy, Violin, and Harpsichord. The present writer's copy is the only one with which he has ever met.

4. *Musica vaga ed artifiziosa di Romano Michieli.* Folio, 1615, Venezia.

5. *Osservazioni di ben regolare il Coro della Cappella Pontificizia, fatte da Andrea Adami.* Quarto, 1714; in Roma.

Any other books of character on the subject will be very acceptable; but when I review the list and see so many thundering folios, I don't expect that any gentleman will bring them in his breeches-pocket, or even in his cloak-bag.[1]

And in 1774 Walpole wrote to Sir William Hamilton, at Naples (whose archaeological explorations were in progress and whose wife was an accomplished musician):

I have just been reading Pliny on ancient music: pray, have you found any silver flutes in Herculaneum or Pompeii? As the edition of the former seems at a stand, would not it be worth your while to send over and publish a mere list of all the utensils, etc., that have been discovered at either? My press is at your service. I should be particularly glad of an account of any new musical instruments or singularities in old ones. A friend of mine is actually employed on such work, and Lady Hamilton is better qualified than anybody to assist you. My best compliments to her.[2]

A number of other friends of Hawkins had been called upon to assist in the great project. His Preface ends as follows:

It remains now that due acknowledgment be made of the assistance with which the author has been favoured and honoured in the course of his work; but as this cannot be done without an enumeration of names, for which he has obtained no permission, he is necessitated to declare his sense of obligation in general terms, with this exception, that having need of assistance in the correction of the music plates, he was in sundry instances eased of that trouble by the kind offices of one, who is both an honour to his profession and his country, Dr. William Boyce; and of the difficulty of decyphering, as it were, and rendering in modern characters the compositions of the greatest antiquity amongst those which he found it necessary to insert, by the

---

[1] Walpole, v. 14, under date 2 Jan. 1761. Walpole had in fact, in 1759, collected notes on English musicians 'for Dr. Hawkins'. The editors of the Yale edition of Walpole's Correspondence say that these notes number about twenty-five and that they were not all used by Hawkins (who made no acknowledgements to Walpole for those that he did use). It may be desirable to state that the above titles of Italian works are textually as they appear in Walpole's letter.   [2] Ibid. Supp. i, 233.

learning and ingenuity of Dr. Cooke, of Westminster Abbey, Mr.
Marmaduke Overend, organist of Isleworth in Middlesex, and Mr.
John Stafford Smith, of the royal chapel.

Of Boyce and Cooke something has been said elsewhere,
and of Overend's musical pedantry (which may, in its way,
have been useful) we have an account by Hawkins's daughter:

I must not omit Mr. Marmaduke Overend, the scientific organist
of Isleworth, who gave theoretic lectures on music in London, in
delivering which he turned his back on his auditors, pointing with a
rod to immense sheets covered with diagrams and series of figures that
defied numeration.

He spoke very unintelligibly at all times; and in this exertion, his
head being very much thrown back, when his progressions led him to
the top of his chart, those who listened to him lost still more than usual
of what he said: added to which, he was sometimes *un peu embrouillé*,
by having mistaken one incalculable total for another, and being therefore under the necessity of beginning again.

He lamented very much the want of taste in the polite world, when
the deceased Countess of Jersey, then in the bloom of beauty's pride,
having subscribed, and heard one lecture, on being warned by the
professor himself that the audience awaited her arrival, sent down word
that she could come to no more.[1]

Of Smith's assistance in one particular there is a record in
the unique 'Mulliner Manuscript' in the British Museum, in
which Smith, who then owned it, has written, 'Lent to Sir
J. Hawkins, 1774'.

Various other people are known to have helped Hawkins
in one way or another. It is from this History (ch. cxlvi) that
we derive the well-known story of how one Gostling, a Chapel
Royal bass with a remarkably deep voice, was taken out by
Charles II with a yachting party, to help to entertain the
company, and how in a dreadful storm they all narrowly
escaped with their lives, and how Gostling, on return, got
Purcell, as organist of the Chapel Royal, to compose the
Anthem, 'They that go down to the sea in ships', with a low

---

[1] *Anecdotes*, 12. *D.N.B.* and Grove's *Dictionary of Music* tell us of the publication
of Overend's lectures in 1783 but say that it 'does not appear that they were ever
delivered'—which, as we see, is incorrect.

solo part for himself.[1] This Gostling's son, the Rev. William Gostling, became (like his father before him) a Minor Canon of Canterbury Cathedral, and Hawkins, with his daughter, made a special visit to Canterbury to get from him 'a prodigious store of information' concerning English music, which had come to him from his father.[2]

Then there was the Dowager Duchess of Newcastle, of whom Hawkins knew that in her younger days she had been 'well acquainted with the *politics* of the musical world' and 'much interested in the feuds and squabbles that excited as keen a party-spirit amongst duchesses and countesses as those of a higher class did amongst Dukes and Earls'. Hawkins, in his magisterial capacity, had to see her concerning 'a question under consideration of removing the Westminster hay-market', but, whilst wishing to take the opportunity of drawing on her musical recollections, recognized 'the difficulty of connecting the subject of music with the market for hay':

At length the interview grew so far sociable, that my father expressed his regret that Twickenham, where we had resided half the year, had lost her Grace as a resident in the Park. 'I was sorry to leave it,' said the Duchess; 'but indeed, Sir John, I inhabited the old house till the boards of the floors played under my feet like the keys of a harpsichord.'

Who could have calculated on such a chance; or looked for such good fortune? The ice was broken, or rather, a bridge was made over it;—conversation now flowed, and communication gushed out; for the Duchess seemed delighted with having a hearer as much interested in listening, as she was in relating what had excited every feeling, when her feelings were most alive. She now entered, not only into the biography of composers and performers of 'her time', but she almost

[1] The story is briefly retold in Grove's *Dictionary of Music*, s.v. 'Gostling, Rev. John'.

[2] Laetitia (in her *Anecdotes*, pp. 245–64) gives many pages to an account of the friendship that grew up between the Hawkins and Gostling families. She says that on the Rev. William Gostling's death her father compiled 'an elaborate catalogue' of his music, which was printed in preparation for the sale of his effects. He also wrote a poem, on Gostling's death, which Boyce set to music and Cooke performed in Westminster Abbey. It appears on p. 262 of the *Anecdotes* (see also p. 229 of that book).

acted the gestures with which rival-patronesses had expressed their zeal for their favourites, and their hostility to opposite patronesses.

The conversation was long, and the information valuable—Sir John was desired to repeat his visit, against which she promised to call up all her recollection; and from that time she enrolled him as one of her accustomed morning-visitors, and, perhaps, with some sincerity of welcome, as the Haymarket business was decided in her favour, and in that of her nephew.[1]

There was also Goldsmith, 'this idiot in the affairs of the world'. Hawkins tells us:

While I was writing the History of Music, he, at the club, communicated to me some curious matter: I desired he would reduce it to writing; he promised me he would, and desired to see me at his chambers: I called on him there; he stepped into a closet, and tore out of a printed book six leaves that contained what he had mentioned to me.[2]

Hawkins's many personal reminiscences and anecdotes of Goldsmith tend to show that he did not hold him in very high esteem. Of his musical ability he is scornful:

He was used to say he could play on the German-flute[3] as well as most men. . . . But, in truth, he understood not the character in which music is written, and played on that instrument, as many of the vulgar do, merely by ear. Roubiliac the sculptor, a merry fellow, once heard him play, and minding to put a trick on him, pretended to be charmed with his performance, as also, that himself was skilled in the art, and intreated him to repeat the air, that he might write it down. Goldsmith readily consenting, Roubiliac called for paper, and scored thereon a few five-lined staves, which having done, Goldsmith proceeded to play, and Roubiliac to write; but his writing was only such random notes on the lines and spaces as any one might set down who had ever inspected a page of music. When they had both done, Roubiliac shewed the paper to Goldsmith, who looking over it with seeming great attention, said, it was very correct, and that if he had not seen him do it, he never could have believed his friend capable of writing music after him.[4]

[1] *Anecdotes*, 241.   [2] Hawkins, *Johnson*, 419.
[3] The 'German' flute is simply the ordinary side-blown one, as distinct from the 'English' flute, i.e. the end-blown flute or recorder.
[4] Hawkins, *Johnson*, 416.

It has been alleged that Hawkins, in both his editions of Walton (see p. 64) and his *History of Music,* was 'somewhat reluctant in admitting his obligations to his friends'. William Oldys, the antiquary, speaks in his diary of visits to Dr. Pepusch, 'to have talks about his rare old musical collections', and in one place states: 'Dr. Pepusch offer'd me any intelligence or assistance from his antient collection of musick for a history of that art and its professors in England.' The diary was in 1861 reproduced in *Notes and Queries*[1] and W. H. Husk, the well-known musicological writer and editor of old music, asks, 'Can any correspondent inform me whether Oldys made any collections for, or progress in such a history?' To this the Editor himself replies:

If Oldys made any collections for a History of Music, they were most probably handed over to Sir John Hawkins. David Erskine Baker, Hawkins, and Oldys, were at this time the leading writers in *The Universal Spectator.* Our musical knight appears to have been somewhat reluctant in acknowledging his obligations to his friends. Oldys, writing to Sir John Hawkins, reminds him that 'the few materials I, long since, with much search, gathered up concerning Izaak Walton, you have seen, and extracted, I hope, what you found necessary for the purpose I intended them'. But on turning to Sir John's *Life* of Walton, the reader will find but a scant acknowledgment for only one statement made by him, respecting some letters of Walton in the Ashmolean Museum.[2]

And, talking of the erudite Pepusch, one recalls a statement sometimes seen to the effect that Hawkins acquired 'the fine collection of theoretical treatises and other works formed by Dr. Pepusch'[3] and soon after the publication of his *History* presented them to the British Museum.

This is probably not quite correct. What Hawkins tells us in his *History,* when discussing Pepusch, is:

The manuscript papers of the Doctor, that is to say his studies for a long course of years, came to the hands of the author of this work,

---

[1] See Ser. II, vol. xi, pp. 102, 122. [2] Ibid. 204.
[3] Grove's *Dictionary of Music* carried this statement in its editions from 1879 to 1940. It probably originates in a badly worded sentence in Hawkins's Preface.

who is sorry to say that, after a very careful selection of them, they appear to contain hardly anything that can tend to the improvement of music, or the gratification of public curiosity.[1]

But there is scattered about the book so much detailed information about Pepusch's own life in England, and about the general London musical life of that half-century, as to make it almost certain that Hawkins had obtained much of this from Pepusch himself. An old man whose recollection of the city's musical life, in its many different phases, went back to about the year 1700, would be able to contribute valuably to the historian's store of information. Pepusch had been in the habit of taking part (with Handel and others) in the famous weekly concerts which were held by the musical 'small-coal' (i.e. charcoal) street hawker, Thomas Britton, in his loft in Clerkenwell. These ceased on Britton's death in 1714, five years before Hawkins's birth, yet he shows the most detailed knowledge of them, accounting for it as follows:

There are some now living who are able to give an account of this extraordinary institution, or the principal persons that performed at his concert, and of the company that frequented it: many of these have been sought out and conversed with, for the purpose of collecting all that could be known of him: inquiries have been made in his neighbourhood, of particulars touching his life, his character, and general deportment; and the result of these will furnish out such a supplement to what has been said of this extraordinary man in print, as can hardly fail to gratify the curiosity of such as take pleasure in this kind of information.[2]

It certainly seems likely that Pepusch, whom Hawkins probably met at the concerts of the Academy of Ancient Music, of which Pepusch was the chief promoter, would talk to Hawkins about the musical activities of his early days in London, and it is clear also that during the many years of preparation of the *History* its intended author was preparing himself by a diligent collection of information wherever it

[1] *History*, ch. cxcvii.
[2] Ibid., ch. clxv.

could be found—to our great enlightenment today. (If any reader cares to look through such a work as Grove's *Dictionary of Music* and to count up the occasions on which some fact about English music is prefaced by a formula such as, 'As Hawkins informs us' he will probably be surprised.) The historian tells us in his Preface that he had done much work in the British Museum and 'the public libraries and repositories of records and public papers in London and Westminster'. He also went to Oxford and Cambridge to see what he could find in the university and college libraries. Such was the vigorous investigator's determination to gather facts that he even pursued his studies 'in cemeteries and other places of sepulture', for the purpose of 'ascertaining facts and dates'. And in addition to all this he carried on active 'correspondence with learned foreigners'.

To Oxford, in 1771, he took two engravers to copy the portraits of musicians in the fine collection of the University's Music School, and these, beautifully reproduced, are scattered through his five volumes. The engravers were Charles Grignion, an artist of high standing whom Hogarth had for a time employed in his own house, and James Caldwell, also a man of prominence in his profession.[1]

It will now have been realized that this ardent historian spared no pains in his efforts to make his monumental work as perfect as he could.

The bookseller-publisher who first agreed to bring out the work was Thomas Davies, of whom we read so much in Boswell's *Johnson*—indeed it was he who first introduced the young Scots advocate to the English sage:

At last, on Monday the 16th of May [1763], when I was sitting in Mr. Davies's back-parlour, after having drunk tea with him and Mrs. Davies, Johnson unexpectedly came into the shop; and Mr. Davies having perceived him through the glass-door in the room in which we were sitting, advancing towards us,—he announced his aweful

---

[1] *D.N.B.* says Hawkins took to Oxford 'an engraver', but some of the reproductions bear one name and some the other. Probably it was found that there was too much work for one man.

approach to me, somewhat in the manner of an actor in the part of
Horatio, when he addresses Hamlet on the appearance of his father's
ghost, 'Look, my Lord, it comes!'[1]

Something happened to prevent Davies carrying out his
intention (probably his approaching bankruptcy had to do
with it) and the bookseller who actually undertook the work
was Thomas Payne—'Honest Tom Payne', in the Mews-
Gate by St. Martin's Church, Trafalgar Square. From what
Laetitia says it seems possible that the financial terms Davies
was able to propose were unacceptable. Yet:

> The author's views in this instance, I can aver, were not avaricious;
> for I have heard my father laughingly declare, that if he got the price
> of a pair of carriage-horses by his fifteen years' labour, he should think
> himself fortunate. One the other side, I have heard Payne say, when
> by Davies's defalcation the contract devolved on him, that he should
> lay by his profits for his daughters.[2]

The shop of 'Honest Tom Payne' was the daily resort of men
of learning and letters. Here were to be met, engaged in
earnest discussion of the wares displayed and of whatever were
the literary topics of the day, Porson, Percy, Malone, Windham, Langton, Hawkins, and, indeed, almost all the men of
note in the world of scholarship and letters who are mentioned
in the present book and a great many others, so that somebody
conferred on the place the nickname of 'The Literary Coffee
House'.

In November 1776 the book's appearance is announced in
the *Gentleman's Magazine* as follows:

> A General History of the Science and Practice of Music, from the
> Establishment of a System thereof to the present Time, &c. &c. By
> Sir John Hawkins, 5 vols. 4to. 6l. 6s. in boards. Payne.

It must be said for Payne that he produced a specimen of
fine printing.

[1] Boswell, *Johnson*, i. 391.
[2] *Anecdotes*, 19.

The great work opened with the following sonorous dedication to one of the country's most ardent music-lovers:

To

GEORGE THE THIRD

KING OF GREAT BRITAIN, ETC.

A PRINCE

NOT MORE DISTINGUISHED

BY HIS PATRONAGE OF THOSE ELEGANT ARTS

WHICH EXALT HUMANITY

AND ADMINISTER TO THE IMAGINATIVE FACULTIES

THE PUREST DELIGHTS,

THAN

HONOURED AND BELOVED

FOR HIS REGAL AND PRIVATE VIRTUES,

THE FOLLOWING HISTORY IS,

WITH ALL DUE REVERENCE

AND GRATITUDE,

DEDICATED

BY HIM WHO ESTEEMS IT

EQUALLY AN HONOUR AND A FELICITY

TO SUBSCRIBE HIMSELF

HIS MAJESTY'S FAITHFUL AND DEVOTED

SUBJECT AND SERVANT,

THE AUTHOR.

Hawkins got his friend Lord Rochford to obtain permission for him personally to present a copy to the dedicatee. This copy was beautifully bound by the well-known binder, Darbishire, and the proud author duly appeared 'not in the usual form at St. James's but in private at the Queen's house' (i.e. Buckingham Palace).

He had asked a very worthy officer of Hicks's Hall, whose meritorious daughter is now one of the first legal ladies in Scotland, to accompany him; and, with this attendant, he awaited the King's coming from the riding-house, and was conversing with Mr. Nicolay, one of the pages, who was a lover of music, when he was most agreeably surprised to see His Majesty enter the apartments, followed by the Queen. Mr. Nicolay received the presented volume from the King's hand, and then ensued a conversation on the subject of the work, and of music in general, in which Her Majesty took a lively part; the King professing his decided taste for what is called *the old school*, and jocularly complaining of his inability to persuade the Queen to prefer it to the modern style.

There was a point, however, in which my father could subscribe to Her Majesty's opinion, without the sacrifice of his own. This was, in condemning the light airs to which modern composers have set sacred words for choral service. She said she was extremely displeased with many anthems which she had heard at the chapel-royal, for their want of devotion; and to bring one to his recollection, she sang the first few bars of it. I think it was Kent's 'O Lord our Governor', an anthem so much a favourite with some fashionable *amateurs*, that half a guinea was often given by a musical man of rank to a chapel-boy for singing it.

With these criticisms, our aimable monarch expressed his fervent admiration of really fine music, and concluded what he had to say, by a sentiment similar to that of Shakespeare, 'that he should not like to meet in the dark, a man who had no love for music'.

The conversation was kept up for more than an hour, when their Majesties withdrew in the most gracious manner.[1]

The Lord Rochford mentioned above was the fourth Earl, who had just resigned his position as Secretary of State for the Southern Department. Laetitia testifies that he was 'very easy of access, very fond of music, and very willing to bestow any leisure moments in conversation'. And this mention of the great man offers an opportunity to enlighten British readers as to the circumstances that brought about a certain now common embellishment of their country. Laetitia is speaking:

His lordship introduced into this country the Lombardy poplar, and told my father that he brought the original sapling from Turin, tied to the pole of his carriage. When the tree was a novelty, it became a general favourite, and was adopted universally wherever a rapid growth of what may be called screenery was desired; but being planted in strait lines, before rows of houses of as quick growth as itself, it became vulgarised, and was treated with neglect equal to the fondness

[1] *Memoirs,* ii. 44.

which had made it common. It now has found its level, and artists who have been in Italy, can admire a *single* Lombardy poplar as a substitute for the more classic cypress.

To any body disposed to seek amusement in familiar objects, few more readily afford it than a row of these bowing gentry in a brisk wind; but it is no subject of merriment to have fifteen of them planted between one's windows and a south-western view of one of the finest curves on the Thames. I speak feelingly.[1]

[1] Ibid. 7. As explaining the sad last sentence let it be mentioned that Laetitia was, at the date she wrote, living at Windsor.

XI. *His 'History' frankly discussed*

LIKE all conscientious book-readers we will study first what the author has written last. In dignified style his Preface opens as follows:

A History of Music by any but a professor of the science, may possibly be looked on as a bold undertaking; and it may appear not a little strange that one, who is perhaps better known to the world as occupying a public station than as a writer, should choose to be the author of a work of this kind, and for which the course of his studies can hardly be supposed to have in any degree qualified him.[1]

In justification of the attempt, and to account for this seeming inconsistency, the reader is to know, that the author having entertained an early love of music, and having in his more advanced age not only become sensible of its worth, but arrived at a full conviction that it was intended by the Almighty for the delight and edification of his rational creatures, had formed a design of some such work as this many years ago, but saw reason to defer the execution thereof to a future period.

From this we pass on to statements as to the general design of the work and the methods adopted to obtain the information necessary to carry out that design, and the comforting assurance that the reader shall not be worried by 'unnecessary technical terms, and fantastical phrases and modes of expression that, comparatively speaking, were invented yesterday and will die to-morrow', which 'make no part of any language, conduce nothing to information, and are, in truth nonsense'.

And so on, until we arrive at the rather meagre acknowledgement of help received to which allusion has already been made (p. 115).

To the Preface succeeds a very extended 'Preliminary

[1] It is worth recalling that some of the most valuable later writers on musical-historical subjects have been amateurs, e.g. Jahn (Professor of Archaeology and Philology), Thayer (in the American diplomatic service), Chappell (music publisher), and Grove (civil engineer).

Discourse' (eighty-four pages). In reading this we get a hint
of the defect we shall quickly find in the body of the book to
follow. It abounds in the evidence of wide reading and deep
thinking but it is difficult to trace any coherent plan in the
way in which the results of those processes are set out.

At the outset we find a psychological and philosophical
discussion of the effects of the various arts, including music.
Then comes a statement as to the attitude to music expressed
in the works of Bacon, Milton, Dryden, Addison, and others.
After this we are involved in a consideration of the introduction of musical notation, harmony, and counterpoint, and
then are launched into a sort of *catalogue raisonné* of previous
theoretical writers on music down to one who is 'previous' by
only a few months, for there is a not ungraceful brief reference
to the recent appearance of the first volume of Burney's *History*.[1]

The Music of the Ancients and that of the Early Christian
Church are now touched upon, and there follows a further
discussion of its treatment by various authors (from Chaucer
to St. Evremond). The affection of Hawkins for the older
English music comes to our notice in a lament on the general
public ignorance of the work of the English Elizabethan composers, ending with an expression of that conservatism which
we shall later find exemplified in the fact that this *History of
Music*, published in 1776, when Haydn was in his forties, brings
its subject no lower than the work of Handel and Geminiani.

We now turn over the pages that follow and find them
quite extraordinary in their chaotic lack of systematic arrangement. There is no Table of Contents; the material in the five
huge volumes is divided into twenty books and these into one
hundred and ninety-seven chapters, without any indication as
to what period is treated in each volume, section, or chapter,
there being no section or chapter headings—or page headings, or, indeed, help of any kind whatever in finding our way
through this vast jungle of historical information other than
an index at the end of the final volume (an index on an excellent system, let us admit, but alas! far from complete, having

[1] Hawkins's name appears in the list of subscribers to Burney's book.

probably about half as many entries as it ought to have).[1] Fétis, in his famous *Biographie des Musiciens* (8 vols.; 1868–70), was not far wrong in alleging—'A proprement parler, le livre de Hawkins n'était point une histoire de la musique, mais un recueil de bonnes matières pour cette histoire.' And much of the material is indeed 'bonne'. To this day the book remains a quarry for other authors seeking building material.

Because Hawkins did not know how to lay out his great work systematically, and also because his index was so incomplete (for a good index is a great help to an author), he has sometimes unwittingly repeated himself. For instance in chapter 175 we read:

About the year 1725, an organ having been erected in the new church of St. George, Hanover-square, Roseingrave offered himself for the place. The parish, being determined to choose the person best qualified, required that each of the candidates should give a specimen of his abilities by a performance, of which Mr. Handel and Geminiani were requested to be judges; the test of which was by them settled to be a point or subject of a fugue, which the performer was to conduct at his pleasure: this kind of trial was so suited to the talents of Roseingrave, that he far exceeded his competitors, and obtained the place, with a salary of fifty pounds a year.

And in chapter 184 we read again:

When an organist was to be chosen for the new church of St. George, Hanover-square, Mr. Handel, who lived in the parish, Geminiani, Dr. Pepusch, and Dr. Croft, were the judges to determine of the pretensions of the candidates; they gave them each the same subject for a fugue; and Roseingrave, who acquitted himself the best in the discussion of it, was elected.

But worse than the repetitions which, after all, are harmless, are the omissions. What an astonishing thing that Hawkins, born in 1719, never so much as mentions the leading English composer of his lifetime, Arne, born only nine years earlier than he, and active in London musical life up to the very period of the publication of this book! (What lies behind that? Can there have been animosity? But even so ——!)

[1] In the two nineteenth-century reprints the index was made somewhat more complete but the original system was unfortunately abandoned.

Nor is there any treatment of the English folk-music. The printed ballad literature of the country is, however, mentioned (as one would expect, the author being a friend of Percy) and the words of about twenty ballads are given. Walpole wrote:

My friend, Sir John, is a matter-of-fact man, and does now and then stoop very low in quest of game. Then he is so exceedingly religious and grave as to abhor mirth, except it is printed in the old black letter, and then he calls the most vulgar ballad pleasant and full of humour.[1]

As for the alleged objection of the Puritans to music we expect it to appear in this *History* ('The fanaticism of the times led many to think music an unchristian recreation', &c.) as it does in Burney's ('The art of music, and indeed all arts but those of killing and canting, and hypocrisy were suppressed'). The one historian like the other never noticed the contradiction between his general statement as to the discouragement and, indeed, suppression of music during the period of Puritan control and his particular instances of its practice during that same period, e.g. in Hawkins, Playford's abundant output of musical publications; Cromwell's employment of Hingston to teach his daughters music and to train boys to sing his favourite vocal music (i.e. 'Deering's Latin songs, which Cromwell greatly delighted to hear and had often performed before him in the Cockpit at Whitehall'); the introduction of opera to London in 1656, and so forth.

To Bach, Hawkins, like Burney, does not do justice. However, he gives information obtained from Bach's son, John Christian (the 'London Bach'), and also reproduces a little keyboard music (three items of the Goldberg Variations). It must be remembered that very little of Bach's music was then obtainable and that it was out of fashion even in his own country.

So one might go on! But adequately to analyse Hawkins's *History* would be a long task and one calling for many pages in the presentation of the result. Let this be said, however— Here is the work not of a professional musician like Burney, who had been articled to the leading English composer of his

---

[1] Letter to the Countess of Upper Ossory, 3 Dec. 1776. In Walpole, ix. 445.

day, whereas Hawkins was articled to an attorney. (If ever he received any formal musical instruction we have no trace of it.) Burney all his life earned his living by the practice of the art; moreover he had travelled the continent extensively in search of materials. Hawkins was occupied in the practice and administration of the law. In music he was by temperament rather an antiquarian than a musician. And so far from travelling abroad he seems hardly ever to have left the neighbourhood of London. Remembering these things the book really does him some credit. It was twice reprinted during the nineteenth century (in 2 vols., 1853 and 1875) and then very largely bought. It will perhaps never be reprinted again but it occurs to one that perhaps a useful compilation of its more valuable portions would be a possibility. (But see note respecting the Rev. Wm. Cole's corrections, on p. 113.)

One merit the book can decidedly claim—its many reproductions of old compositions (nearly 150 of them), very few indeed of which were at that time, or for long after, available in any other form.[1]

Let us close this chapter with one of our historian's lighter touches. He has just mentioned Handel's song 'Spera si' in his opera *Admetus*, and footnotes it with this happy untruth:

Of this air the late Mr. John Lockman relates the following story, assuring his reader that himself was an eye-witness of it, viz., That being at the house of Mr. Lee, a gentleman in Cheshire, whose daughter was a very fine performer on the harpsichord, he saw a pigeon, which, whenever the young lady played this song, and this only, would fly from an adjacent dove-house to the window in the parlour, where she sat, and listen to it with the most pleasing emotions, and the instant the song was over would return to the dove-house.[2]

[1] Seventy years after the *History* first appeared the *Athenaeum* pointed out that Hawkins had reproduced a fugue of Kerl without calling attention to the fact that Handel's chorus, 'Egypt was glad' in *Israel in Egypt* is, note for note, a plagiarism of it. This, of course, reflects not only on Hawkins but also on his helpers, Boyce, Cooke, and Stafford Smith.

[2] *History*, ch. cxcvii. The anecdote comes from 'Reflexions concerning Operas', by John Lockman, prefixed to his *Rosalinda, a Musical Drama* (1740). Lockman was a member of the Johnson circle (see Hawkins, *Johnson*, 516 n.). Boswell's note on him is 'Secretary of the British Herring Fishery, remarkable for an extraordinary number of occasional verses, not of eminent merit' (Boswell, iii. 6, n. 1). He was the translator of Voltaire's *La Henriade*.

XII. *How was the 'History' received?*

How was it received? Not well! And poor Hawkins must have felt very inadequately repaid for his sixteen years of toil laboriously spent in acquiring and putting together material for over three thousand pages, amounting to well over a million words.

The attacks on the *History* seem to have been begun by George Steevens, who was notorious for disloyalty to his friends. Laetitia recalls an instance of his dishonest treatment of her father. Shortly before the appearance of the *History* the opening of hostilities in America had prompted the Middlesex magistrates to address the throne with 'patriotic offers of their services'. Laetitia had been employed by her father in making a copy of the address. This copy was left on the library table. Steevens was shown in and on his departure it was missed, so that she had to make another. Next morning the address appeared in *The St. James's Chronicle*, with which Steevens was connected.[1]

Steevens had for the previous six years been on very intimate terms with Hawkins and constantly in his London house, often arriving there from Hampstead before breakfast. Hawkins had helped him with his 1773 edition of Shakespeare and he, on his part, had helped Hawkins, for Laetitia tells us, 'There are in the last volume of the *History of Music* some proofs of his prompt genius, for which the compiler of such a work could not but feel very much obliged.' Yet when the *History* appeared he became, it is said, its secret enemy. The following is the tradition:

Sir John Hawkins published his History of Music with Tom Payne,

[1] *Memoirs*, i. 265. These dates should be kept in mind. First shots at Lexington, Apr. 1775; Bunker Hill, June 1775; Declaration of Independence, July 1775; the incident just recounted 1775; publication of Hawkins's *History*, Dec. 1776.

of the Mews Gate, the celebrated dealer in old books, who seldom
printed on his own account; but on this occasion, was induced by the
literary reputation of the knight, and by the friendship which had
long subsisted between them. The printing of so voluminous a work
involved a considerable capital; and Payne's future comfort, as a man
of business, depended on its success. The author happening to be very
intimate with George Steevens, the annotator on Shakespeare, Steevens
persuaded Hawkins to permit him to read the sheets while the work was
still in the press. Steevens, at that time, was a writer in the Monthly
Review; and his love of wit and sarcasm transcending his sentiments of friendship and honor, he availed himself of the use of the
sheets, to write a laboured and severe commentary on the work
for the Review; and took care that it should appear a few days
after Payne's publication.

The elaborate and sarcastic character of the criticism, and its
simultaneous appearance with a production from which much had
been expected, led to a prodigious increase in the demand for the
Review; but utterly prevented the success of Hawkins's History.
Steevens, of course, kept in the background: the article in the Review
was ascribed to various persons; and, among others, to Dr. Burney,
then known to be a writer in the same Review, and supposed to be
actuated by feelings of rival authorship. The public question was, how
an article could have been prepared and printed with such apparent
despatch? and it was some time before the chagrin of Hawkins led
him to expose the bad faith of his friend. But, when he did so, Steevens
was sent to Coventry, in the literary circles of the metropolis, and
honest Tom Payne sunk, in a dead stock, the whole of his precious
capital.[1]

George Steevens attacked the *History* in a poem in the
St. James's Chronicle. Hawkins's interest in music was treated
with a sneer. Its sounds, it was said, 'Play round the head, but
never reach his heart'. And a charge of pride was supported

---

[1] Busby, *Concert Room and Orchestra Anecdotes* (1825), i. 133. See also Nichols,
Illustrations, v. 428. The allegation against Steevens is of dubious authenticity.
Griffiths, the Editor of the *Monthly Review*, identified the contributors' initials in
his office copy, now in the Bodleian Library, and Steevens's initials do not occur.
The notice of Hawkins's *History* was by Burney's close friend, William Bewley, of
Massingham, one of Griffiths' principal reviewers (see Nangle, *The Monthly Review*,
1st series, 1934, p. 4). It has been attributed to Burney, whose contributions to the
Review, however, are supplied with the indication, 'Dr. B', or 'Dr. B—y', or
'Dr. Burney'.

by the allegation that he: 'Scarce deign'd to kneel when knighted by the crown.'

If, as we are told, Steevens was one of the proprietors of the *Chronicle* it was remarkably fair-minded of its editor to insert Hawkins's poetical rejoinder:

> The dark designing villain's art,
> His teeming brain, his ranc'rous heart,
>   Great Shakespeare to unfold,
> Iago's horrid portrait draws,
> In breach of friendship's sacred laws,
>   And fiend-like malice bold.
>
> His muse, assuming humour's guise,
> Laughs at PAROLLES, and blinds his eyes
>   While he betrays his lord;
> A liar, coward, braggart vain,
> The soldier's scorn, of arms the stain,
>   A scoundrel on record!
>
> Our EDITOR the poet's page
> Illustrates, and to teach the age
>   A truth but little known,
> That two such characters may meet,
> And in one bosom fix their seat,
>   Unites them in his own.[1]

Apparently it was about this time that Steevens was also guilty of creating some trouble between Garrick and Hawkins. A document had come into the hands of one of Hawkins's sons, Laetitia tells us, which proved Steevens's guilt in this matter also, and Hawkins's wrath at last boiled up:

Everything was now prepared to inflict on Steevens the punishment he merited; and I was in the act of copying a statement of grievances, when, at his usual very early hour, he entered the room where he was generally received. My father met him with the paper, which he was

1 *Memoirs*, i. 268. There is allusion throughout this effusion to Steevens's editions of Shakespeare and other Shakespearian publications, as also to the commission Steevens held in the Essex militia. A good account of Steevens's malicious tricks appears in Isaac Disraeli's *Curiosities of Literature* (several passages; see the book's index).

preparing, in his hand, and verbally taxed him with being the cause of hostility between him, Garrick, and Murphy. I heard him, with guilt in his countenance, deny it, and offer 'to take the Sacrament' on the truth of what he asserted. I remember my father's saying—'A pretty fellow you to talk of taking the Sacrament!' and then by the collar turning him out at the house-door.[1]

Another enemy to the *History* was the satirical 'Peter Pindar'—the Rev. John Wolcot, whom Boswell, in a footnote to his *Johnson*, calls 'a contemptible scribbler, of whom I have learned no more than that, after having disgraced . . . the clerical character, he picks up in London a scanty livelihood by scurrilous lampoons under a feigned name'. Peter Pindar's epigrammatic rancour finds expression as follows:[2]

> Sir John, renown'd for musical palavers,
> The Prince, the King, the Emperor of Quavers,
> Sharp in solfeggi as the sharpest needle,
> Great in the noble art of tweedle tweedle,
> Of Music's College form'd to be a Fellow
> Fit for Mus.D. or Maestro di Capella,
> Whose volume, though it here and there offends,
> Boasts German merit—makes by bulk amends.
>
> High plac'd the venerable quarto sits
> Superior, frowning o'er octavo wits
> And duodecimos, ignoble scum,
> Poor prostitutes to ev'ry vulgar thumb!
> Whilst undefil'd by literary rage,
> He bears a spotless leaf from age to age.

[1] For the relations between Hawkins and Steevens see *Anecdotes*, 37–40 (from which this passage has been taken), and *Memoirs*, i. 258–68 and 273–5.

In view of all the above facts it is curious that Sir Sidney Lee in the *D.N.B.* should state that Steevens later contributed a 'collection of anecdotes to Johnson's 'Works', as edited by Hawkins. It is, however, a fact that Hawkins, in his vol. xi of the 'Works' included in the 'Apophthegms, Sentiments, Opinions, etc.' a number of these taken from the collection Steevens had published in the *European Magazine* for 1785 (whether Steevens was a party to this seems doubtful, especially as we know that Hawkins, as author and editor, was not very scrupulous).

[2] For the poem of which this is an extract see p. 202. Wolcot is, by the way, reported to have been a good musician. He once published a poetical eulogy of the composer William Jackson (of Exeter).

The attacks on poor Hawkins's *magnum opus* long continued. There appeared in the *Gentleman's Magazine* for
August, September, and October 1787 a 'Panegyrical Epistle
on Hawkins v. Johnson'. Sir John's *Life of Samuel Johnson,
LL.D.* had just come from the press and in this bitterly
satirical treatment of it the anonymous author (known to
have been the great Greek scholar, Porson) strays momentarily from his direct path to get in a hit at the *History of Music*,
which had appeared eleven years before.

Of the reviews at the time of the *History's* appearance one,
at least, was entirely favourable. The *Critical Review* gave it
no less than forty pages spread over five issues.[1] Mostly these
consist of quotation but they include praise for the author's
'uncommon industry', his 'judgement', and his book's 'entertaining qualities': the statement as to the industry is supported
by a list of the libraries searched, then going on admiringly
as follows:

> Even the mansions of the dead have been entered under the direction
> of the industrious learned author, for the purpose of ascertaining facts
> and dates by sepulchral and monumental inscriptions.

This journal actually goes so far as to praise the book where it
is most open to blame, saying that its author 'has arranged his
materials in distinct order'.

William Bewley in the *Monthly Review*,[2] on the other hand,
declares:

> We have seldom met with a performance so pregnant with confusion
> as the present: and yet the Author has not bestowed upon it even a
> simple table of contents; nor has the bewildered reader any clue to
> lead him to any particular part of this extensive wilderness, except
> a solitary index placed at the end of the fifth volume. Nevertheless the
> work is formally divided into books and chapters; but why it is thus
> divided, we cannot discover; as it is not easy, in general, to find a
> reason why a particular book or chapter begins where it does, rather
> than anywhere else: neither is there a title prefixed to any of them,
> notwithstanding the various and heterogeneous matter contained in

[1] Between June 1777 and Jan. 1778.
[2] Feb. and Apr. and Aug. 1777.

many of them. In short, these nominal divisions carry the specious appearance of *direction posts*; but the traveller will generally find them put down and in the wrong places without any direction upon them. Indeed these *dumb* guides point to so many and such winding paths, that it would be difficult to contrive a proper title for the greatest part of them.

The author's preoccupation with what is ancient is condemned ('To begin with the most early period of his history he has not spared a single cobweb of antiquity that lay within his reach'). The reviewer, however, frankly admits a possible personal bias due to his having noticed in Hawkins's edition of Walton's *Angler* a footnote lauding the English Elizabethan composers at the expense of later ones:

We were in hopes, however, that, in the course of sixteen years, our Historian might have acquired a little taste, or at least one somewhat more congenial with our own — but had soon the mortification of finding him maintaining the same tramontane and Gothic opinions, and even speaking in the most irreverent terms of the music of the present day.

The book is scoffed at for its repetitions, the writer pointing out that readers are twice (at a distance of two hundred and fifty pages) given the important information as to the precise spot in the City of London where stood the shop of Mr. Samuel Jeacock, a baker (cf. p. 20).

The writer of these criticisms lays down one of his kindly principles by maintaining that: 'The diversion of baiting an author has the sanction of all ages and nations, and is more lawful than the sport of baiting other animals, because, for the most part, he comes voluntarily to the stake.'

The *Gentleman's Magazine* mostly occupies its space with quotations and with a list of corrections suggested for a second edition should such be called for. It concludes pleasantly:

From the above epitome of this most curious History the reader will see what a variety of entertainment he may expect; and we cannot dismiss it without expressing our surprise that the author should be able to collect so many flowers and so much harmony among the thorns of the law and the discord of Hicks's Hall.

Unquestionably Hawkins's social unpopularity had something to do with the general ill reception of his greatest work. And undoubtedly his lack of interest in all contemporary composers offended some readers, for the whole of the musical activities of a quarter-century immediately previous to the publication of his work was completely ignored, and, after all, the intelligent reader *is* interested in the history of his own times. (When Burney's final volume appeared, in 1789, it brought its account down to one musician who 'died November 1st 1788, whilst this sheet was printing'.)

Hawkins's attitude to the music of the period in which he was writing is bluntly summed up at the end of his *History*, where he expressed a faint hope that better times may yet come. He has been deploring 'the gradual declination from the practice and example of the ablest proficients in harmony discoverable in the compositions of the present day, which, as they abound in noise and clamour, are totally void of energy'. Music of this kind, he says, being 'constructed without art or elegance, awakens no passion': the general uproar of a modern symphony or overture 'neither engages the attention, nor interrupts conversation'. And in that spirit he plods along to the final paragraph of his five volumes, in which he assures his late-eighteenth-century readers that a return to true principles will bring '*a conviction of the vanity and emptiness of that music with which we are now pleased, and produce a change in the public taste, that, whenever it takes place, can hardly fail to be for the better.*'

We can understand how such a pronouncement was, in itself, sufficient to irritate many keen music-lovers of the day (and especially younger ones), but, frankly, one big factor in the opposition to Hawkins seems to have been personal partizanship for Burney. How bitterly Burney himself felt towards his rival we shall see in a moment, and no doubt his general popularity in musical circles and in society prompted many to take his side against his rival. The present writer cannot affirm that Porson and Burney ever met, but Porson and that other great Greek scholar, Burney's son Charles, were intimate friends and five years after Porson's sly attack on Hawkins's *History* appeared we find Charles Burney, junior, setting on foot a subscription to buy an annuity for the impoverished Porson.[1] May not friendship with the Burneys have had some influence in promoting or making more acute the antagonism to Hawkins shown by Porson and others—an antagonism that, by the way, was long maintained, as we realize when we sing (if we *do* still sing it) the long-popular catch of Burney's friend, J. W. Callcott.[2]

It would appear that Hawkins had an idea that at some future date a new demand for his *History* might possibly arise and a second issue of it become possible. In Francis Douce's copy, now in the Bodleian Library, there is a page inserted at the opening on which its owner has written that Payne sold the plates and blocks to Hawkins for £30 ('after they had been ineffectually exposed to public auction'):

> But when the boxes that were supposed to contain the latter were opened many of the blocks used in Newbery's chap-books were found, which the printer had sent to Payne by mistake. It turned out that Hawkins's blocks had been burned in a fire that consumed the printer's warehouse.

Rather surprisingly the *History*, as already mentioned, *did* enjoy a resurrection—in 1853, when it was republished (in two volumes of text and one of portraits) by Alfred Novello. In this edition there were incorporated some manuscript notes from the author's own copy in the British Museum. A 'Life of Sir John Hawkins, compiled from original sources' was prefixed: it is interesting but includes several errors. The book was passed through the press under the care of Mrs. Cowden Clarke (Mary Novello), and she provided the index. This edition was reprinted in 1875.

---

[1] *Diary and Letters of Madame D'Arblay*, Austin Dobson's edn. v, 108.
[2] For this catch see Appendix 5.

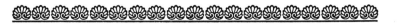

XIII. *The rival historians—Burney and Hawkins*

THE rivalry between the country's two musical histories, those of Hawkins and of Burney, had begun before they were published. Both were announced well in advance of publication and the many friends the two men shared were probably watching with interest the race to appear and discussing the relative chances of success of the competitors. About three years before publication took place (i.e. in 1773) Boswell and Johnson were talking about them, and Boswell records the conversation as follows:

Both Sir John Hawkins's and Dr. Burney's *History of Musick* had then been advertised. I asked if this was not unlucky: would not they hurt one another? JOHNSON. 'No, Sir. They will do good to one another. Some will buy the one, some the other, and compare them; and so a talk is made about a thing, and the books are sold.'[1]

In the same year Burney, writing to his friend, the Rev. Thomas Twining (a keen musician who gave him valuable help with some parts of his *History*) discusses the 'Hatton Garden Knight' very freely and shows a good deal of annoyance at his rivalry and of contempt for his abilities.[2]

A few months before Burney's first volume came before the public his daughter, Fanny, recorded in her diary one of Garrick's early morning visits, in which (as usual on these occasions), unable to refrain from acting, he set himself to amuse the Burney family. The account concludes:

'Doctor, when shall we have the History out? Do let me know in time, that I may prepare to blow the trumpet of Fame.' He then put

[1] Boswell, *Tour to the Hebrides*, 20th August. What led to this conversation was probably the fact that Hawkins's work had, about a month before (17 July 1773), been announced in the *Public Advertiser* as in a state of 'great forwardness', it being added that the 3rd volume (it was then intended that there should be only four) was 'now in the Press'.   [2] See Appendix 1 for extracts from these letters.

his stick to his mouth, and in Raree-show-man's voice, cried, '*Here is the only true History, Gentlemen; please to buy, please to buy. Gad, Sir; I shall blow it in the very ear of yon scurvy magistrate.*'[1]

And forty years after the 'scurvy magistrate's' big book had appeared, quickly to succumb before the competition with its rival, Hawkins's daughter, on her side, quietly expresses her natural loyal partizanship:

Without disparaging anyone, it may be observed, how much more closely my father appears to have adhered to the title of his work, than those who, in giving out that they write a history of what is deep in its own essence, make it their principal aim to amuse.[2]

Burney himself certainly talked disparagingly of Hawkins in the Thrale household which he so much frequented, for Mrs. Thrale, four years after Hawkins's work had appeared, makes a diary entry in which is found an allusion to Burney's feelings towards its author:

How happy, how skilful, how elegant is that dear Creature's [Burney's] Pen! but his Mind is so elegant, every thing that comes from it, partakes of the Flavour: yet there is no Perfection to be found in Character: Burney is narrow enough about his own Art: envious of Hawkins, jealous of Piozzi; till I listened a little after Musick, I thought he had not a fault but Obsequiousness: *that* however is a *Vice de Profession*—so God a Mercy Burney! I do love the Man; he is so much to my natural Taste.[3]

How bitter was Burney's antipathy to Hawkins (how ferocious, one might even say) is realized as one plods through a long satirical poem in which he freely expressed himself. In this are no less than a thousand lines, and every one of them heavily tinctured with wormwood and gall.

This poem, now in the John Rylands Library, Manchester, was almost certainly given by Burney to Mrs. Thrale, for it forms part of a collection of manuscript material once owned by Mrs. Thrale's adopted son, Sir John Piozzi Salusbury.

[1] Fanny Burney's *Early Diary*, 26 Mar. 1775, ii. 29.
[2] *Anecdotes*, 45.
[3] *Thraliana*, ed. Balderston, 458, under date Sept. 1780.

Its existence seems to have been quite unknown until Mr. W. Wright Roberts, the Assistant Librarian, in 1933, called attention to it in an article in the Library's Bulletin.[1] It is in Burney's own handwriting, in a small notebook such as he was accustomed to use for his numerous private records, and of this it occupies over forty pages.

The title of the poem is *The Trial of Midas the Second*, and it is a modern adaptation of the general theme of the classical legend. There are three Cantos, of which the first opens with a sort of prologue:

> Within the magic circle of the Arts,
> Where Genius only draws and knows the Charts,
> What Mortal, uninspir'd, who entrance found,
> The Rocks cd. clamber, or the Caverns sound?
> Pursue the Labyrinths, the Wilds explore,
> Or Navigate the Seas from shore to shore?
> If bright Apollo, parent of the Day,
> Grant not the aid of one celestial Ray,
> One Sacred Spark of his immortal Fire,
> 'Tis vain for Man at science to aspire;
> The roads, wch. Reason's Light can scarcely find,
> Are all impervious to the Vulgar Kind.—
> —So sings the Muse, from whose recording page
> I now the Ills recount, that wait on Gothic Rage.

Then the story begins:

> Around Apollo's radiant throne, a crowd
> Has late assembled, clamorous and loud;
> Complaining of a certain Scribe malign,
> Unlicenc'd by the God or Muse divine;
> Unauthoris'd by Judgement, Talents, Taste,
> Unprincipled in present Lore or Past;
> Without or Ear to hear, or Soul to feel,
> Without a Mask his malice to conceal;
> Who dared traduce his sons of high renown
> And try to blast each well-earn'd Laurel-crown;
> Denying all the feeling world allows,
> Who bind with never-fading wreaths their brows;

[1] Reprinted in *Music and Letters* in Oct. of the same year.

> Whate'er they play, whate'er they write is *Trash*
> And, most divine, it most provokes his Lash.

Hawkins's magisterial function is now alluded to:

> 'And who is this same scrivner, cries the God,
> That thus to scourge my sons, assumes the Rod?'
> 'Oh 'tis his trade, they all reply, to chace
> The Sons and Daughters of celestial Race:
> The offspring of thy kindred, great Apollo!
> Their occupation ne'er in Peace can follow;
> Sly Hermes' sons, abt. their business running,
> All dread his Myrmidons, as still more cunning;
> No tender Nymph, kind Soul! throughout the Strand
> But Nightly trembles at his cruel hand;
> And these, and all the Votaries of Venus,
> Are not less lash'd than those of old Silenus,
> Who ne'er perform their Rites with pious Zeal,
> But strait his unrelenting rage they feel.'

'That is all very well!' replies, in effect, the God, '*But why
. . . should this new Midas thus on all lay hands, And indis-
criminately seize and flog, My Children, With each drunkard,
w—e, and rogue?*'

The complainants then, with apparent honesty, try to
minimize the guilt of the offender—in the course of this effort,
however, only further blackening his character. They dwell
upon his antiquarian tastes:

> Then thus the agriev'd Complainants strait reply;
> 'In this, Great Pow'r! To exculpate him we'll try;
> For though the blood be black wch. fills his heart
> Yet ignorance in his award has part;
> False principles and prejudice combine
> To thwart his purpose, if he well design;
> For he, alas! long since so stuff'd his head
> *With all such reading as was never read;*
> With Canons, Madrigals, Motets, and Fugues,
> With Points, Conundrums, and such useless drugs;
> So oft in Cobwebs poked his Nose and Broom,
> For Good, in house or head he left no room.

Hence, ev'ry Rule he draws from Gothic works,
From barb'rous Jargon, and unmeaning Quirks,
Produc'd in impious and ill-fated Days
When all thy sacred altars ceas'd to blaze,
Thy Priests to sing, thy incence to expand,
And not a Muse was worship'd thro' the Land!
Black-Lettered Chains his cold Ideas bind
Nor let Conviction beam upon his Mind;
Eager with Fire and Faggot to pursue
Whate'er is graceful, elegant, or new—
And shall great Clio ever deign impart
To *him* the Records of thy fav'rite Art?'

Apollo is not altogether impressed with the danger the complainants feel to exist:

> 'Such feeble efforts ne'er
> Can the just honours of my sons impair.'

The complainants, however, persist in their appeal to the God to take action:

'The elder Midas, both in Heav'n and Earth
By his award excited only Mirth;
For when the Lydian King the Satyr crown'd
He far more stupid than malign was found;
Nor shd. the opinions of the younger fright,
While only built on Ignorance, and spite.—
Oh! Mighty Pow'r!' they cry, 'whose active rays
Pervade our Minds as well as gild our Days,
Let not this Remnant of the Iron Age
Eternal War with Taste and Feeling wage;
Nor try, unpunish'd, Doctrine to restore
Which damp'd thy Fires, and shamed us heretofore;
Again Repel us to uncultur'd ground,
Feed us on acorns, after Corn is found;
To second Childhood make us back return,
And all the Arts of Goths and Vandals learn!
O prove at once thy wrath and pow'r divine
And strait to chastisem^t the wretch consign!
If the first Midas had his Ears made long
When less thy strains he priz'd than Pan's rude song,

> The Second, hating ev'ry one that sings,
> Shd. have his lopped, at least, as useless things.'

Apollo holds his ground: The culprit is beneath his notice, he declares:

> 'My vengeance too much honour wd. bestow
> Were I to punish so obscure a Foe.
> The Lydian Judge, whose sentence damn'd his Fame,
> Tho' Music's Pow'r his breast cd. ne'er inflame,
> An Empire ruled on the terrestrial Ball,
> But *This* is only King of Hicks's Hall.
> I ne'er rewards bestow, or weild the Rod
> But on Occasions, worthy of a God:
> Try him yourselves, and as his Crimes appear
> Be mild, my sons, your sentence, or severe.'
> — — This said, Apollo vanish'd from the crowd
> Wrapt in the splendor of a golden Cloud.

And so ends the first Canto. In the next one there takes place a vigorous discussion as to the form the trial shall take—whether by judge and jury, and according to what laws. In the end an unexpected decision is arrived at—to leave the whole conduct of the trial to Boyce:

> As Rome endanger'd by a Foe, or Traytor;
> Among her chiefs elected a Dictator:
> To judge this self-elected judge, the choice,
> Almost unanimously, fell on Boyce:
> A man whose Probity was bias proof,
> And Music, like his Manners, bold and rough.
> In both, tho' new refinem^t he withstood,
> His heart and Harmony were sound and Good;

This we may call an unexpected decision. For Boyce, as we know, was a friend of Hawkins and had helped him in the preparation of this very *History* (see p. 115). The poem, however, seems to hint that the friendship between Hawkins and Boyce had ceased, and a strange reason is given for this:

> The Pris'ner's Friend he seemed in former days,
> Before he had disgrac'd him with his Praise.

DRS. CHRISTOPHER PEPUSCH and WILLIAM BOYCE. Pepusch lived in England from about 1700 and his intimate knowledge of half-a-century of London's musical life supplied Hawkins with much useful information (see p. 120). Dr. William Boyce, Organist of St. Paul's Cathedral and Master of the King's Band, helped by 'decyphering and rendering into modern character' some of the old music Hawkins wished to reproduce (see p. 115).

GEORGE STEEVENS and DR. CHARLES BURNEY. George Steevens, long a frequenter of Hawkins's house, slyly attacked the *History of Music* in an anonymous poem in the *St. James's Chronicle*, and was, in turn, attacked by Hawkins in another (see pp. 131 et seq.). The generally so urbane Burney, on his part, wrote a long and bitter poetical-satirical attack on the book and its author—but apparently merely for private circulation.

(Portraits by George Dance)

In the Practise of Chanting a Melody consisting of Breves and Semibreves, amounting to ... of in Number is applyed ... ... crimately long or short to the Verses of the Psalms: these form the measure ... in respect of Time for each Verse Where the Clause is short the Intonation is necessary protracted, where it is long the Intonation is by the like Necessity accelerated resembling the Beds of Procrustes which those whom he laid on them ... by Stretching or amputating respectively their Limbs, were made to fit.

In ridicule of this Practise a merry Fellow adapted the following Words to the Notes of the Invocation in Tally's Litany

And was not Pharaoh &c

And was not Phar - aoh a pi - ti - ful Ras - cal who

would not suf - fer the child - ren of Is - rael their Wives and their lit - tle ones

their Flocks and their Herds with their Ox - en and Ass - es to trav - el three Days

jour - ney in - to the Wild - er - ness to sol - em - nize the Pas - chal

A MANUSCRIPT FOOTNOTE IN HAWKINS'S OWN COPY OF HIS HISTORY
(Now in the British Museum

But, so far from in any marked manner praising Boyce, the *History* (it is one of its several glaring lacunae) almost totally ignores him, since apart from the Preface's mention of his help we find merely one short sentence, plus a few passing allusions to the presence in his great collection of *Cathedral Music* of some work whose composer is being discussed. Presumably the 'praise' referred to is the following: Weldon has been referred to as 'a very sweet and elegant composer of church music' and then we are informed that:

His successor in his places in the royal chapel is one whose merits will ever endear him to the lovers and judges of harmony, and particularly, of cathedral music, Dr. William Boyce.

If that brief instance of praise was capable, in itself, of offending Boyce he was not the genial, good-humoured man we are led by other writers to believe that he was![1] If Boyce felt disgraced by Hawkins's treatment of him in the *History* it must surely rather have been on the grounds of neglect. He was the composer not only of church and choral music of solid value, but also of a good deal of excellent instrumental music (music that has in our days, by the way, too much fallen out of sight and hearing).

Had Boyce and Hawkins quarrelled? The following by Laetitia Hawkins does not suggest it. It refers to a period two or three years after the publication of the *History*.

Dr. Boyce had laboured hard in the duties of his profession, and had achieved a task, which I should have supposed would have been a fortune to those who inherited his property,—the compilation of his magnificent volumes of Cathedral-Music. On his death, my father interested himself most warmly in the disposal of the plates for the benefit of his family. *I* never was more astonished, nor did I ever see my father more indignant, than when he was offered by one of the principal music-sellers in London, the value of the pewter only!

On subsequent application to Mr. Ashley, father of the celebrated performer of that name, he immediately offered one hundred guineas,

[1] See, for instance, the *D.N.B.*: 'Personally Boyce was a most amiable and estimable man. . . . He seems to have been a universal favourite with all with whom he came in contact.'

which, though compared with *my* expectation small, yet set against the previous offer, was such as was chearfully accepted.[1]

Apparently we shall have to pass on without having been able to explain in any satisfactory way Burney's allusion to the relations between Boyce and Hawkins. Perhaps he was labouring under some misapprehension on the subject, though that seems unlikely.

An account of the trial follows, with the indictment and the evidence of many witnesses. So ends the second Canto.

The last Canto continues the evidence, which includes long lists of names of composers to whom the *History* has not done justice, and (as we begin to weary of such an unrelieved recital of guilt) at last the jury's verdict of 'Guilty', and the judge's sentence:

> 'For me nought now remains
> But the dread sentence wch. the Law ordains;
> Which to pronounce my soul o'erwhelms with grief,
> Yet from this Court's award there's no relief.—
> On Laws of Science, Taste and Wit, you've trampl'd
> With Fury fell, and Malice unexampl'd;
> The dearest sons of Fame have tried to Slay
> In such Felonious, such a Murd'rous way,
> That precedents no human Laws provide
> (The Romans long had none for parricide)
> How Crimes like yours to punish or Chastise
> And, by Example, others make more Wise.
> Had you for social virtues been belov'd
> Your Book, tho' bad, a milder fate had prov'd
> And though your Frailties long have been reveal'd,
> A Noble Work your pardon wd. have seal'd:
> Learn hence, Ye Scribes! The World can never brook
> At once a hated Man, and worthless Book.
> Uncommon as your deeds and fell Intent
> O Midas! now must be your punishment!

[1] *Anecdotes*, 243. Boyce died in Feb. 1779. A second edition of the *Cathedral Music* appeared in 1788 and for this Hawkins wrote a preliminary Memoir, so, in a measure, atoning for his neglect, in his *History*, to give information about his old friend.

To rid the World at once of such a name,
And choke the Trumpet harsh of Evil Fame,
To both I now consign a dirty Niche
Deep in the darkest part of loath'd Fleet-Ditch.'

The crowd flocks out of the court room:

    The People seek their Homes
    Till the dread day of Execution comes.

And then arrives the end:

    In effigy a Figure quite Ideal
    Is brought for Midas as his presence real,
    This, with his Volumes five, in sable clad,
    Befitting well their situation sad,
    Are placed upon a sledge and drawn along
    With Leisure mete, amid the grinning throng.
    The Executioner, Jack-Catch yclep'd
    Between the Culprits his dread station kept.
    The Sheriff and his men attend to see
    Justice perform'd with due Solemnity.

    Thus the Procession moves in Sober Mood
    Close to the Margin of the Ebon Flood;
    When Tyburn's Lord, with public approbation,
    Inflicts, by means uncommon, suffocation.
    Tho' hard it seems such boyant things to drown,
    (No reader ever yet cd. get them down)
    Yet, spite of Cobwebs, Sweepings, Idle Stories,
    Foundations weak of Midas' future Glories
    With so much Lead about him and his work,
    They must have sunk in Jackets made of Cork.
    And when, as sentenced, in Fleet Ditch they are hurl'd,
    The Lake Oblivion of this upper World,
    Where all the Refuse of Terrestrial things,
    Hateful to sense, each neighb'ring Mortal flings,
    No Force Centrifugal creates a pause;
    With speed exceeding Gravitation's Laws,
    Through Water, Mud, and Dirt, they rapid pass,
    And penetrate the most obdurate Mass;
    Each diff'rent strata [sic] of the Globe they enter,
    Nor stop one Instant till they reach the Centre.

And so (not too soon!) we reach the close of Burney's not very dignified attack on his rival. The age was one of vigorous satire and Burney was a man of his age. And we may remember that the thing was probably intended for nothing more than private reading amongst its writer's friends.

It is, by the way, perhaps just worth mentioning that when, in the early days of the nineteenth century, Burney wrote the musical articles for Rees's great forty-volume *Cyclopaedia*, whilst he included biographical treatments of many lesser writers on music, he omitted Hawkins.[1]

---

[1] There have from time to time been allegations that Burney (in his second and subsequent volumes) took facts from Hawkins's work, without acknowledging his source. See, for instance, *The Musical World*, 7 and 21 June 1838; Chappell, *Popular Music of the Olden Time*, 1st edn., Introduction, ix; Welch, *Six Lectures on the Recorder*, 116 (the allegation in this last case being founded on information supplied by Hawkins's grandson, Colonel Hawkins).

It is, by the way, rather surprising to realize for how long a period the literature of the history of music remained little more than a re-compilation from Hawkins and Burney. Thus Busby's *General History of Music* (1818) is announced on its title-page as 'Condensed from the Works of Hawkins and Burney', and the tardy earliest American work of this sort, Joseph Bird's *Gleanings from the History of Music* (1850) in its preface frankly acknowledges its debt, admitting: 'From these two works we have taken what seems to us most useful and pleasing, trusting that what was most so to us would be so to others.'

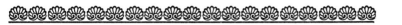

XIV. *His removal to Westminster* (1770) *and the Gordon Riots* (1780)

THREE successive attempts at burglary seem to have suggested that the Hatton Garden house, in which the Hawkins family had lived since 1763, was in some odd way particularly unsafe; these burglaries, we are told, occurred with intervals of only one or two nights between, and the natural result was the resolve on a removal. Temporarily this was to St. James's Place, and then the family settled in an old house (formerly that of Admiral Vernon) in a street leading to Queen's Square, Westminster.[1] Here they remained for the next five years.

They now attended the church of St. Margaret's, Westminster. In 1778 Hawkins, ever protective of public rights (cf. pp. 62, 69), took action to defend the church from the inconsiderate intentions of a surveyor to the Board of Ordnance who, in defiance of a proviso in his lease, had planned a building to be placed at the end of the church where it would spoil the window. The said surveyor was duly routed.

And now, in 1780, came to the Hawkins family, as to innumerable London and provincial families, the great excitement of violent disorder at their very door. In Laetitia Hawkins's *Memoirs* she gives us a pretty full account of the activities of her father in his magisterial capacity during the period of those 'riots called Lord George Gordon's'—which 'disgraced the metropolis and spread contagion or terror over the whole kingdom'.

The first hint of anything unusual came when her mother and she, in 2 June 1780, returning in their carriage from a morning visit in the south of London, noticed a great crowd

[1] Chalmers.

in St. George's Fields. They decided it must be 'a bean-feast, or some such accumulation of persons', and quietly proceeded home to dress for a party at the house of their family friend, Bennet Langton.

Then there returned Laetitia's lawyer brother, Henry, who had been in the thick of the disturbance created by that 'accumulation of persons' when, marching from St. George's Fields, it reached Westminster. Evidently his sister later got him to write down his account of what he had experienced. It begins as follows:

> On the day when the riots began, I was in Westminster Hall, and the tumult became so great, that Mr. Dunning, who was then speaking in the Court of King's Bench, was unable to go on; and, as the Hall was then filling with an immense crowd, who were making their way to block up all the avenues to the House of Lords, the Court adjourned. I afterwards saw the mob in regular procession marching up Charing Cross, and driving back every nobleman's carriage that was on its way to the House. Some noblemen who were thought to be friendly to the opinions of the mob were treated more gently than the rest; Lord Fortescue, if I mistake not, was taken out of his carriage by them, and kissed by the old women who had mixed with the throng. The Lord Chancellor only met with sarcastic pity; the mob crying out not to touch his head, in a way that showed that they would insinuate that that was his weakest part.

Despite this serious report the two ladies thought they might safely go to their party:

> We still had no idea of further danger, and should have gone out, had not the coachman come in to say, that a lady, who lived very near us, had been stopped in her carriage by the mob at Charing Cross, and compelled to huzza for Lord George, and cry out 'No Popery!' on pain of being dragged out.
>
> The next day we heard that the guards were preparing for duty; but all reliance in them was destroyed, by its being said that they were heard to declare, if ordered to fire, it should be over the heads of the mob that they would discharge their pieces.

It now became necessary for Sir John and his colleagues to attend in turn at the Guildhall. A day or two later his family

were alarmed by his non-return and by his sending them word
that he would be engaged on his duties all night. He had
received a message from the Lord Chief Justice, Lord Mansfield, begging him to come at once to his house in Bloomsbury
Square:

My father went thither directly on foot, attended by constables,
and found his lordship in the most tumultuous state of feelings, and
utterly at a loss to know what to do. The mob had given notice of their
intention to visit him and a great concourse of people was assembling
as spectators of the impending mischief. Sir J. was cool and firm: he
advised sending for a military force; and while this was carrying into
effect, Lord Mansfield asked him to go to the Archbishop of York, who
lived in the adjoining house, and was under the same terror. The
Archbishop, however, was more himself.

The soldiers arrived but Lord Mansfield, unfortunately,
'insisted on their not remaining on the spot, but going to
a little distance and holding themselves ready to return if
summoned'. Hawkins and the officer commanding protested,
but had to fall in with this suggestion, and the soldiers
were placed in the vestry of St. George's church—not
very far away, but too far for quick action should it be
called for.

The result is well known to those who had the misfortune to witness
the scenes of this time. The mob kept their promise; and, in a space
of time inconceivably short, his house had only its walls standing.
One of the young ladies of the family staid long enough to see her
grand piano-forte thrown into a bonfire made of the furniture; and
such was the *noble spirit* of these *protestant heroes*, that a large silver
tankard was thrown into the blaze with a considerable quantity of
guineas in it. A cry was then set up, from the tone and temper of
which it was conjectured that *all* the mob were not of the same
description; the audible words were, 'If there are any *females* in the
house, send them away.' Having given time for the execution of this
charitable order, and consequently the evacuation of the house, they
proceeded with the work of demolition.

Before this happened a message had come to Hawkins from
the Duke of Northumberland, begging him to accompany the

messenger to Northumberland House, in the Strand, there to give his advice:

In the way they met a large party of the rioters, who were just then in all the exultation of a successful attack on the gaol of Newgate, and were preceded by the deep-toned bell which was part of the spoil. But, contrary to all expectation and probability, they proceeded on their course, and suffered the guardians of the peace which they were destroying to do so also, who reached Northumberland House, happily for us who were so deeply interested, in safety.

Soldiers had been called in here also and Hawkins's advice was that they should be drawn up 'in the courtyard, with their faces towards the Strand, and on the first summons to open the gates; and then, after due form, should they [the mob] not retreat, to suffer the soldiers to fire over their heads'.

The Duke asked my father if he would stay with him. He replied, 'Certainly, for he could do no good at Lord Mansfield's.'

They sat down to supper. News came of the demolition of Lord Mansfield's; but day dawned, and no attack was attempted on Northumberland House. The Duke then proposed retiring to rest, and very politely said to Sir J. 'Lord Percy's bed is ready for you.' My father accepted the offer of rest, but lay down in his clothes.

Meantime Hawkins's family in Westminster, alarmed by the terrible rumours that came to them, were too anxious to feel able to go to bed.

At seven next morning Sir John arrived home, bringing with him the curate of the parish, whom he had met and who had reported that he had heard that the Hawkins's house was to be demolished. The curate offered to take charge of any portable valuables and did so. Other neighbours made similar offers:

One offer of assistance which we received was from a lady, whose stables in the neighbourhood afforded abundant room for furniture, and this encouraged us to attempt saving the best. We had but recently settled ourselves in this dwelling, and the newness of the carpets and other articles exciting the *tenderness* of our servants, they exerted themselves vigorously; our wardrobes were stript, and their contents thrown into chests, the books were packed in boxes, and by

THE GORDON RIOTS (June 1780)

THE DESTRUCTION OF NEWGATE PRISON. Hawkins, on his way from Blooms-bury to the Strand (see p. 152), met '*a large party of rioters, who were just then in all the exultation of a successful attack on the gaol of Newgate and were preceded by a deep-toned bell which was part of the spoil*'. This contemporary engraving shows that attack.

FIRING ON THE MOB. To this day there is a relic of the Riots in the piquet of twenty-four men of one of the Guards regiments who every evening are to be seen marching with fixed bayonets to take up their duties within the walls of the Bank of England.

the hour at which we were to abandon our condemned house, not an article remained for the bonfire, but bedsteads and fixtures.

The empty house was then abandoned and the family set out for Clapton, where they had a promise of hospitality. It seems to be a reflection on Hawkins's sense of duty that he accompanied his household. Why, at such a time, did not he (from the office he held one of the men of greatest responsibility) remain within the zone of danger, ready to give the magisterial authorization should it become necessary in any part of London for the military to open fire?[1]

Even in Clapton, three miles or so from the centre of disturbance, safety was not assured. 'The *protestant* spirit had outgone us,' says Laetitia; 'everywhere we saw blue ribbons hung out of the windows,[2] and our appearance among the inhabitants of Clapton gave rise to a supposition that we must be Roman Catholics who had fled our house in danger from our religion'. Laetitia, on going to bed, looked out of the window towards London, and counted seven fires then blazing.

But the next day brought comfort:

Those who went in town in the morning, returned with news that the military power was constituted the guardian of the peace, and that the public offices were converted into barracks. Vigorous exertions soon brought the rioters under control; and, bad as this tremendous convulsion had been, we stood and still stand indebted to it for a better order of things.

There exist many eye-witness accounts of the doings of those unhappy days.[3] Some of them are much more detailed

---

[1] His rival, Sir John Fielding, staunchly stood his ground and committed several rioters to Newgate. His house was destroyed. John Wilkes, as an alderman, was also active. For the parts Fielding and Wilkes played in suppressing the riots see Wilkes's diary (British Museum, Add. MS. 30866, ff. 239 foll.), which is quoted at some length by Dr. L. F. Powell (Boswell, iii, App. F, 537–9).

[2] Burney says that Gordon and his friends had distributed '£2500 worth of blue ribbon' (see the present author's *The Great Dr. Burney*, i. 375).

[3] As for instance Burney's above mentioned; and, of course, Dickens, in *Barnaby Rudge* (drawing upon contemporary documents, of which he had made a study in the British Museum), is very graphic.

(and also more exciting) than Laetitia's, but still she seems to be worth quotation as bringing before us something of the spirit of consternation that took possession of the more respectable part of London's population.

She follows her account with a verbatim reproduction of 'Sir J.H's Charge to the Grand Jury after these riots'. This is a very thorough discussion of the principles of English justice and of the powers and duty of the jury in defending and promoting such principles, especially in times of tumult, but it runs to about thirty solemn pages and the reader shall be spared!

And now that we have Laetitia's account of her father's conduct during the riots it is proper to ask ourselves what other records exist which would enable us to check it—just in case filial respect may have led to a treatment of the subject too favourable to the Chairman of the Middlesex Quarter Sessions? There is, at any rate, a letter from the Archbishop of York to his son in the navy which mentions Hawkins. He deplores Lord Mansfield's refusal to have the soldiers in his house, and then seems to throw the blame on Hawkins and his colleagues both for the departure of the soldiers and for their not being called back when required:

I applied however for a guard, and at about nine 40 men were sent, 20 for Lord Mansfield, and 20 for me, with a young ensign. If he could be persuaded to take them into his house, we should both have been safe; but those whom I found with him had given him an opinion that the intelligence might probably be false, and that his having soldiers might provoke an attack which was not intended. They were accordingly marched off as far as Bloomsbury church, to be there in readiness; and some justices promised that they would be with us in a moment if necessary; but when they were wanted, they were not to be found. They were most of them frightened out of their wits, as some of their houses had already been burnt for having acted.

I must tell you too, that a fatal error had prevailed among the military, that they could not in any way act without the orders of a civil magistrate: which is the case when a great mob is assembled, but has not yet proceeded to acts of violence; but when they have begun to commit felonies, every subject, and the military among the rest, are justified in common law in using all methods to prevent illegal acts.[1]

Apart from those two conflicting accounts there seems to be none remaining of the part Hawkins played in the Gordon Riots.

As for his leaving Lord Mansfield's house for the Duke of Northumberland's, Dr. Dorothy George, in the article afore-mentioned (p. 108), is first congratulatory and then cutting:

He was indeed lucky, as this proved to be the one occasion during the riots when a magistrate read the Riot Act, and Hawkins, if present, might have incurred the same public shame as poor Brackley Kennett, the Lord Mayor, who watched the mob burning and plundering without making any effort to stop them, or allowing the Guards to act. There could be few safer spots in London than Northumberland House, with its court-yard and great gates, behind which soldiers were drawn up. . . .

The story of the 'message' from the duke recalls a drawing by the author of *Vice Versa* of a knight riding *ventre à terre* away from a dragon—he is not, as one might suppose, running away, but is going to fetch his pocket-handkerchief. Much must be allowed for filial piety and family legend, but in the light of our knowledge of the aged Lord Mansfield's courage and misfortunes, the contrast drawn by Laetitia Hawkins between his lordship's fear and her father's 'casting vote' for 'active exertion' would be odious if it were not ludicrous.

There the matter must rest—and what the exact truth of it is nobody, presumably, will ever know. But it may be remembered that Hawkins's friend, Johnson, had no very high opinion of the conduct of the magistracy on this occasion. Writing to Mrs. Thrale, and alluding to the fact that at last the King stepped in, 'put the soldiers in motion, and saved the town from calamities such as a rabble's government must naturally produce', he alludes to this royal action having been taken 'without the concurrence of his ministers, *or the assistance of the civil magistrates*'.[2] And, of course, all our historians

[1] *History of the Markham Family*—known in its 2nd edition (1913) as *Markham Memorials*.

[2] Boswell, iii. 430. It should, however, be remembered that the Lord Mayor was induced by John Wilkes to raise the *Posse Comitatus* (Boswell, iii, App. F, 538).

take somewhat that same general view. As Sir John Fortescue
has put it:

When in the first week of June 1780 the Gordon rioters carried
on their orgy of anarchy and destruction in London, ministers and
magistrates were utterly supine, and the situation was only saved by the
use of the military at the express injunction of the King.[1]

---

[1] *Johnson's England,* ed. Professor Turberville (1933); chapter on 'The Army'
i. 69. We have seen that not all the magistrates were 'utterly supine'.

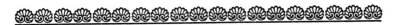

XV. *Some of his Westminster friendships*

In 1771, or thereabouts, Hawkins had left Twickenham. His father, who was fond of visiting him there, was now dead and probably it was felt that the upkeep of the town house was sufficient and that there was little justification for the frequent moving backwards and forwards from the one house to the other. Hawkins had been driven out of his house in Hatton Garden by burglaries. In 1785 he was driven out of his new house near Queen's Square, Westminster, by a disastrous fire—which, amongst other losses, entailed that of his valuable collection of books and prints. He then removed to a house in Broad Sanctuary, Westminster, and this remained his home to the end of his life.

Residence in these two successive houses under the shadow of the Abbey offered Hawkins an admirable opportunity, which he greatly appreciated, of enjoying the best church music. The Abbey's organist, Dr. Benjamin Cooke, was a close friend. Laetitia gives us a very pleasant account of some of his characteristics, one of which, as we shall see, was rather comical:

Every thing agreeable is connected with the remembrance of Dr. Cooke. He was one of the worthiest and best-tempered men that ever existed; and though at an early period of life he had obtained a very high rank in his profession, he had escaped all the ills connected with music and prosperity. Being of a rather taciturn disposition in general society, or rather, I may say, too modest to enter into conversation unless called on, his peculiar talent for humour was not generally known, but it was genuine and of the best description.

No one was ever less vain of superior excellence in an art, or rather, less sensible of it: he certainly supposed that every body could do what he did, 'if they would but try;' When seated at the organ of Westminster Abbey, where it will be acknowledged by his many still-existing scholars, no one ever excelled him in accompanying an anthem, he would press every hand that could be useful, into his service; and even at the risk of addressing himself to persons ignorant of the first principles of music, he would say to any lad who had strolled into the church and found his way up to the organ, 'Young gentleman, can't you lend us a hand here?' To his boys he would say, 'Come, come, don't stand idle: put in one hand here, under my arm.'[1]

It will be remembered that, long years before, Hawkins had supplied the poems for eleven Vauxhall cantatas to which his friend, Stanley, wrote the music. He had, in fact, written twelve, but had withdrawn one of them in favour of one by a friend of his, Foster Webbe. Now of Cooke's 'readiness to oblige by the loan of his talents' there are, says Laetitia, 'many proofs in the sweet harmony he would bestow on a friend's poetry'. Hawkins, then, had little trouble in persuading him to set the poem that remained over from that long-past period. It may be interesting to readers to see this specimen of Hawkins as Poet: it is very distinctly a product of its period but it will probably be admitted that, then and since then, many a worse poem has been set to music.

RECITATIVE

Fearing that he must resign
The care-dispelling joys of wine,
And the soft distresses prove
Which fill the souls of those who love,
Young Lycidas besought the wingèd boy
Who wields the never-erring dart
To wound some other heart,
More prone to love and am'rous joy;
Prostrate on the ground he laid,
And thus he pray'd:

AIR

Wanton God, who dost inspire
Am'rous thought and gay desire,
O! forbear my soul to move
With that tormenting passion, love:

[1] *Anecdotes*, 229 (some degree of exaggeration here, surely?).

Nor draw me from gay Bacchus' shrine,
At Haughty Cynthia's feet to pine.

RECITATIVE

The God beheld the foolish swain
Idly waste his youthful days,
And in a gently-chiding strain
To nobler joys thus sought his soul to raise:

AIR

Vain mortal, no more
Thus fondly adore
    Plump Bacchus the drowsy and stupid;
Let the charms of the fair
Employ all thy care,
    And kneel to the gentle god Cupid.

My gold-pointed dart,
When aimed at her heart,
    Shall force the coy maid to comply;
With joy thou shalt bless
My pow'r, and confess
    That to love is to live, but to drink is to die.[1]

If the composer himself took part in the performance of his setting of this romantic poem he must have done so in a sympathetic manner, for 'to love is to live' was apparently part of his creed and he was an expressive vocalist:

Dr. Cooke had married early, and was an excellent husband—had a large family, and was a most affectionate parent; so affectionate, as on the early death of a son to be most alarmingly grieved. His feelings at all times, and in their natural state, were very tender. He would sing his part in the beautiful Scotch song 'Farewell to Lochaber', but never could do it without the tears standing in his eyes.[2]

This friendly man, it seems, was friendly to all the world:

His cordiality, though it never led him into imprudence, was such as kept his door almost always open; and many times have I seen him come home from business, when he had been waited for in his

<hr>

[1] Ibid. 230.   [2] Ibid. 231.

dining-parlour and study, and his drawing-room has received him into a circle that has obliged him make his hasty compliments all round.

In the streets he was perpetually stopt: it is impossible to describe the humour with which he would apologize for any delay in giving a lesson, which was, to do him justice, not frequent;—he had a peculiar action of his elbow while he was recovering his breath and his fingers were unconsciously preluding the finest modulations on a keyed-instrument; and with a laugh that indicated some humorous re-collection, he would say, 'I was just stopt a few minutes as I came along'. . . .

One instance of his regard to the ease of others occurs to remem-brance. In the frequent invitations which he would give to his friends and neighbours, to be present at the performance of a little music, if, in the vocal parts, the words were not familiar to any one person or more, he always read them over, or lent them round, that no one might be at a loss.[1]

One of Cooke's choirboys was James Bartleman. With him the Hawkins family became acquainted and they made him welcome in their home (this would be from about 1780 onwards). Laetitia becomes eloquent in recalling his good nature: and his 'mellifluous notes':

I have always wished that those who knew and justly admired Bartleman as a bass-singer, had known him, as I did, when a pupil of Dr. Cooke, and in the choir of Westminster-Abbey. Living, as my father did, for the sake of enjoying the choral service, very near the Abbey, 'Bat', as my mother called him, would sometimes spend the leisure part of the whole day in our house; and his good nature was such, that on my father's bringing out of his library a volume of music, putting it before him, and saying 'Bat, will you try if you can sing that for me?' he would answer 'Yes, Sir, if I can I will;'—then *sotto voce* he would say to my brothers, to whom perhaps he had the minute before been telling something very ludicrous—as, 'how many pan-cakes some boy had eaten', or some such great event, 'I will tell you the rest presently.' Then, before the smile was off his countenance, he would clear his voice, and with the sweetness of a lark, would pour forth his tender mellifluous notes.

We always knew by the archness of his look, when a long shake was coming. In his natural simplicity, it was an exertion which he

[1] *Anecdotes*, 231–2, 234.

esteemed as he would have done any that presents itself in boys' sports; and, as if for what boys call 'fun', he would hold out to the utmost of an *ad libitum*. But when called upon to sing a solo-part of an anthem, then it was that he most shone and most delighted. I have heard him, times without number,—nay now I seem to hear him, sing—Kent's *Hear my prayer*, and Greene's *Acquaint thyself with God*, and may I never forget the impression of these sounds!

He was fine, I confess, very fine, as a bass-singer; but I have heard as fine a voice—never accompanied by so fine a taste; and this taste, this nice discretion as it may be called, in the use of his powers, was either natural to him or showed itself so early, as to make it appear so; under Dr. Cooke's tuition it met with every encouragement; and while the state of his voice allowed him to retain his situation in the Abbey, I think it must be acknowledged by all who ever heard him, that excepting the lark, 'Singing up to Heav'n's gate', nothing more melodious ever warbled in the air. Astonished was I, when he came forward with so firm, so grand a *bass* voice.

As boy and man Bartleman evidently enjoyed the high admiration of the Hawkins family. Laetitia recounts an anecdote of the period when, his voice having broken and not yet re-settled, he was for a period not a member of the Abbey choir:

An instance of his nice feeling I call to mind. My father had made him a present, annexing to the gift the condition that he should copy out some music for him. 'Bat' undertook it cheerfully; but just afterwards, having reached a point in his musical studies which left him less leisure, he found he had not time to do that which he had promised. Having detained what he was to copy, long enough to make the experiment, he returned that and what he had received, with an extremely well-penned note, saying, that 'as he could not perform the task, it was not just to accept the reward'. . . .

I do not at this moment recollect any further particulars respecting Bartleman. I can only add with pride and acknowledgment, that in the goodness of his nature, he never forgot where he had spent many of his boyish hours, and that whatever time elapsed without our meeting, he was always on every occasion prompt to show and cordial in expressing the continuance of his regard. Success never altered him, applause never elevated him; and he died, I am confident, as he had lived, beloved beyond the usual degree of love bestowed on those whose excellence, to use Wordsworth's beautiful words respecting longevity, 'has no companion'.

One of the ways in which the adult Bartleman showed his continued affection for the Hawkins family was in a certain delicate attention he paid to its head during the services at the Abbey. We gather from the following that the weekday congregation was very small and that the musical arrangements were of a somewhat free-and-easy nature—even to the point of decision during the service itself as to what the anthem should be—and no doubt Dr. Cooke's friendship with a certain member of the congregation had something to do with the choice sometimes being left to that member:

Though Bartleman for years attracted crowds as a bass-singer, he sung to almsmen and paupers in that which was his school, except that he knew where to find my father in his snug corner, almost daily at the afternoon-service, when he either quitted the bars to tell him what the anthem was, or to know what he wished it to be.[1]

One of the Hawkins's Westminster neighbours and friends was Lady Lucy Meyrick, 'by birth Lady Lucy Pitt, daughter of the Earl of Londonderry, and sister of the last who bore that title'. She had lived in Westminster before—as a girl, with her uncle, who was her guardian, and Laetitia was interested in a romantic story of her early residence there. It seems that the uncle had a daughter a little older than Lucy herself:

The young ladies, who had formed a strict friendship, were kept under great restraint, which they bore as two lively girls may be supposed to have done. Their endurances soon reached the ear of two Westminster scholars, of one of the Welch families of Meyrick, who, in the true spirit of knight-errantry, concerted with them a plan for escaping, which they carried into effect. Having gone thus far, there was nothing for the courteous knights to do, but to marry the fair

---

[1] *Anecdotes*, 271. We are enabled to gather the meaning of that expression 'quitted the bars' on turning back a few pages in Laetitia's extended discussion of cathedral music in her day. She complains of choirs where one sees 'conversation only suspended to make the responses, and those made by persons negligently clad in soiled vestments', and 'junior performers' by whom 'nuts are cracked and marbles trucked "within the bars"'.

damsels to whom they had rendered this essential service;—and for this purpose, they took them to the Fleet, or to May-Fair, in both which places marriages were solemnized with the utmost privacy. Here the two couples presented themselves, a baker's wife attending upon the ladies.

Lady Lucy was then, and to the end of her life, one of the smallest women I ever saw; she was, at the time, not more than fourteen years of age, and being in the dress of a child, the person officiating objected to performing the ceremony for her. This extraordinary scrupulosity was distressing; but her ladyship met it by a lively reply, that her cousin might be married first and then lend her her gown, which would make her look more womanly; but I suppose her right of precedence was regarded, for she used to say herself, that she was at last married in the baker's wife's gown.

Yet even now, if report be true, an obstacle intervened: the young ladies turned fickle,—not, indeed, on the question 'to be or not to be' married, but on their choice of partners; and I was assured that they actually changed, Lady Lucy taking to herself, or acquiescing in taking, the elder brother.

When the school broke up for the holidays and the boys went home, troubles began. A newly arrived guest from London, being asked 'What news from town?' told 'an odd story of two Westminster scholars, names unknown, who had, it was said, married two girls in the neighbourhood of the school'. The boys, taken by surprise, allowed their faces to betray that they knew something of the matter, and, on being questioned, they confessed.

Lady Lucy was fetched to the house of her father-in-law. His lady, seeing her so very much a child in appearance, said, on receiving her, in a tone of vexation, 'Why child, what can we do with you? Such a baby as you are, what can you know?' With equal humility and frankness Lady Lucy replied, 'It is very true, Madam, that I am very young and very ignorant; but whatever you teach me, I will learn.'

All the good lady's prejudice was now overcome, and Lady Lucy's conduct proved the sincerity of her submission. She lived seven years in Wales, under the tuition of her mother-in-law, conforming to the manners, tempers, and prejudices of her new relations.[1]

[1] Ibid. 182 et seq. Cf. *Complete Peerage*, 1932, viii. 109 n., where we learn that the young husband was Pierce Meyrick, youngest son of Owen Meyrick of Bodorgan, Anglesey.

And, after this probation, it seems, married life began, and so far as we can guess from what we are told, the couple who had 'married in haste' did not 'repent at leisure'. They had a son and a daughter, and let us hope that these, whilst being less impulsive in matrimony, inherited from their mother those fine qualities which Laetitia reports her as possessing, for she testifies that:

More perfect integrity and sincerity,—more attachment to friends, —or more strict endeavour to do right, without in any way decrying the practice of others, no tuition could have given her.

In addition to frequenting Cooke's musical home Hawkins, in the earlier part of the Westminster period, was often to be found in that of Boyce at Kensington Gore, and Laetitia is amusing in her description of how when her father and mother and she were out in the family carriage 'for *a street airing*', he would alight at Boyce's house 'just to speak a word', leaving the ladies in the carriage at the door to a late hour.

The same sort of thing happened when Hawkins had, by arrangement, to be fetched from the house of his friend, the great city merchant, Mr. Mathias. Here, however, on one occasion 'some accident betrayed us and the master of the house would not suffer us to lie hidden'.

Laetitia was dazzled by what she saw in this 'city palace' and especially by 'a set of silver candlesticks of the best taste I ever saw', with real wax candles, 'made of wax (not such as the best demi-tallow demi-wax that now pass for such'), which 'lighted the room nobly':

But this goodly show was not the whole of our entertainment:— the gentlemen kindly repeated some of the most agreeable of the glees they had sung; and Sir John Hawkins was not at home at all the sooner for his wife's fetching him.[1]

Says Laetitia 'other friends of my father's I can recollect coeval with those I have mentioned, some of whom he had the pleasure of meeting frequently, together with others not of his previous acquaintance, at that most choice of all tables,

[1] *Anecdotes*, 286.

"the Chaplains' table" (at St. James's Palace)', and writing half-a-century later, she laments the change which came over this 'rallying point' of good men and true:

I felt jealous and grieved when I heard of unworthy persons, or at least such as did no honour to the choice, as engrafted into this select band, and consequently knew that guests who would have been as well seated any where else, sate round that table, and probably on the identical chairs that had held men of such distinguished gravity, or such correct cheerfulness, as those whom my father, on his return home, would pourtray.[1]

Much has been recounted in this book of Hawkins's un-popularity but it is clear that he did have *some* friends!

[1] Ibid. 301.

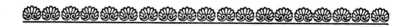

XVI. *Johnson's revival of his Ivy Lane Club and his foundation of the Essex Head Club* (1783)

HAWKINS relates a pathetic incident of 1783 concerning his old friend Johnson—an attempt to revive the pleasant conviviality of the Ivy Lane Club, which had first gathered a third of a century before (1749), had continued to meet for seven years, and had then dropped:

It has been already related that, being seized with a paralysis about the month of June 1783, he was so far recovered therefrom, as to entertain a hope, that he had nearly worn out all his disorders. 'What a man am I!' said he to me, in the month of November following, 'who have got the better of three diseases, the palsy, the gout, and the asthma, and can now enjoy the conversation of my friends, without the interruptions of weakness or pain!'—To these flattering testimonies I must add, that in this seeming springtide of his health and spirits, he wrote me the following note:

Dear Sir,

As Mr. Ryland was talking with me of old friends and past times, we warmed ourselves into a wish, that all who remained of the club should meet and dine at the house which once was Horseman's, in Ivy Lane. I have undertaken to solicit you, and therefore desire you to tell on what day next week you can conveniently meet your old friends.

I am, Sir,
Your most humble servant,

Bolt Court, Nov. 22, 1783.[1]   SAM. JOHNSON.

Ryland, apparently, was deputed to make the arrangements. He found 'the old house' shut up, and fixed upon the Queen's Arms, in St. Paul's Churchyard, as the meeting place. Johnson then sent Hawkins a letter inviting his attendance. Another meeting took place at the Queen's Arms, and then

---

[1] Hawkins, *Johnson*, 562.

one at Johnson's house; and that was the last meeting of the Club's surviving members, for serious illness came upon Johnson:

A few days after, he sent for me, and informed me, that he had discovered in himself the symptoms of a dropsy, and, indeed, his very much increased bulk, and the swoln appearance of his legs, seemed to indicate no less. He told me, that he was desirous of making a will, and requested me to be one of his executors: upon my consenting to take on me the office, he gave me to understand, that he meant to make a provision for his servant Frank, of about £70 a year for life, and concerted with me a plan for investing a sum sufficient for the purpose: at the same time he opened to me the state of his circumstances, and the amount of what he had to dispose of.[1]

Then follows the sad account of Johnson's dejection. Sending for Hawkins:

He bade me draw near him, and said, he wanted to enter into a serious conversation with me; and, upon my expressing a willingness to join in it, he, with a look that cut me to the heart, told me, that he had the prospect of death before him, and that he dreaded to meet his Saviour. I could not but be astonished at such a declaration, and advised him, as I had done once before, to reflect on the course of his life, and the services he had rendered to the cause of religion and virtue, as well by his example, as his writings; to which he answered, that he had written as a philosopher, but had not lived like one. In the estimation of his offences, he reasoned thus—'Every man knows his own sins, and also, what grace he has resisted. But, to those of others, and the circumstances under which they were committed, he is a stranger: he is, therefore to look on himself as the greatest sinner that he knows of.' At the conclusion of this argument, which he strongly enforced, he uttered this passionate exclamation,—'Shall I, who have been a teacher of others, myself be a castaway?'

Much to the same purpose passed between us in this and other conversations that I had with him, in all which I could not but wonder, as much at the freedom with which he opened his mind, and the compunction he seemed to feel for the errors of his past life, as I did, at his making choice of me for his confessor, knowing full well how meanly qualified I was for such an office.[2]

[1] Ibid. 564.　　　　　　　　　　　[2] Ibid. 564-5.

Johnson now prepared himself for the end. He spent a day in 'fasting, humiliation and such other devotional exercises as became a man in his situation':

On the Saturday following, I made him a visit, and, upon entering his room, observed in his countenance such a serenity, as indicated that some remarkable crisis of his disorder had produced a change in his feelings. He told me, that, pursuant to the resolution he had mentioned to me, he had spent the preceding day in an abstraction from all worldly concerns; that, to prevent interruption, he had, in the morning, ordered Frank not to admit any one to him, and, the better to enforce the charge, had added these awful words, 'For your master is preparing himself to die.' He then mentioned to me, that, in the course of this exercise, he found himself relieved from that disorder that had been growing on him, and was become very oppressing, the dropsy, by a gradual evacuation of water to the amount of twenty pints, a like instance whereof he had never before experienced, and asked me what I thought of it.

I was well aware of the lengths that superstition and enthusiasm will lead men, and how ready some are to attribute favourable events to supernatural causes, and said, that it might savour of presumption to say that, in this instance, God had wrought a miracle; yet, as divines recognize certain dispensations of his providence, recorded in the Scripture by the denomination of returns of prayer, and his omnipotence is now the same as ever, I thought it would be little less than criminal, to ascribe his late relief to causes merely natural, and, that the safer opinion was, that he had not in vain humbled himself before his Maker. He seemed to acquiesce in all that I said on this important subject, and, several times, while I was discoursing with him, cried out, 'It is wonderful, very wonderful!'[1]

It is a curious circumstance that later in the very month when Johnson revived his Ivy Lane Club, and then passed through these severe trials of bodily ill health and mental oppression, he was impelled to found a new club. And considering how especially close Hawkins was to him at this particular time it seems, on the face of it, odd that he was deliberately left out of the membership of this new

[1] Hawkins, *Johnson*, 565–6.

companionship and even of early knowledge of what was
projected:

He had no sooner experienced the ease and comfort which followed
from the remarkable event above-mentioned, than he began to entertain a hope, that he had got the better of the disease which most
oppressed him, and that length of days might yet be his portion; he,
therefore, sought for a relief from that solitude, to which the loss of
Mrs. Williams and others of his domestic companions, seemed to have
doomed him; and, in the same spirit that induced him to attempt the
revival of the Ivy Lane club, set about the establishment of another.

I was not made privy to this his intention, but, all circumstances
considered, it was no matter of surprise to me when I heard, as I did
from a friend of mine, that the great Dr. Johnson had, in the month
of December 1783, formed a sixpenny club, at an ale-house in Essex-
street, and that, though some of the members there were persons of
note, strangers, under restrictions, for three pence each night, might,
three nights in a week, hear him talk, and partake of his conversation.

I soon afterwards learned from the doctor, the nature of, as also the
motives to this institution, which, as to him, was novel, in this respect,
that, as the presidency passed in rotation, he was oftener excluded
from, than entitled to enjoy, that pre-eminence which, at all times, and
in all convivial assemblies, was considered as his right.[1]

In relating these circumstances Hawkins, forgetting his
voluntary retirement from the Literary Club, which Johnson
probably had in mind, shows some not unnatural pique at his
exclusion:

The more intimate of Johnson's friends looked on this establishment, both as a sorry expedient to kill time, and a degradation of those
powers which had administered delight to circles, composed of persons,
of both sexes, distinguished as well by their rank, as by their talents
for polite conversation. It was a mortification to them, to associate in
idea the clink of the tankard, with moral disquisition and literary
investigation; and many of them were led to question whether that
pleasure could be very great, which he had rendered so cheap: they,
however, concealed their sentiments, and, from motives of mere
compassion, suffered him to enjoy a comfort, which was now become
almost the only one of which he was capable; and this he did for the

[1] Ibid. 567.

short space of about ten months, when the increase of his complaints obliged him to forego it.[1]

Boswell, in recording Johnson's invitation to Reynolds to join the new club, tells us:

> It did not suit Sir Joshua to be one of this Club. But when I mention only Mr. Daines Barrington, Dr. Brocklesby, Mr. Murphy, Mr. John Nichols, Mr. Cooke, Mr. Joddrel, Mr. Paradise, Dr. [Bishop] Horsley, Mr. Windham, I shall sufficiently obviate the misrepresentation of it by Sir John Hawkins, as if it had been a low ale-house association, by which Johnson was degraded.[2]

Laetitia Hawkins, habitually so loyal in her support of her father, is very candid in her comments on his account of the formation of this club:

> Boswell was well justified in his resentment of my father's designation of this same Essex-Head Club, as a sixpenny-club, meeting at an ale-house; for in what respect was it inferior to that which he formed in 1749, at a beef steak house in Ivy Lane? The rate of admission could be no consideration in a society to which neither wealth nor rank could introduce; and whatever it was as a *house*, Johnson's presence would have absolved it from indignity. Perhaps it was, of eligible places, the nearest to his residence, and, therefore, gave the best chance for his ability to meet his friends. As to 'a presidency in rotation', the fable of 'the Lion and the other beasts hunting' solves every difficulty. Woe had betided the president who should presume to preside when Johnson was there.
>
> I am sorry my father suffered himself to seem pettish on the subject: honestly speaking, I dare say he did not like being passed over, and I am sure he never construed Johnson's secrecy as I do. It is my fault that the passage stood: had I said to him what I do here, it would have been struck out of the manuscript.[3]

Laetitia takes the trouble to assure her readers that though Johnson did not see fit to invite Hawkins to join his last club

---

[1] Hawkins, *Johnson*, 567.

[2] Boswell, *Johnson*, iv. 254. See C. R. Leslie and Tom Taylor, *Life and Times of Sir Joshua Reynolds*, ii. 434 and Hill's *Johnsonian Miscellanies*, ii. 221. Barry, the painter, was apparently one of the persons invited to join this club, and, as he had grossly attacked Reynolds, a wish to avoid meeting him may have been Reynolds's motive in declining the invitation.   [3] *Memoirs*, i. 103.

he went out of his way to soften the omission. It will be remembered that Hawkins wrote, 'I was not made privy to this his intention', and that he heard of the project only 'from a friend'. This very secrecy, Laetitia tells her readers, she herself understood as a testimony of 'respect and esteem', and she describes the means Johnson took for reducing the impact of the blow to his friend's pride that he realized had been delivered:

If I may be allowed to prove Johnson's respect and esteem for my father, from his having acted clandestinely by him, I should quote the secrecy with which he established the 'Essex Street Club', in 1783, exactly one year before his death, and after he had held the most serious conversations with him on the most important subjects, and had talked on the fitness of abstraction from the world.

I remember, after this shadow of conviviality had been got up, his inviting my father and mother to spend an evening with him, and positively on 'club-night': and I never shall forget one of his adulators calling in, in his way to this right honourably designated meeting, 'just', as he said, 'to have the pleasure of informing the club of the state of his health'. Johnson listened as he might have done to a deputation from the cats; and got rid of the enquiry to resume his conversation on the irritability of Warburton, and the better spirit of Sir Matthew Hale.[1]

That close friend of the Hawkins family, Richard Clark, whom Hawkins had introduced to Johnson long years before (see p. 44) and to whom he had transferred his legal practice, was a member of the club. Boswell prints a letter of Johnson to him:

To RICHARD CLARK ESQ.

Dear Sir,

You will receive a requisition, according to the rules of the Club, to be at the house as President of the night. This turn comes once a month, and the member is obliged to attend, or send another in his place. You were enrolled in the Club by my invitation, and I ought to introduce you; but as I am hindered by sickness, Mr. Hoole will very properly supply my place as introductor, or yours as President. I hope in milder weather to be a very constant attendant.

I am, Sir, &c.

Jan. 27, 1784.   SAM. JOHNSON.

[1] Ibid. i. 102.

You ought to be informed that the forfeits began with the year, and that every night of non-attendance incurs the mulct of three-pence, that is nine-pence a week.

In the document by Clark himself quoted on p. 44 he states that 'the last time he enjoyed the company of this great and good man was at the Essex Head Club, of which, by the Doctor's invitation he became a member'.

William Cook's *The Pleasures of Conversation—a Poem*, in its 4th edition (1815) and later editions, offers poetical portraits of the principal characters of the clubs founded by 'Johnson, the Socrates of modern days'—apparently merging those of the Literary Club and those of the Essex Head Club. The following is an extract:

> Burke, whose omniscient eye surveyed around
> All that in learning—morals—taste were found,
> Reynolds, whom nature from his earliest hour
> Endued with all her fascinating power,
> Goldsmith, whose moral, sweet, descriptive quill,
> Pure as the fount on Aganippe's Hill. . . .
> Twinned with this sister art 'twas Burney's skill
> To paint the powers of music at his will.
> Nor Wyndham's merits should be left unsung.
> Whilst memory has a note—or praise a tongue—
> O Garrick! who can praise thy various powers
> To cheer and vivify the social hours?
> Near Garrick's shrine let modest Farmer stand,
> Truth in his voice—decision in his hand.
> Next Boswell came, whose roving fancy sought
> By turn—the choruses of pleasantry and thought.
> Lo! Horsley, champion of the church's cause
> And Barrington, the guard of British Laws.

Cook was one of Johnson's earliest biographers (see p. 189).

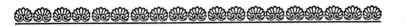

XVII. *The death of Johnson; Hawkins as executor* (1784)

WE come now to a period in Hawkins's life that makes sad reading—the period in which he was attending on the dying Johnson. In reading of his devotion to his suffering friend we may recall that for some years they had been seeing comparatively little of one another. Soon after the formation of the 'Literary Club' Johnson had begun to grow intimate with the Thrales and at length he had fallen into the habit of spending the greater part of his week with them at Streatham. Thus he tended to be less in touch with his old friends in London. Hawkins was not a member of the Streatham circle and did not care to make any attempt to push himself into it. Laetitia tells us of his feelings on the matter:

> Others might merely lament this monopoly—many would have sought the opportunity of self-introduction. My father was indignant; but this feeling was not deep; he remembered what Johnson had been, and as eagerly caught at opportunities of hearing of him, as a brother would have done under a separation, on *his* part painful.[1]

Then, on the death of Mr. Thrale and Johnson's estrangement from Mrs. Thrale owing to her infatuation with the musician Piozzi and her evident intention of marrying this man supposed to be socially so much 'beneath her', Johnson had, to the pleasure of Hawkins and his family, resumed his intimate relations with them:

> On a sudden he came out again, and sought my father with kind eagerness. Calls were exchanged; he would now take his tea with us; and in one of those evening visits, which were the pleasantest periods of my knowledge of him, saying, when taking leave, that he was leaving

[1] *Memoirs,* i. 96.

London, Lady H. said, 'I suppose you are going to Bath.' 'Why should you suppose so?' said he. 'Because,' said my mother, 'I hear Mrs. Thrale is gone there.' '*I* know nothing of Mrs. Thrale,' he roared out; 'good evening to you.'[1]

That must have been in 1782 or 1783, and in 1784 Johnson's end was clearly in sight.

As we turn almost any page of Hawkins's own account of the period we feel oppressed, as we have done before (see p. 167), by both our inevitable sympathetic participation in his friend's bodily sufferings and our sense of an all-pervading fear of death and judgement. Consider that combination of maladies—asthma, palsy, gout, dropsy, emphysema of the lungs, and granular disease of the kidneys; reflect on his deadening his pain by repeated resort to opium, on his appealing to his surgeon to scarify his leg, and when that had little effect, and his servant refused to bring him a lancet, seizing 'a pair of scissors that lay in a drawer by him' and plunging them 'deep in the calf of each leg'! And as for his mental state, how sorry a thing it is that throughout Christian history believers of so many varieties of creed have pictured a God in heaven whose mercy is far inferior to that which their own code, as they have learnt it from the Son of God, requires them to show to their fellows on earth. Is it not pathetic to read of the devout Johnson's confessing to his future biographer how deeply he was troubled by 'the thought of meeting his Saviour', and faintly expressing his 'hope that he would not reject him'?

His belief in God and his justice was, however, unshaken, and it was at Hawkins's suggestion that, for the instruction of his fellows, he at length decided to leave in writing 'an explicit declaration of his belief', such as might obviate all suspicion that he was other than a Christian:

He thanked me for the hint, and, calling for paper, wrote on a slip, that I had in my hand and gave him, the following words: 'I humbly commit to the infinite and eternal goodness of Almighty God, my soul

---

[1] *Memoirs*, i. 96. It is worth remarking that when Hawkins came to write his *Life of Johnson* he practically ignored the whole Streatham connexion—important as it is.

polluted with many sins; but, as I hope, purified by repentance, and redeemed, as I trust, by the death of Jesus Christ'; and, returning it to me, said, 'This I commit to your custody.'[1]

In William Roberts's *Memoirs of the Life and Correspondence of Hannah More*[2] is an account of a conversation with the Rev. Mr. Storry of Colchester:

We were riding together near Colchester, when I asked Mr. Storry whether he had ever heard that Dr. Johnson expressed great dissatisfaction with himself on the approach of death, and that in reply to friends, who, in order to comfort him, spoke of his writings in defence of virtue and religion, he had said, 'admitting all you urge to be true, how can I tell when I have done enough?'

Mr. S. assured me that what I had just mentioned was perfectly correct; and then added the following interesting particulars.

Dr. Johnson, said he, did feel as you describe, and was not to be comforted by the ordinary topics of consolation which were addressed to him. In consequence he desired to see a clergyman, and particularly described the views and character of the person whom he wished to consult. After some consideration a Mr. Winstanley was named, and the Dr. requested Sir John Hawkins to write a note in his name, requesting Mr. W.'s attendance as a minister.

Mr. W. who was in a very weak state of health, was quite overpowered on receiving the note, and felt appalled by the very thought of encountering the talents and learning of Dr. Johnson. In his embarrassment he went to his friend Colonel Pownall, and told him what had happened, asking, at the same time, for his advice how to act. The Colonel, who was a pious man, urged him immediately to follow what appeared to be a remarkable leading of providence, and for the time argued his friend out of his nervous apprehension: but after he had left Colonel Pownall, Mr. W.'s fears returned in so great a degree as to prevail upon him to abandon the thought of a personal interview with the Dr. He determined in consequence to write him a letter: that letter I think Mr. Storry said he had seen,—at least a copy of it, and part of it he repeated to me as follows:—

Sir—I beg to acknowledge the honour of your note, and am very

---

[1] The quotations given in this chapter, unless otherwise indicated, come from Hawkins's *Johnson*, 581 et seq. A close parallel account of Johnson's last days, in some details amplifying Hawkins's, is that of his friend John Hoole in *The European Magazine*, Sept. 1799, 153 (reprinted in Hill's *Johnsonian Miscellanies*, ii. 145 et seq.).
[2] i. 376.

sorry that the state of my health prevents my compliance with your request; but my nerves are so shattered that I feel as if I should be quite confounded by your presence, and instead of promoting, should only injure the cause in which you desire my aid. Permit me therefore to write what I should wish to say were I present. I can easily conceive what would be the subjects of your inquiry. I can conceive that the views of yourself have changed with your condition, and that on the near approach of death, what you once considered mere peccadillos have risen into mountains of guilt, while your best actions have dwindled into nothing. On whichever side you look you see only positive transgressions or defective obedience; and hence, in self-despair, are eagerly inquiring, 'What shall I do to be saved?' I say to you, in the language of the Baptist, 'Behold the Lamb of God!' &c. &c.

When Sir John Hawkins came to this part of Mr. W.'s letter, the Dr. interrupted him, anxiously asking, '*Does he say so?* Read it again! Sir John.' Sir John complied: upon which the Dr. said, 'I must see that man; write again to him.' A second note was accordingly sent: but even this repeated solicitation could not prevail over Mr. Winstanley's fears. He was led, however, by it to write again to the Doctor, renewing and enlarging upon the subject of his first letter; and these communications, together with the conversation of the late Mr. Latrobe, who was a particular friend of Dr. Johnson, appear to have been blessed by God in bringing this great man to the renunciation of self, and a simple reliance on Jesus as his Saviour, thus also communicating to him that peace which he had found the world could not give, and which when the world was fading from his view, was to fill the void, and dissipate the gloom, even of the valley of the shadow of death.[1]

[1] The 'late Mr. Latrobe' (1728–86) was a bishop in the Moravian church. An American scholar, after thorough investigation of the account, inclines to think it mythical. He has identified Mr. Storry (who died in 1814), Mr. Winstanley (who died in 1789), and Colonel Pownall, but expresses the opinion that 'Merely to identify the various persons mentioned in the letter does not prove that its contentions are trustworthy. . . . Obviously the letter raises many questions. Through what channels did the obscure Mr. Storry hear the report? Why should Johnson have sought religious advice from Winstanley, who was unknown to him, when he could easily have called upon one of his orthodox and Evangelical acquaintances among the clergy? Finally, if there's any truth in the tale, why did neither Boswell nor Hawkins, who allegedly sent for Winstanley, never mention the man in connexion with Johnson? Our inability to answer those questions only serves to strengthen the impression that the whole account is mythical. Nevertheless, the fact that all the persons mentioned were real characters who conceivably could have played the parts assigned to them makes one hesitate to brand the report as a clear fabrication' (Prof. M. J. Quinlan, in *Review of Religion*, Mar. 1948, 255).

There seemed to Hawkins to be a danger of his friend dying intestate, and so giving occasion for litigation amongst his relations. Hawkins called at his home to put before him his fear of that happening, but found that he had gone to spend the day with their friend the Reverend Mr. Strahan, of Islington. Hawkins followed him there:

He told me, that he had signed and sealed the paper I left him;—but that, said I, had blanks in it, which, as it seems, you have not filled up with the names of the executors.—'You should have filled them up yourself', answered he.—I replied that such an act would have looked as if I meant to prevent his choice of a fitter person.—'Sir', said he, 'these minor virtues are not to be exercised in matters of such importance as this.'—At length, he said, that on his return home, he would send for a clerk, and dictate a will to him.—You will then, said I, be inops consilii; rather do it now. With Mr. Strahan's permission, I will be his guest at dinner; and, if Mr. Hoole will please to hold the pen, I will, in a few words, make such a disposition of your estate as you shall direct.—To this he assented; but such a paroxysm of the asthma seized him, as prevented our going on. As the fire burned up, he found himself relieved, and grew chearful. 'The fit', said he, 'was very sharp; but I am now easy.' . . . Having executed the will with the necessary formalities he would have come home, but being press'd by Mr. and Mrs. Strahan to stay, he consented, and we all dined together. Towards the evening, he grew chearful, and I having promised to take him in my coach, Mr. Strahan and Mr. Ryland would accompany him to Bolt-court. In the way thither he appeared much at ease, and told stories. At eight I set him down, and Mr. Strahan and Mr. Ryland betook themselves to their respective homes.

And so, from 27 November to 13 December, Hawkins, who evidently kept a diary-record of all that passed, gives us a day-by-day account of the downhill progress to the inevitable end, which came on Monday the thirteenth:[1]

On Sunday, 5 December, had occurred an incident of which Hawkins's own account (which it seems reasonable to believe) is as follows. This incident occurred whilst Johnson

---

[1] Here he has the advantage over his coming rival as biographer, as Boswell was in Scotland during the last six months of Johnson's life, so that his account of the period is based on information acquired at second-hand.

was dressing for the solemnity of the Sacrament of the Last Supper which Mr. Strahan administered to him with 'Mr. Langton, and other of his friends, as many as nearly filled the room':

While he was dressing and preparing for this solemnity, an accident happened which went very near to disarrange his mind. He had mislaid, and was very anxious to find a paper that contained private instructions to his executors; and myself, Mr. Strahan, Mr. Langton, Mr. Hoole, Frank, and I believe some others that were about him, went into his bed-chamber to seek it.

In our search, I laid my hands on a parchment-covered book, into which I imagined it might have slipped. Upon opening the book, I found it to be meditations and reflections, in Johnson's own handwriting; and having been told a day or two before by Frank, that a person formerly intimately connected with this matter, a joint proprietor of a newspaper, well known among the booksellers [Steevens; cf. p. 133] and of whom Mrs. Williams once told me she had often cautioned him to beware; I say, having been told that this person had lately been very importunate to get access to him, indeed to such a degree as that, when he was told that the doctor was not to be seen, he would push his way upstairs; and having stronger reasons than I need here mention, to suspect that this man might find and make an ill use of the book, I put it, and a less of the same kind, into my pocket; at the same time telling those around me, and particularly Mr. Langton and Mr. Strahan, that I had got them both, with my reasons for thus securing them.

After the ceremony was over, Johnson took me aside, and told me that I had a book of his in my pocket; I answered that I had two, and that to prevent their falling into the hands of a person who had attempted to force his way into the house, I had done as I conceived a friendly act, but not without telling his friends of it, and also my reasons. He then asked me what ground I had for my suspicion of the man I mentioned: I told him his great importunity to get admittance; and farther, that immediately after a visit which he had made me, in the year 1775, I missed a paper of a public nature, and of great importance; and that a day or two after, and before it could be put to its intended use, I saw it in the news-papers.

At the mention of this circumstance Johnson paused; but recovering himself, said, 'You should not have laid hands on the book; for had

I missed it, and not known you had it, I should have roared for my book, as Othello did for his handkerchief, and probably have run mad.'

I gave him time, till the next day, to compose himself, and then wrote him a letter, apologising, and assigning at large the reasons for my conduct; and received a verbal answer by Mr. Langton, which, were I to repeat it, would render me suspected of inexcusable vanity; it concluded with these words, 'If I was not satisfied with this, I must be a savage.'

By Johnson's will (a revised copy of which was made five days before his death) Hawkins became one of his executors, with, as colleagues, Sir Joshua Reynolds and Dr. Scott (Johnson's companion on his journey to Edinburgh eleven years before; the future Lord Stowell, Advocate-General, &c.). To each of them he left a few books—to Hawkins 'the Annales Ecclesiastici of Baronius and Holingshead's and Stowe's Chronicles, and also an octavo Common Prayer Book'.

Of the three executors it was apparently Hawkins who took the lead in settling the estate, and we find hints of a little callousness on his part, such as the following:

Dr. Samuel Johnson . . . died this year; and during the time the surgeon was engaged in opening his body, Sir John Hawkins, Knight, was in the adjoining room seeing to the weighing of the Doctor's tea-pot, in the presence of a silversmith, whom Sir John, as an executor, had called upon to purchase it.[1]

A clause of the will to which Hawkins felt an objection was the following:

The rest of the aforesaid sums of money and property, together with my books, plate, and household-furniture, I leave to the before-mentioned Sir Joshua Reynolds, Sir John Hawkins, and Dr. William Scott, also in trust, to be applied, after paying my debts, to the use of Francis Barber, my man-servant, a negro, in such manner as they shall judge most fit and available to his benefit.

This meant that Barber, whom Johnson had adopted over thirty years before, whom he had had educated, and who had

[1] J. T. Smith, *A Book for a Rainy Day.*

since then (with one or two small interruptions) served him as valet and general factotum, would receive, by the arrangement of the executors, a life annuity on which a man of his class might comfortably live. The following incident which lies behind this bequest is well known:

Having no near relations, it had been for some time Johnson's intention to make a liberal provision for his faithful servant, Mr. Francis Barber, whom he looked upon as particularly under his protection, and whom he had all along treated truly as a humble friend. Having asked Dr. Brocklesby what would be a proper annuity to a favourite servant, and being answered that it must depend on the circumstances of the master; and, that in the case of a nobleman, fifty pounds a year was considered as an adequate reward for many years' faithful service; 'Then, (said Johnson) shall I be *nobilissimus*, for I mean to leave Frank seventy pounds a year, and I desire you to tell him so.'[1]

All this Hawkins regarded as 'ill-directed benevolence' and he discusses it very unfavourably in the course of the last pages of his *Life of Johnson*. He was of opinion that one Humphrey Heely, whom he describes as a 'relative' of Johnson, should have received mention in the will and he even tried to persuade Barber to supply the wants of Heely, who with his wife had, at Johnson's instance, been accommodated in an almshouse ('an old man and lame, having one leg much shorter than the other but of an excellent understanding', as Hawkins describes him).[2] Barber very naturally replied '*I cannot afford it*', which evidence of parsimony on the part of the legatee evidently shocked the wealthy executor. But Boswell surely puts the case very fairly:

And here I am enabled fully to refute a very unjust reflection, by Sir John Hawkins, both against Dr. Johnson, and his faithful servant, Mr. Francis Barber; as if both of them had been guilty of culpable

---

[1] Boswell, iv. 401.

[2] Having 'one leg much shorter than the other but of an excellent *understanding*'. Were we not accustomed to the habitual seriousness in Hawkins's writings one might imagine him indulging in a kind of pun. (But this is an unworthy thought!)

Laetitia, by the way, says 'Heely was a wonderful man, and my father was fond of his society' (*Anecdotes*, 163). Laetitia is violent on her father's side in all this affair (*Memoirs*, i. 153, 222 and *Anecdotes*, 163).

neglect towards a person of the name of Heely, whom Sir John chooses to call a *relation* of Dr. Johnson's. The fact is, that Mr. Heely was not his relation; he had indeed been married to one of his cousins, but she had died without having children, and he had married another woman; so that even the slight connection which there once had been by *alliance* was dissolved. Dr. Johnson, who had shewn very great liberality to this man while his first wife was alive, as has appeared in a former part of this work, was humane and charitable enough to continue his bounty to him occasionally; but surely there was no strong call of duty upon him or upon his legatee, to do more.[1]

There exists a letter of Boswell in London to Barber at Lichfield, dated 29 June 1787, as follows:

Dear Sir,

Sir John Hawkins having done gross injustice to the character of the great and good Dr. Johnson, and having written so injuriously of you and Mrs. Barber, as to deserve severe animadversion, and perhaps to be brought before the spiritual court, I cannot doubt of your inclination to afford me all the help you can to state the truth fairly, in the work I am now preparing for the Press.

I therefore beg that you will without delay write three Copies of the Letter No. 1 which I enclose, directing one to Sir Joshua Reynolds, one to Dr. Scott, and one to Sir John Hawkins, putting to each the *date* on which you write, and enclose them to me, together with a Letter in the words of No. 2. I have mentioned the business to Sir Joshua and Dr. Scott. When I have received the said letters distinctly written out by you, I shall proceed in an effectual manner.

Please to enclose your packet under cover of the Honourable William Ward, M.P., London.

You may at the same time let me have a private letter informing me

---

[1] Boswell, *Johnson*, iv. 370. This passage is followed by a letter of Johnson's arranging for some small financial relief for Heely. The account of Johnson's bounty 'in a former part of this work' includes a letter in which Johnson authorizes a friend to pay Heely ten pounds and says, 'What I could do I would do for the woman, having no good reason to pay much regard to Heely himself.'

As regards Hawkins calling Heely a 'relation' of Johnson, it may be pointed out that Johnson himself, in taking steps to secure Heely's admission to the almshouse, called him 'a poor relation of mine'. When in 1796 Strahan published the third edition of Johnson's *Prayers and Meditations* he stated in it, 'The profits of the second edition have been distributed among Dr. Johnson's poor relations and connexions, all of whom are since dead, except Humphrey Hely. . . . This poor man, who has seen better days, is now a tenant of Whicher's Alms-houses, Chapel Street, Westminster' (Boswell, iv. 547).

how you are, and mentioning any thing that occurs to yourself. Be assured that I am ever sincerely concerned for your welfare. I send my compliments to Mrs. Barber and am with much regard

Dear Sir

Your steady friend

James Boswell

And over seven months later (20 Mar. 1788) Boswell wrote to Barber again, asking him for a letter in these terms:

Sir,

I hereby authorise you to demand from Sir John Hawkins all books or papers of any sort which belonged to the late Dr. Samuel Johnson, that may be in his possession, and your receipt to him shall be sufficient on my account as residuary legatee.[1]

A few days before Johnson's death he asked Hawkins, 'where he should be buried' and received the reply, 'Doubtless in Westminster Abbey'—as to which Boswell records that he 'seemed to feel a satisfaction very natural to any man of imagination who has no family sepulchre in which he can be laid with his fellows'.

But there was little satisfaction amongst Johnson's friends as to the manner in which the proceedings in the Abbey were conducted. The Burneys, perhaps naturally, placed all the blame for this on the shoulders of one of the three executors. Dr. Charles Burney, senior, wrote a week later to his friend Twining, as follows (and it will be seen that he mentions the Dean and Chapter as considering Hawkins responsible):

The Dean and Chapter of Westminster Abbey lay all the blame on Sir John Hawkins for suffering Johnson to be so unworthily interred. The Knight's first inquiry at the Abbey in giving orders, as the most acting executor, was—'What would be the difference in expense between a public and private funeral?' and was told only a few pounds to the prebendaries, and about ninety pairs of gloves to the choir and attendants; and he then determined that, 'As Dr. Johnson had no music in him, he should choose the cheapest manner of interment.'

---

[1] These letters are in the Lomax Collection at the Johnson Birthplace, Lichfield. They have been published by Aleyn Lyell Reade in his *Johnsonian Gleanings*, Pt. II (1912).

And for this reason there was no organ heard, or burial service sung; for which he suffers the Dean and Chapter to be abused in all the newspapers, and joins in their abuse when the subject is mentioned in conversation.

And Dr. Charles Burney, junior, was equally blunt, for in a letter to Parr he said:

The executor, Sir John Hawkins, did not manage things well, for there was no anthem or choir service performed—no lesson—but merely what is read over every old woman that is buried by the parish. Dr. Taylor read the service, but so-so.[1]

Tyers, in the *Gentleman's Magazine*,[2] indicates that the dissatisfaction was widespread, but condones the economy practised:

It must be told that a dissatisfaction was expressed in the public papers, that he was not buried with all possible funeral rites and honours. In all processions and solemnities, something will be forgotten or omitted. Here no disrespect was intended. The executors did not think themselves justified in doing more than they did. For only a little cathedral service, accompanied with lights and music, would have raised the price of interment. In this matter, fees run high: they could not be excused; and the expences were to be paid from the property of the deceased. His funeral expences amounted to more than two hundred pounds. Future monumental charges may be defrayed by the generosity of subscription: the whole cost will be more than the last mentioned sum.

And there we may leave the question.

In 1785,[3] when Hawkins was sixty-six, he was pressed to have his portrait painted. Laetitia's story of this is as follows:

My father had always refused, even to my mother's request, to sit for his picture. He treated such solicitude for being remembered, as foppery, for which he entertained the most unqualified contempt. We had therefore nothing approaching nearer to a portrait, than an outline taken by a friend by candlelight.

But at length Dr. Hayes of Oxford, strongly urged him to sit to a young artist whose interests he was anxious to promote, and adding

---

[1] Johnstone, *Works of Samuel Parr . . . and a Selection from his Correspondence* (1828), i. 535. Dr. John Taylor, Prebendary of Westminster, was Johnson's old schoolfellow of Lichfield days and his lifelong friend.

[2] 1785, p. 86.   [3] This date is given by *D.N.B.*

that he was influenced likewise by another motive, his wish to place the picture in the music-school at Oxford. My father then complied, and he submitted to be painted as he never looked, dressed as he never dressed, and employed as he never was employed; for he is represented smirking in a velvet coat, with a volume in his hand which certainly, by its external, must be one of the last new novels then printed.

The artist vowed it was 'a capital likeness', and we young folk, delighted with the prospect of having a portrait of our parent, determined on subscribing to have it copied. I believe it was my mother who advised seeing with our own eyes the original;—we did so, and withdrew our commission.[1]

The 'young artist' mentioned was James Roberts, who must at that date have been in his early thirties. He had just settled in Oxford, which, presumably, was how Hayes knew him. Possibly Hawkins visited Oxford then and advantage was taken of this to put the commission in the hands of Hayes's protégé.

Roberts had a reputation as a portrait painter—especially of actors in character. His portrait of Hawkins is still in the University's Music Faculty collection. It is not first-rate but is the only one we possess (for the 'outline', or silhouette, mentioned by Laetitia and used by her as the frontispiece of her *Anecdotes* is of no significance whatever). An engraving of the Oxford portrait, by R. Clamp, from a drawing of it by Silvester Harding, was published nineteen years after Hawkins's death by E. and S. Harding, of Pall Mall, and was reproduced in the mid-nineteenth-century editions of Hawkins's *History*.[2]

[1] *Anecdotes*, 137.
[2] Roberts made a pencil sketch of Johnson when he was on his last visit to Dr. Adams, Master of Pembroke College, Oxford. This is at Painswick House, Stroud, Glos. (formerly the home of Dr. Adams's daughter), and the circumstances under which it was drawn are given in the Hill-Powell edition of Boswell, iv. 533–4.

XVIII. *His 'Life and Works of Johnson'* (1787–9)

WHATEVER blame may have found expresssion as to the manner in which Johnson's funeral was conducted there is no doubt that during the days immediately preceding it, as during the days of the last illness, Hawkins showed great devotion to his old friend. His daughter's account of the period insists on this:

> Few persons know what my father went through in performing these last acts of steady, unobtrusive friendship. They were called for in the depth of one of the two severest winters that ever I remember, immediately following one another, and with little intervention of summer; the snow had fallen in October, and an unrelenting frost intruded so far into the spring, that on the first of May, not a leaf had opened on the trees in St. James's Park; on the fifth they were in foliage!
> Again the snow came, if I recollect rightly in October, and in December, when Johnson died, none but hackney-horses could be risked in the streets. My father disregarded everything; he was little at home in the day, and if he returned at midnight, only giving fresh orders for the morning, we were happy.[1]

And then she goes on to tell us that 'immediately on his emancipation from this severe attendance' she heard her father say, 'He has left me his executor, and I will write his life'. An invitation to do this, and also to become responsible for a complete edition of Johnson's works, came immediately:

> A very few hours after, perhaps not more than four, two gentlemen came to him. Wanting me to write, he ordered me to be called into his study, and on my entering the room, he named these visitors to me as Mr. Strahan and Mr. Cadell.

[1] *Memoirs*, i. 154.

Considering Johnson's professed or real antipathy to the Scots there is a little irony in the fact that the chief of the two publishers who so promptly presented themselves on this mission was one. Strahan (father of the Rev. George Strahan who had just attended Johnson on his deathbed, cf. pp. 177–8) had been partly responsible for the publication of the great Dictionary and had often served as business adviser to Johnson and as his banker: he combined with the commercial ability of his race a literary acumen which had often enabled him to move in such circles as brought him in touch with able writers, and when his business success became such that he was in a position to set up his coach Johnson proudly claimed this as 'a credit to literature'. As for Cadell (here is another Scots name, by the way, though this particular Cadell was born in Bristol), he also was a friend of Johnson's and, years before, had offered him a large sum if he would write a volume of Devotional Exercises (a task which Johnson did not feel he should undertake). Strahan and Cadell were partners in business but approached Hawkins as a delegation from a large body of bookseller-publishers, for, according to the common custom of the day, the 'Life and Works' were to be published by a syndicate (the various firms' names on the title-page of the volumes when they appeared numbered nearly fifty).

The choice of Hawkins for this project seemed to be a quite natural one. He had been long a recognized author; he had been for over a third of a century in close touch with Johnson;[1] any documents that had been left were at that moment in his hands, and it may have been known, moreover, that these included certain small books of a diary nature, from which facts concerning Johnson, and a record of some of his thoughts, could be drawn.

---

[1] It may seem temerarious to differ from that very complete Johnsonian, Professor Joseph Wood Krutch, but the present author cannot accept his statement in his admirable *Samuel Johnson* (p. 171 in the 1948 British edition), 'Hawkins was never really intimate with him'. Hawkins's membership of the Ivy Lane and Literary Clubs, and Johnson's apparently frequent visits to his house (see Laetitia Hawkins *passim*) and dependence on him during his last days seem to conflict with this view.

The remuneration offered strikes one as extremely modest. 'Considering the necessary expenses of such an undertaking,' says Laetitia, 'they had offered him £200, which allowed him to employ an amanuensis, and to turn over the correction of the proofs to others.' (But surely that £200 cannot have been the whole of what Hawkins was to receive for writing the *Life* and editing the works: if it was then Hawkins comes under Johnson's own condemnation as recorded by Boswell, 'No man but a blockhead ever wrote but for money'. Perhaps it is merely an expenses allowance and there was some arrangement apart from it as to the actual remuneration). As regards the *Life* that was to precede the volumes of *Works* Hawkins's usual amanuensis was ready to hand. Laetitia goes on:

He added a question whether *I* would undertake the labour, saying, 'It will be a large octavo volume of 600 or 700 pages: it is a trifling job to *you*; and as for that part of the corrections [of the proofs] with which I shall concern myself, you are so used to it, that it will be nothing.'

I think at that time a new edition of the Complete Angler found me employment [there was none between 1784 and 1792]; but I would have undertaken any thing even without pay, for the various knowledge I gained. My father was no ungenerous exactor: he had often repeated to us the axiom, that no one had a right to the gratuitous service of another; and the caveat of the Jewish law against muzzling the ox while treading out the corn, was so constantly in his mind, that he never suffered me even to peel an orange for him, without giving me what, as children, we called 'two pigs'. He, therefore, in this spirit, offered me at the time such a remuneration as I joyfully accepted, and eventually trebled it—I had forty pounds!

In addition to her duty as amanuensis Laetitia had a more important duty allotted to her. Johnson's diary-like books have just been mentioned. She says:

It was my business to select from his little books of self-examination, which came into my father's hands, the passages that should be printed as specimens; and I rejected, as subject to wild surmises, those which contained marks known only in their significations by himself.[1]

[1] *Memoirs*, i. 188.

Moreover (and this is rather surprising) Laetitia and her brothers, as the work proceeded, were constantly consulted and their candid criticism taken in good part:

Of the life, as my father wrote it, I have no occasion to speak, and *for* it, even *he* would not expect me to say any thing. We, to our shame be it spoken! were most unmerciful critics; he gave up everything—'tis too little to say to our *judgment*, though his expression often was, as he threw his rough draught amongst us, 'What you would have it make it';—it was given up to our *ferocity*: the façon of our hard work was often merriment, and his good-humour admitted of our receiving the flying leaves, with 'Come, let us see'; and when we objected, we condescended to say, 'We would see what we could make of it.'

In *general*, I must say, my father's disposition to give up while thus employed was incredible. With the History of Music, we dared not take liberties; and there were times in the course even of this *minor* undertaking, when the best judgment amongst us could not prevail.[1]

But others besides Hawkins were already engaging in this topical enterprise of Johnsonian biography. On 5 May 1785 we find the Rev. Dr. Lort, Prebendary of St. Paul's, writing to Bishop Percy:

Your old friend Johnson's death afforded a fruitful topic of conversation for a fortnight or three weeks, and called forth an abundance of anecdotes relative to his life, which have been carefully gleaned up, and have [been] or will be retailed in due time to the public at large. One Cooke, a writer employed by Kearsley, had prepared and printed a life, which I believe was published a day after he expired. Mr. Tyers followed in two subsequent Gentleman's Magazines; and Sir John Hawkins, Dr. Kippis, and Mrs Piozzi, have announced by advertisements in the papers their intentions of treating the world with all they know or can collect concerning him. The lady has honoured me with a letter dated Milan, March 22, in which she mentions this design, and begs me to collect for her. I am told the foundation of her work will be Johnson's letters to her. . . .

To Johnson's biographers I should have added Boswell, who has for many years been committing to paper all that fell from his lips when they were together. Sir Joshua Reynolds has opened a subscription for a monument.[2]

---

[1] *Memoirs,* i. 159.   [2] Nichols, *Illustrations,* vii. 467.

The 'One Cooke' mentioned was William Cook, a member of Johnson's Essex Head Club (commonly known as 'Conversation Cook' from his poem, *Conversation*, which retails club anecdotes—see p. 172). He was quickly off the mark with his *Life of Samuel Johnson, LL.D.*, if not quite so quickly as Dr. Lort states, his preface being dated 28 December 1784 and the date on the title-page 1785. His book appeared anonymously,[1] as did another the same year, attributed to William Shaw, the Gaelic scholar and Johnson's supporter in the Ossian controversy. Johnson had written for Shaw his 'Proposals' for *An Analysis of the Scotch Celtick Language*, and had also persuaded him to abandon his orders in the Scottish Presbyterian Church and to become an Anglican clergyman. His *Memoirs of the Life and Writings of Dr. Samuel Johnson . . . authenticated by living evidence* is now somewhat rare. Mrs. Piozzi's *Anecdotes of the Late Samuel Johnson, LL.D.*, appeared in 1786.

Hawkins's book, in 1787, which has no actual Preface, opens nevertheless with a sonorous prefatorial passage:

The general sense of mankind and the practice of the learned in all ages, have given a sanction to biographical history, and concurred to recommend that precept of the wise son of Sirach, in which we are exhorted to 'praise famous men, such as by their counsels and by their knowledge of learning were meet for the people,—and were wise and eloquent in their instructions,—and such as recited verses in writing'. In each of these faculties did the person, whose history I am about to write, so greatly excel, that, except for my presumption in the attempt to display his worth, the undertaking may be thought to need no apology; especially if we contemplate, together with his mental endowments, those moral qualities which distinguished him, and reflect that, in an age when literary acquisitions and scientific improvements are rated at their utmost value, he rested not in the applause which these procured him; but adorned the character of a scholar and a philosopher with that of a christian.

---

[1] *D.N.B.* does not mention it in its list of his writings. Austin Dobson, in his essay *Boswell's Predecessors*, speaks of him as the 'supposed author'. Colonel F. Grant, in the extensive bibliography at the end of his short *Life of Johnson* (1887), attaches no name to the title.

Then follows the reasonable request of the biographer to be excused if he has used the first person more often 'than the practice of some writers will warrant'. As to this, says he:

By the office I have undertaken I stand engaged to relate facts to which I was a witness, conversations in which I was a party, and to record memorable sayings uttered only to myself. Whoever attends to these circumstances, must, besides the disgust which such an affectation of humility would excite, be convinced, that in some instances, the avoiding of egotisms had been extremely difficult, and in many impossible.

As a matter of fact it is just the passages so alluded to that are nowadays the most interesting: indeed it may perhaps be said that it is these scattered passages that most make the work still worth perusal, for it is, in the main, like the *History of Music*, a monument of incompetence in planning (if it can, indeed, be said to show evidence of any planning at all), so that its value as a connected 'life' is not very high.

Hawkins, like his daughter, was incapable of deciding on a route and keeping to it. He was perpetually led up bypaths which beguiled him into forests in which he wandered not knowing how to find his way out, or into morasses in which he floundered, unable within any reasonable time to get his feet again on to dry land. Of this discursiveness Sir Edward Boyle, in an article *Johnson and Sir John Hawkins*, has given a brief summary:

There is an account of a Portuguese Mission to Abyssinia, and a dissertation on the decline of British watchmaking. Long quotations are given from Urquhart's *Life of the Admirable Crichton*, and a statement as to the respective rights of debtor and creditor. We are given the author's views as to the proportions of columns, and as to the respective merits and defects of Fielding, Smollett and Richardson. Among other things dealt with—sometimes in considerable detail—are the humanity of the law and its tenderness to felons, life in St. Kilda, the weakness and difficulties of the medical profession, the first Prayer Book of Edward VI, the gradual improvement in public morals, the failings of authors, Jonas Hanway's *Essay on Tea* (in which he asserts 'that the practice of drinking tea is productive of harm among the lower classes of people'), the genius of Sterne, and a per-ambulation of London. The mention of Johnson's lack of appreciation of Milton in his *Lives of the Poets* is made the excuse for eight pages regarding an attack on Milton's memory and reputation in another quarter. As instances of the Parliamentary Reports contributed by Johnson to Cave's *Magazine*, he occupies no less than twelve pages in giving Lord Hardwicke's speech on Carteret's Address to the Crown praying for the removal of Walpole, and about nine in setting out Chesterfield's speech in regard to the retailing of liquor.

No book was ever so outrageously padded. Out of its 600 pages, not more than half can truthfully be described as having any direct bearing on the life of Johnson.[1]

This statement, as a matter of fact, could be considerably extended. It is too kindly! Not only does Hawkins often stray into some bypath, he is apt then to stray from that one into another. Thus a passage on a visit Johnson received from Dodington leads to a remark that amongst the 'men of genius' who enjoyed Dodington's favour was Paul Whitehead, who, says Hawkins, for 'many years was my neighbour in the country', and so we are let in for no fewer than seven pages on the said Paul Whitehead, with digressions inside digres-sions (on the principle of a set of Chinese boxes) on people more or less associated with Whitehead, such as Amherst, Strutt, 'the celebrated Mrs. Teresa Constantia Phillips', and Dr. Thompson. A reference to the fact that people used to go to Johnson for advice suggests to Hawkins the parallel case of Richardson, who was equally sought after by people in per-plexity, and this in its turn leads to a footnote relating how Hawkins once happened to travel with Richardson in the Fulham stage coach and found him an unsociable companion.

Hawkins's footnotes are formidable! As an example—he makes 'mention of three persons, his contemporaries, all eminent in literature', but in some ways differing from John-son in their practice of it, one being the Rev. Dr. Thomas Birch, of whom a long account follows. Now Birch, it seems, was a great walker, and what can be more appropriate for a

[1] *National Review*, Mar. 1926, 85; reprinted in *Biographical Essays, 1790–1890* (Oxford University Press, 1936).

walker than a footnote? And so we are given about a page of small-type account of how Birch once 'had the curiosity to measure the circuit of London by a perambulation thereof'. His route is given in detail and when at last we find him back at his house in Norfolk Street, Strand, having 'according to his rate of walking, computed the circuit of London at twenty miles', we are favoured with a further computation, on Hawkins's own part, that 'with the buildings erected since, it may be supposed to have encreased five miles', and the reflection that 'if that is so, the present circumference of this great metropolis is about half that of ancient Rome'!

There are places in this book where a mere two or three lines of text at the top of a page suggest to its voluble author forty or more lines of footnotes. Many of the footnotes are, indeed, carried on from page to page. There is at least one footnote which is the equivalent of five pages of normal text.

The lack of any constructive sense in Hawkins's literary mind is indeed phenomenal, and the effect is sometimes positively crazy. There are moments when we feel almost impelled to cry, '*Was this writer perfectly sane?*'

There are, of course, also a certain number of errors in the book and (as we would expect from Hawkins) some uncharitable judgements. The account that is given of Johnson's relations with his wife, for instance, merits condemnation under both these heads. Laetitia, however, supports her father in this last matter. She has no belief in the reality of Johnson's so often expressed affection for his wife, and very tartly concludes a long (and, it may be admitted, thoughtful) passage on the subject thus: 'The kitten-ing, the Tetty-ing, and all this contemptible puerility, is to the last degree unaccountable'.[1]

Naturally Hawkins's big *Life* of the friend to whom he was so much attached, like the previous history of the art he loved, brought a chorus of disapproval. Partly, of course, this was due to personal enmity on the part of various people, but,

---

[1] *Memoirs*, i. 208.

3

Sir,

I send you herewith three portions of Johnson's life, reserving the fourth to be printed, under my direction, by Mr. Hughs. You will take care so to manage that the pages of his part are made to catch with the last page of the foregoing parts, as also finally to correct what is here sent you. If any difficulty occurs in the reading, you will of course apply to me. I have softened every expression that might tend to reflect on the memory of Mr. Cave.

Your humble Servant

John Hawkins

8th April 1787

Sir John Hawkins, agreeable to Mr. Nichols's desire, returns enclosed the original Manuscript of Dr. Johnson, which contains the account of money received for the translation of Father Paul.

The first Volume of the Political State was returned, after keeping it a very few days, to Mr. as were also, as soon as they could conveniently used and made use of, all the volumes of Magazine &c with which he favored Sir John.

[This is the Handwriting of Sir John Sec. John Sidney Hawkins by J. N.]

23. May 1787

The first of these communications would seem to show that two different printers were employed on Hawkins's *Life of Johnson*. The 'translation of Father Paul' mentioned in the communication to Nichols was a project of 1738–9 which was dropped, as another author (curiously, of the same name) had undertaken such a translation. However, Johnson's *Life of Father Paul* appeared in the *Gentleman's Magazine* (1739).

as has been seen, it was largely deserved. The following pretty well represents general contemporary opinion:

'The Life of Samuel Johnson, LL.D. By Sir John Hawkins, knight,' consists of a vast mass of heterogeneous matter, from which it is no easy task to separate the parts which properly belong to the hero of the story. Beside the life of Johnson, our author has entered into a number of tedious digressions, in which he has introduced an account of all his contemporaries of whom he had any knowledge, and various unconnected fragments of criticism, politics, and legal decisions.

With respect to Johnson's life, Sir John has added little, if anything, to the information of which we were before possessed: and, we are sorry to observe, that he has shown no more tenderness, no more justice to the memory of his friend, than any of his former biographers.

From many of the anecdotes respecting the contemporaries of Johnson, and the literary clubs of which he was a member, we have received considerable entertainment. But we have been disgusted with the unjust and rancorous abuse which he has wantonly poured on several excellent characters, whose names and merits will not soon be forgotten. Of the Knight's critical powers, the specimens which we have in the volume before us do not lead us to entertain the highest estimation; and the opinions which he delivers on the subjects of politics and morals, are too crude and dogmatic to receive our implicit assent.

On the whole, though this miscellaneous composition abounds in materials and facts which may prove of use to the patient historical enquirer, it is too complex, irregular, and inelegant, to please the general reader, or to insure its author even a moderate share of celebrity.[1]

The *Gentleman's Magazine* in March, April, May, August, September, and October accorded it no less than twenty-three columns of its tiny print—over nine thousand words, and not one of them of the nature of a compliment. The last three of these articles, signed by a *nom de plume*, are known to have been by Porson, and this was Porson in his mood of bitterest sarcasm—which is saying a good deal!

It is proposed here, on grounds of limited space and exhausted patience, to invite any reader who does not happen

---

[1] *New Annual Register*, 1787, 254.

to be short of the latter quality to read for himself the Magazine's twenty-three columns,[1] contenting with just one example of the Porsonian humour those readers less liberally endowed by nature. This humour, it may be explained, subtly takes throughout the colour of unrestrained panegyric:

> The witlings and critics of the day combined to run down that excellent book the 'History of Music' in five volumes quarto, and their malice prevailed so effectually, for some time, that people who had any regard for their reputation were ashamed to have the book, or to know anything about it. But Sir John was steady to his resolution; *he wrote on as he had written before*; and presented the publick with this last best gift, which not only sells itself, but is the cause of selling the Knight's other works. . . .
>
> I am credibly informed, that since the publication of this Life, a copy of the 'History of Music' has risen first from half a guinea to twelve and sixpence, next to fifteen shillings, nay, that even a guinea has been paid for a set handsomely bound in morocco. So that the book-seller, instead of losing two hundred and fifty pounds is likely to lose not above two hundred and thirty, or two hundred and forty, at most.— I beg pardon, Mr. Urban, for this rapture. But I cannot govern my imagination, whenever I think or speak of that great man. However, as I disapprove of general criticism, I will try to check my enthusiasm, and point out some few of the numberless beauties that shine through this inimitable performance.

Hawkins, who in general was 'proof against criticism' and 'considered this indifference as absolutely necessary to exertion', for once departed from his lofty principle, and called on the Editor and complained. He later learnt, it appears, that the Editor had, in conversation with a common friend, defended himself by asking, 'What business had Sir J.H. to say anything against the writings of Sterne?' (which writings Hawkins had described as 'abounding in wit and humour of the licentious kind').

Boswell's *Life*, when it appeared, four years after that of Hawkins, was found to be exceedingly plainspoken about its

---

[1] 1787, pp. 253, 285, 345, 419, 435, 521, 652, 751, 847.

predecessor—and not altogether fair. The first allusion to it opens as follows:

> Since my work was announced several Lives and Memoirs of Dr. Johnson have been published, the most voluminous of which is one compiled by Sir John Hawkins, Knight, a man, whom, during my long intimacy with Dr. Johnson, I never saw in his company but once, and I am sure not above twice.

As a statement this is open to question and as an implication is certainly quite unfair. That Boswell saw Johnson and Hawkins together not more often than twice is just possible yet surprising: however we must remember that Boswell did not make Johnson's acquaintance until 1763, and that the occasions on which the Edinburgh advocate could have seen Johnson and Hawkins together were limited to the periods of his visits to London (unless we read Boswell with a careful attention to dates we are all in danger of getting a wrong idea of the amount of time he spent in his hero's company). As for the suggestion that Hawkins was not much in Johnson's company, that really is quite unjustified. From incidents related in Laetitia's two books we learn not only that (at some periods, at any rate) Johnson was a fairly frequent visitor to her parents' house, but also that Johnson was in the habit of consulting Hawkins on business or legal matters.[1] Johnson's choice of Hawkins as a foundation member of his clubs in 1749 and 1764, and his reliance upon him during the most trying period of his life, make quite clear to us that, whatever criticism he may sometimes have expressed, there was solid esteem, based on close acquaintance. Hawkins was a member of the Johnson circle for at least fourteen or fifteen years before Boswell first entered it—possibly, indeed, a good deal more: he was in touch with Johnson over a period of not less than thirty-five years, whereas Boswell was in touch with him for only twenty-one years. We may admit that the friendship between Johnson and Boswell became of a more closely intimate character than that between Johnson and

---

[1] See *Anecdotes* and *Memoirs* passim.

Hawkins, but we can do this without accepting Boswell's suggestion that meetings between Johnson and Hawkins had been extremely rare, thus making Hawkins's undertaking of his *Life* a piece of presumption on his part.

After that unfair opening Boswell proceeds in a manner rather more justifiable (contriving to bring in, at the end, a slight hit at another of his rivals, Mrs. Piozzi—formerly Mrs. Thrale):

Johnson might have esteemed him for his decent, religious demeanour, and his knowledge of books and literary history; but from the rigid formality of his manners, it is evident that they never could have lived together with companionable ease and familiarity; nor had Sir John Hawkins that nice perception which was necessary to mark the finer and less obvious parts of Johnson's character. His being appointed one of his executors, gave him an opportunity of taking possession of such fragments of a diary and other papers as were left; of which, before delivering them up to the residuary legatee, whose property they were, he endeavoured to extract the substance. In this he has not been very successful, as I have found upon a perusal of those papers, which have since been transferred to me.

Sir John Hawkins's ponderous labours, I must acknowledge, exhibit a *farrago*, of which a considerable portion is not devoid of entertainment to the lovers of literary gossiping; but besides its being swelled out with long unnecessary extracts from various works (even one of several leaves from Osborne's Harleian Catalogue, and those not compiled by Johnson, but by Oldys), a very small part of it relates to the person who is the subject of the book; and, in that, there is such an inaccuracy in the statement of facts, as in so solemn an authour is hardly excusable, and certainly makes his narrative very unsatisfactory.

But what is still worse, there is throughout the whole of it a dark uncharitable cast, by which the most unfavourable construction is put upon almost every circumstance in the character and conduct of my illustrious friend; who, I trust, will, by a true and fair delineation, be vindicated both from the injurious misrepresentations of this authour, and from the slighter aspersions of a lady who once lived in great intimacy with him.

Boswell, of course, corrects a large number of errors to be found in his predecessor's *Life* and he differs, quite legitimately, from him in many matters of opinion (for instance, Hawkins's allusion to Johnson's 'enmity towards Milton'). But he need hardly have gone so far as to declare that 'Sir John's carelessness to ascertain fact is very remarkable' and to speak of 'our poor Sir John Hawkins, who is *unlucky on all occasions*',[1] and it is with pleasure that one finds at last the admission that 'In Sir John Hawkins's compilation there are some passages concerning Johnson which have unquestionable merit'.[2] We even find the following attempt at apology:

The greatest part of this book was written while Sir John Hawkins was alive; and I avow, that one object of my strictures was to make him feel some compunction for his illiberal treatment of Dr. Johnson. Since his decease, I have suppressed several of my remarks upon his work. But though I would not 'war with the dead'[3] *offensively*, I think it necessary to be strenuous in *defence* of my illustrious friend, which I cannot be without strong animadversions upon a writer who has greatly injured him.

Let me add, that though I doubt I should not have been very prompt to gratify Sir John Hawkins with any compliment in his life-time, I do now frankly acknowledge, that, in my opinion, his volume, however inadequate and improper as a life of Dr. Johnson, and however discredited by unpardonable inaccuracies in other respects, contains a collection of curious anecdotes and observations, which few men but its author could have brought together.[4]

So Croker, who published his edition of Boswell in 1831, could have made at any rate an exception or two from his statement that 'Mr. Boswell is habitually unjust to Sir John Hawkins'.

---

[1] Boswell, iii. 229, quotes Johnson on 'the frequency of false information', 'confused memories', and 'habitual inaccuracy', and adds—'Had he lived to read what Sir John Hawkins and Mrs. Piozzi have related concerning himself, how much would he have found his observation illustrated.' [2] iv. 371.

[3] As to this expression cf. p. 213. It comes originally from Pope's translation of Homer and was used by Johnson in a prologue to a play. There is a letter of Boswell to his friend the Rev. William Temple, of 5 Mar. 1789, in which he says: 'Pray (by return of post) help me with a word. In censuring Hawkins's book I say, "There is throughout the whole of it a dark uncharitable cast which puts the most unfavourable construction on every circumstance of my illustrious friend's conduct." Malone maintains *cast* will not do. He will have *malignancy*. Is not that too strong ? How would *disposition* do ? Hawkins is, no doubt, very malevolent. Observe how he speaks of me as quite unknown' (but cf. p. 198, note).

[4] Boswell, i. 27, n. 1.

Critics who followed Boswell were no kinder to Hawkins than he in general was, e.g. Malone speaks of 'the malignant prejudice of that shallow author' and when Murphy was called upon to re-edit Johnson's works (his edition was published in 1792) he cast aside the *Life of Johnson*, which had formed the volume introductory to Hawkins's edition of the works, and replaced it with a long 'Essay on the Life and Genius' of Johnson, in which he repeatedly attacked Hawkins's 'malignant remarks', 'misrepresentations', and 'injustices', and complained of 'the prodigious variety of foreign matter, introduced into the performance', which 'seemed to overload the memory of Dr. Johnson, and, in the account of his own life to leave him hardly visible'.

Laetitia tells an amusing story of Boswell's pique at the undistinguished way in which he was mentioned in her father's book. We need not take very seriously every detail of what she relates, but some incident of the sort must evidently have occurred:

My father and Boswell grew a little acquainted; and when the Life of their friend came out, Boswell showed himself very uneasy under an injury, which he was much embarrassed in defining. He called on my father, and being admitted, complained of the manner in which he was enrolled amongst Johnson's friends, which was as Mr. James Boswell of Auchinleck.

Where was the offence? It was one of those which a complainant hardly dares to embody in words: he would only repeat, 'Well, but *Mr. James Boswell!* surely, surely, *Mr. James Boswell*!!...'

'I know,' said my father, 'Mr. Boswell, what you mean; you would have had me say that Johnson undertook this tour with THE BOSWELL.'

He could not indeed absolutely covet this mode of proclamation; he would perhaps have been content with 'the celebrated', or 'the well-known', but he could not confess quite so much; he therefore acquiesced in the amendment proposed, but he was forced to depart without any promise of correction in a subsequent edition.[1]

As to Boswell and Hawkins 'getting a little acquainted',

---

[1] *Memoirs*, i. 235, 237. The reference in Hawkins's *Johnson* is not, as stated, to 'Mr. James Boswell of Auchinleck' but to 'Mr. James Boswell, a native of Scotland' (this is so in both editions).

Hawkins had for some years, apparently, been avoiding this. He had, early in Boswell's friendship with Johnson, 'enquired of Mr. Langton who this novel performer was, meaning rather, I believe, to be on good terms with him, as a frequenter of Bolt Court, but had received a caution against opening his door to him', since 'not only were his visits described to be long, but he was known to carry, as was said, perhaps by way of metaphor, his night-cap in his pocket'.[1]

When the opportunity came for Boswell to 'get his own back' he seized it. In mentioning in his own *Life of Johnson* the names of the members of Johnson's Ivy Lane Club he included not 'Mr. Hawkins, later well-known as Sir John Hawkins, and destined to become one of the early biographers of Johnson and editor of his works', or anything like that, but simply—'Mr. John Hawkins, an Attorney'.

It is interesting to note the judgements of Laetitia Hawkins on her father's *Life of Johnson*. She evidently felt that as Boswell was known to have the intention of writing a life it might with propriety have been waited for and accepted as what we may call the official one:

Whether, of all Dr. Johnson's friends, my father was the most or the least competent to be his biographer, is a question which I am very willing to leave doubtful. Were I to vote on the subject, I should myself hesitate. Their friendship was indeed of long standing, and had therefore commenced sufficiently early to give Sir J.H. opportunity of studying his character under various lights: this, his powers enabled him to do on an enlarged scale.

The London booksellers certainly thought my father the fittest person, or they would not have sent a deputation to him, to ask him to undertake the labour. But I shall never cease to wonder at their doing so, for Boswell's views were, I think, suspected, if not declared.[2]

As for the literary style of her father's book ('the very worst thing he ever gave to the public') she is equally candid:

I have said in this volume, that I considered the style of Sir J.H.'s Life of Johnson as not his own original style: it may be inferred from

---

[1] *Memoirs*, i. 233.   [2] Ibid. 226.

this that I cannot praise it. That it is far better than his daughter's, I willingly admit, and could, alas! bring many to testify.[1]

But as to that last modest opinion we need not quite agree. To be frank with Laetitia both her literary style and that of her father are regrettable, but though we may admit that whilst parent and child share the vicious habit of far-ranging digression, on the whole the daughter's naïve manner of expression is easier on the reader than poor Sir John's long-winded sentences and pompous phraseology, which almost justify the quip of one of the contemporary London newspapers:

> A gentleman, lately arrived in town, has been for several days affected with a lethargy owing to the perusal of three chapters in Hawkins's *Life of Johnson*.[2]

As for the ten volumes of Johnson's Works, Porson points out errors in those also, and some other writers have not shown the highest esteem of Hawkins as their editor. We shall see later (p. 217) Hawkins's irresponsible attitude to his editorship.

Some changes were introduced in the *Lives of the Poets*. An example is mentioned by Laetitia:

> Lord Palmerston, in consequence of Young's connection by marriage with his family, was very solicitous to get some errors corrected in the republication of the poet's Life. This concern, I know, brought his Lordship frequently to our house; and I believe he took on himself to make the alterations he wished for.[3]

The Lord Palmerston mentioned was the Second Viscount (father of the Victorian statesman). It is possible that he and Hawkins had musical associations with one another, for Palmerston was a singer (a member of the Catch Club). Burney, at a slightly later period, frequented his house.[4]

---

[1] *Memoirs*, i. 230, 314.
[2] Quoted by Clifford, in his *H. L. Piozzi*, from Samuel Lysons's Scrap-book, now in the possession of Professor C. B. Tinker. See also *The World*, 22 Mar. 1788.
[3] *Memoirs*, i. 170.
[4] See the *Memoirs of Doctor Burney*, iii. 271–2.

He was elected a member of the Literary Club in 1784, having been blackballed, against Johnson's opinion, the previous year.[1]

The *Life* had one further edition in the same year. This was 'revised and corrected'—not very considerably. After that it was never republished and one can guess that it never will be.

[1] Boswell, iv. 232.

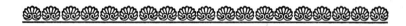

XIX. *Two satires on Hawkins as author*

AT the period at which we have now arrived there appeared
satirical treatments in verse of Hawkins's two major works—
his *Life of Johnson* and his *History of Music*.

The one on the *Life of Johnson* was by 'Peter Pindar'. It is
called *Bozzy and Piozzi, or the British Biographers; a Town
Eclogue* (first published 1786). It opens with an allusion to the
excited efforts of several of Johnson's friends to become the
first of his biographers:

> Strong 'midst the Rambler's cronies was the rage
> To fill with saws, bon-mots and tales the page.

The competition is, for the purposes of this poem, narrowed to
Boswell and Mrs. Piozzi, formerly Mrs. Thrale:

> At length rush'd forth two Candidates for fame,
> A Scotsman one, and one a London dame.
> That, by th' emphatic JOHNSON christen'd BOZZY,
> This, by the Bishop's licence, Dame Piozzi,
> Whose widow'd name, by topers loved, was Thrale,
> Bright in the annals of election ale.
> Forth rush'd to light their books—but who should say
> WHICH bore the palm of anecdote away?

The contestants are then represented as having appointed
Hawkins as adjudicator:

> Like schoolboys, lo! before a two-armed chair
> That held the KNIGHT wise judging, stood the PAIR.

Here follows the passage quoted in a previous chapter (p. 134)
poking sly fun at Hawkins's *History of Music*.

Now begins the strife between the two competitors. In turn
each attempts to demonstrate the importance of his or her
collection and the folly of the rival one by recounting an

anecdote, and so they continue, turn-and-turn-about, until we have had no fewer than thirty anecdotes—these naturally the most trivial the poet could find in their respective books, and not made any the less trivial by his manner of repeating them.

At last the Judge finds his patience reaching its end. In an impassioned aside, he exclaims:

> What have I done, inform me, gracious Lord!
> That thus my ears with nonsense should be bor'd?
>
> . . . .
>
> Ah! ten times happier was my lot of yore,
> When, rais'd to *consequence*, that all adore,
> I sat, each session, king-like in the chair,
> Aw'd ev'ry rank, and made the million stare.
>
> . . . .
>
> Return[1] return again thou glorious hour,
> That to my grasp once gave my idol bow'r;
> When at my feet the humble knave would fall,
> The *thund'ring Jupiter* of Hicks's Hall'.
>
> ————————
>
> The KNIGHT then finishing his speech so fair
> Sleep pulled him gently backwards in his chair,
> Op'd wide his mouth that oft on jail-birds *swore*,
> Then rais'd his nasal *organ* to a roar,
> That actually surpass'd, in tone and grace,
> The grumbl'd ditties of his fav'rite bass.[2]

So ends the poem's Part I. Part II opens with his dream. Johnson appears:

> Wake, HAWKINS (growl'd the Doctor with a frown)
> And knock that fellow and that woman down:
> Bid them with Johnson's life proceed no further;
> Enough already they have dealt in murther.
> Say, to their tales that little truth belongs,
> If fame they mean me, bid them hold their tongues.

[1] The poet adds a footnote here—'Sir John wishes in vain—his hour of insolence returns no more.'

[2] The poet's note—'The violoncello, on which the Knight is a performer.'

Alas! The intolerable string of anecdotes is resumed—thirty-six more of them. And then Hawkins, thoroughly roused at last, thunders forth:

> Instead of adding *splendour* to his name,
> Your books are downright *gibbets* to his fame.
> Of those your anecdotes—may I be curst
> If I can tell you which of them is worst.

> Thus spoke the Judge; then leaping from his chair
> He left, in consternation lost, the Pair.

He resolves to write the life himself and, says the poet, *'The Knight's volume is reported to be in great forwardness and likely to distance his formidable competitors.'*[1]

We now come to the other satirical publication in which Hawkins appears. In 1785 the Poet-Laureate, William Whitehead, died, and the choice of a successor became an interesting matter of speculation in literary and social circles. That successor proved to be the prolific Dr. Thomas Warton, who had been Professor of Poetry at Oxford twenty years earlier and now, in this year, was appointed Camden Professor of History. The occasion was seized, by a sort of syndicate of wits,[2] for the publication of a volume of mock *Probationary Odes for the Laureatship*, preceded by a mock *Preliminary Discourse by Sir John Hawkins, Knt.*

This went into a good many editions (three in the first year, five more in the following two years and then one or two others) but has long since dropped out of the sight of the general reader, to whom a few words of explanation may be welcome.

---

[1] This may refer in part to Boswell, whose claim to be Johnson's biographer was known and who had already published the *Tour to the Hebrides* (1785).

[2] These included Tickell, George Ellis, the Rev. Dudley Bate, Joseph Richardson (under whose name the collection is to be found in library catalogues), Brumell (Secretary to Lord North), the Hon. John Townshend, Richard Fitzpatrick, Dr. French Laurence, General Burgoyne, Isaac Reed (possibly), and the Rev. Thos. O'Byrne (afterwards Bishop of Meath). There is a marginal note by Dr. French Laurence in Rigaud's copy in the Bodleian (8vo. X, 377, B.S.) as follows: 'The first suggestion of the vehicle of the Probationary Odes for the Laureatship came as I understand (for I was not present) from the Rev. Dudley Bate.'

The wits just mentioned were Whigs. Their party was in opposition, having been heavily defeated at the election of 1784 by Pitt and the Tories. They set themselves to make life, for their political enemies, as uncomfortable as possible by the publication of three successive series of satires—*Criticism on the Rolliad*, the *Probationary Odes* just mentioned, and *Poetical Miscellanies*.

In the *Criticism on the Rolliad* the work criticized was a mythical epic concerned with the deeds of a prominent Tory M.P. and his ancestors—John Rolle, Member for Devonshire. The criticism took the form of ingeniously constructed poems by various (anonymous) members of what has just been called the 'syndicate', which bore the name of the 'Esto Perpetua Club'.

This collection appeared piecemeal in the *Morning Herald* and the *Daily Advertiser* and then as a book (in which form it eventually reached a twenty-second edition).

Following *Criticisms on the Rolliad* came the similar *Probationary Odes*. The ideas behind these were that, the laureatship being vacant, all sorts of well-known public men (not only acknowledged poets, but politicians and divines) were standing as candidates, each of them submitting an Ode, as a specimen of what he could do. The odes thus accounted for are extremely ingenious and varied in metres, rhymes, and ideas. Their fun has now largely evaporated, since so many of the topics and topical allusions lack significance to others than specialist students of eighteenth-century English history, but there is no denying that they are extremely clever.

Why the promoters of this clever set of political 'skits' chose Hawkins as the imaginary writer of their 'Preliminary Discourse' is not very clear perhaps. But (*a*) he had developed into a deep-dyed Tory, which made him fair game; (*b*) his name and fame were, presumably through his magisterial functions, known to a wide public, and (*c*) he had opened his *History of Music* of nine years before, with a 'Preliminary Discourse' whose rather solemn and self-important style lent itself to burlesque parody such as the following opening passage:

Having, in the year seventeen hundred and seventy-six, put forth
A HISTORY OF MUSIC, in five volumes quarto, (which buy) notwithstanding my then avocations as Justice of the Peace for the county of
Middlesex and city and liberty of Westminster; I, Sir John Hawkins,
of Queen-square, Westminster, Knight, do now, being still of sound
health and understanding, esteem it my bounden duty to step forward
as Editor and Reviser of THE PROBATIONARY ODES. My grand reason
for undertaking so arduous a task is this; I do, from my soul believe
that Lyric Poetry is the own, if not the twin-sister of Music; wherefore,
as I had before gathered together every thing that any way relates to
the one, with what consistency could I forbear to collate the best
effusions of the other?—I should premise, that in volume the first of
my quarto history, chap. I. page 7, I lay it down as a principle never to
be departed from, that '*The Lyre is the prototype of the fidicinal species*'.
And accordingly I have therein discussed at large, both the origin, and
various improvements of the Lyre, from the Tortoise-shell scooped
and strung by Mercury on the banks of the Nile, to the Testudo,
exquisitely polished by Terpander, and exhibited to the Ægyptian
Priests. I have added also many choice engravings of the various
antique Lyres, viz. the Lyre of Goats-horns, the Lyre of Bulls-horns,
the Lyre of Shells, and the Lyre of both Shells and Horns compounded;
from all which I flatter myself, I have indubitably proved the Lyre
to be very far superior to the shank bone of a Crane, or any other Pipe,
Fistula, or Calamus, either of Orpheus's or Linus's invention; aye, or
even the best of those pulsatile instruments, commonly known by the
denomination of the drum.

And now, he goes on, as 'all this was finally proved and
established by my History, I say I hold it now no alien task to
somewhat turn my thoughts to the late divine specimens of
Lyric Minstrelsey':

For although I may be deemed the legal guardian of MUSIC alone,
and consequently not in strictness bound to any farther duty than that
of her immediate Wardship (See Burns's Justice, article Guardian),
yet surely, in equity and liberal feelings, I cannot but think myself
very forcibly incited to extend this tutelage of her next of kin; in which
degree I hold every individual follower of THE LYRIC MUSE, but more
especially all such part of them as have devoted, or do devote their
strains to the celebration of those best of themes, the reigning King and
the current Year; or, in other words, of all Citharistae Regis, Versi-

ficatores Coronae, Court Poets, or as we now term them, Poets
Laureats.

There follows a discussion of the institution of the Laureateship, 'a very kingly settlement', for 'one hundred a year,
together with a tierce of Canary, or a butt of sack, are surely
most princely endowments for the honour of literature, and
the advancement of poetical genius'.

So proceeds this ten-page 'Preliminary Discourse', at last
coming to an end as follows:

The Authors whose Compositions I collect for public notice are
twenty-three. The odds of survivorship, according to Doctor Price[1]
are, that thirteen of these will outlive me, myself being in class III of
his ingenious tables.—Surely, therefore, it is no mark of that sanguine
disposition which my enemies have been pleased to ascribe to me, if I
deem it possible that some one of the same thirteen will requite my
protection of their harmonious effusions with a strain of elegiac
gratitude, saying, possibly (pardon me, ye Survivors that may be, for
presuming to hint the thought to minds so richly fraught as yours are)
saying, I say,

> Here lies Sir John Hawkins,
> Without his shoes or stockings!

(Said Survivors are not bound to said Rhime, if not agreeable).

Before we reach the poetical effusions we find, as we turn
the pages, some *Thoughts on Ode Writing*, attributed to
Warton, and a number of 'Recommendatory Testimonies'
(for one of which Burney is made responsible), and then we
come to an account of the 'Laureat Election', and a 'Hasty
Sketch of Wednesday's Business at the Lord Chamberlain's
office'. The list of competitors in this election, twenty-one in
number, opens, we find, with the Archbishop of York and the
Lord High Chancellor, and, as already mentioned, includes
many men well known either in the political or the poetical
world.

Space must be found here for just one brief specimen of the
ingenious versification of these Odes. There is little to choose

---

[1] Richard Price, *An Essay on the Population of England* (1780).

amongst them and the following passage is taken, almost at random, from the middle of the one *For the King's Birthday*, *by Sir George Howard, K.B.*:

> Mighty Sov'reign! Mighty Master!
> George is content with lath and plaister!
>   At his own palace-gate
> In a poor porter's lodge, by Chambers plann'd,
> See him, with Jenky,[1] hand in hand,
>   In serious mood,
> Talking! talking! talking! talking!
> Talking of affairs of State,
>   All for his country's good!
> Oh! Europe's pride! Britannia's hope!
>   To view his turnips and potatoes,
> Down his fair Kitchen-garden's slope
>   The victor monarch walks like Cincinnatus,
> See, heavenly Muse! I vow to God
> 'Twas thus the laurel'd hero trod—
> Sweet rural joys! delights without compare!
>   Pleasure shines in his eyes
>   While George with surprize,
>   Sees his cabbages rise,
> And his 'sparagus wave in the air!
>
> But hark! I hear the sound of coaches,
>   The Levee's hour approaches—
> Haste, ye Postillions! o'er the turnpike road;
> Back to St. James's bear your royal load!
> 'Tis done—his smoaking wheels scarce touch'd the ground—
>   By the Old Magpye and the New,
>   By Colnbrook, Hounslow, Brentford, Kew,
>   Half choak'd with dust the monarch flew,
> And now, behold, he's landed safe and sound—
> Hail to the blest who tread this hallow'd ground!

In the course of the setting forth of the poems of all these candidates is interpolated an *Address to Sir John Hawkins*,

---

[1] 'Chambers' is Sir William Chambers, Architect to the King. 'Jenky' is Charles Jenkinson, Baron Hawkesbury, Secretary at War.

Bart. (the 'Bart' presumably being a joke), ostensibly by his 'most obedient humble servant the Archbishop of York', who complains that his Ode, in a sort of blank verse, was not admitted to the competition, as being 'nothing but prose, written in an odd manner'. Here is its 'Strophe I':

> The priestly mind what virtue so approves,
> And testifies the pure prelatic spirit,
>> As loyal gratitude?
> More to my King, than to my God, I owe;
>> God and my father made me man,
> Yet not without my mother's added aid;
>> But GEORGE, without, or God, or man,
> With grace endow'd, and hallow'd me Archbishop.

The volume closes with the King's proclamation, 'To all Christian People', of the appointment of Warton to the Laureateship and a ridiculous 'Table of Instructions' to him, supposed to be provided by the Lord Chamberlain.

The assignment to any particular writer of any poem in the *Criticism on the Rolliad* and the *Probationary Odes* has always been regarded as highly speculative. Various attempts have been made.[1] The 'Preliminary Discourse' has been attributed to George Ellis, the authority on Early English Poetry and friend of Sir Walter Scott, as it has also to Richard Tickell, the playwright and political pamphleteer, brother-in-law of Sheridan. It appeared in the first nine editions (1785–91) and then, Hawkins being dead, was omitted from the editions which followed.[2] Just one remark about the association of Hawkins's name with this 'Discourse': The whole thing culminates in the choice of Warton as the new Poet-Laureate

[1] See *Notes and Queries*, Ser. I, vol. ii (1850), 115, 242, 373, 439; vol. iii (1851), 129, 276, 333.

[2] Malone, in a marginal note in his copy of the *Probationary Odes* 1785 (vet. A5 e, 417 in the Bodleian), says. 'All the Preliminary matter prefixed to the Probationary Odes was written by Richard Tickell and Joseph Richardson'. His information was ultimately derived from Richardson himself. On the other hand Dr. French Laurence, one of the chief contributors, thought that George Ellis and Tickell were the authors (marginal note to another Bodleian copy: (8vo. X, 377, B.S.). It is in the 1795 collected edition of the *Rolliad, Probationary Odes*, and *Political Miscellanies*.

and it seems possible that Hawkins was known to be a keen
admirer of Warton. Laetitia tells us:

My father's taste in poetry was of the same degree of critical
acumen as that he had acquired in music, painting, sculpture, architecture, and the belles lettres in general; he consequently was most
feelingly alive to the gigantic excellence of Thomas Warton; but of
him I remember only the eager expectation of his odes, and the absence
of all graces in his person.[1]

[1] *Anecdotes,* 17.

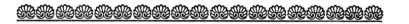

XX. *The end of a busy life* (1789)

Of the last illness and death of Hawkins the fullest account is that (obviously supplied by some member of his family) in Chalmers's *Biographical Dictionary* (1812–17). After telling us that in May 1788, having for some years devoted much time to theological studies, he made his will (it is dated 23 May) and began to study more closely and to prepare himself for the ending of his life, it goes on:

> In this manner he spent his time till about the month of May 1789, when, finding his appetite fail him in a greater degree than usual, he had recourse, as he had sometimes had before on the same occasions, to the waters of Islington Spa [about three miles from his home]. These he drank for a few mornings; but on the 14th of that month, while he was there, he was, it is supposed, seized with a paralytic affection, as on his returning to his carriage, which waited for him, his servants perceived a visible alteration in him.
>
> On his arrival at home he went to bed, but got up a few hours after, intending to receive an old friend from whom he expected a visit in the evening. At dinner, however, his disorder returning, he was led up to bed, from which he never rose, for, being afterwards, accompanied with an apoplexy, it put an end to his life, on the 21st of the same month, about two in the morning.

He was buried in the cloisters of Westminster Abbey and the stone placed over his grave bore merely his initials, the date of his death, and his age: this, as we shall see in a moment, was done on his own instructions, and is an item of evidence against the truth of the charge of pompous self-importance which has often been made and of which in the course of this account of his life we have sometimes seemed to see instances. His will is stated to have been proved on 22 May 1789 (which seems quick work since he died on the 21st: something wrong here!). Probate was granted to his widow and elder son.

After the customary pious prelude he directs that his body may be interned without ostentation or needless expense in the Cloister of the Collegiate Church of St. Peter, Westminster and with no other memorials of me than the initials of my name and the day of my death inscribed on a black marble slab.

He leaves sundry house property and land in Highgate and Hornsey to his three children and the house in Hatton Garden and another on Saffron Hill to his widow, with remainder to his 'dear son Henry'. Bank Stock, to the amount of nearly £5,000, he leaves to his widow with remainder of part of it to his daughter. To his son Henry he leaves as much Bank Stock as may be found necessary for the 'purchase of an elegible seat in the Chancery, where he is now in part provided for', this purchase to be effected when a good opportunity arises. To three cousins and four servants he leaves £10 apiece. To twenty friends whom he names he leaves rings (amongst these friends are three members of the Gostling family: see p. 117). As executors he appoints his widow and his elder son, John Sidney Hawkins.

It is doubtful if Hawkins's loss was, by anyone but his family, very strongly regretted. The *Gentleman's Magazine*[1] praises him for his *History of Music*, disparages his *Life of Johnson*, and just mentions the magisterial position he so long held and his knighthood:

At his house in the Great Sanctuary, Westminster, in his 71st year, Sir John Hawkins, knt.; to whom the publick are infinitely indebted for the many valuable anecdotes recorded in his 'History of Music'. See our vol. xlvi, p. 522, xlvii, pp. 29, 78, 125, 219, 229, 273, lv. 875. His Biography of Johnson, it must be confessed, was undertaken in an evil hour; but 'we war not with the dead'; and enough, perhaps too much, has been said already on that subject. He was elected chairman of the sessions for Middlesex, Sept. 19, 1765; in which capacity he published 'A Charge to the Grand Jury, Jan. 8, 1770'; see vol. xl. p. 37; and received the honour of knighthood Oct. 23, 1772.

[1] May 1789, 273.

One phrase here is probably intended to recall Johnson's prologue to Hugh Kelly's *A Word to the Wise*, produced at Covent Garden in 1777 for the benefit of Kelly's widow and five children, as quoted in Hawkins's *Life of Johnson* (518). It opens:

> This night presents a play, which public rage,
> Or right or wrong, once hooted from the stage:
> From zeal or malice, now no more we dread,
> For English vengeance wars not with the dead.[1]

The Public Advertiser (23 May) was hardly more cordial to the memory of the departed:

Thursday morning, died at his house in Westminster, Sir John Hawkins, Knt., one of his Majesty's Justices of the Peace, and, as he often tells us in his Life of Johnson, sometime Chairman at the Quarter Sessions. Sir John's literary abilities are known principally by *reports*, very few people having read his bulky performances. His last was the Life of Dr. Johnson which the trade very oddly employed him to write; it makes the first volume of Johnson's Works, and has been very aptly compared to a *mill-stone* hung about his neck—Sir John, however, as a man and a magistrate, was irreproachable.

Because of Hawkins being at Islington Spa when the fatal phase of his illness began, a mistake has crept into various books of reference. The early nineteenth century *Biographie Universelle* of the brothers Michaud and, after it, the *Biographie Universelle des Musiciens* of Fétis (1869), speak of the place of death as 'Spa' (i.e. in Belgium). So does Brown & Stratton's valuable *British Musical Biography* (1897).

Sir John left a widow, two sons, and the daughter to whom this present book is indebted for so much information otherwise unobtainable.

Lady Hawkins survived her husband four years, dying in 1793. Despite the 'penurious' character of her husband she had always been a charitable woman and after her death a slip of paper was found in her desk enjoining her children to keep up her benefactions to those whom she had been in the habit of helping—the last of whom died thirty years later.[2]

---

[1] See p. 197 for Boswell's use of the same phrase.   [2] *Memoirs*, i. 225.

XXI. *The next generation—John Sidney, Henry, and Laetitia Hawkins*

SIR JOHN and Lady Hawkins's three children all had literary leanings—and as to literary skill, about as much as their father.

The elder son, JOHN SIDNEY HAWKINS, born in 1758 when his father was thirty-nine, survived his father by over half a century, dying at Brompton in 1842. For fifteen years he followed the law.[1] He was an antiquary (a fellow of the Society of Antiquaries), and as such a considerable author (see the bibliography at the end of the present book).

His most important achievement was an edition (in 1787) of a Latin comedy of the early seventeenth century, Ruggle's *Ignoramus*. A laudatory review of it in the *Gentleman's Magazine* (17 Apr. 1784) opens with a very businesslike letter of Johnson to John Nichols, publisher and editor of that magazine and of many important books, submitting a proposal that he should undertake publication and suggesting terms. The edition, he says in a long account enclosed, is to include portions of the work previously unpublished, annotations, and a glossary.[2]

In J. T. Smith's *Nollekens and his Times* (1829) is an allusion to his own *Antiquities of Westminster* (1807), the task of

[1] See his statement in the *Gentleman's Magazine*, Jan. 1814, 5 and 1817, 9.

[2] Johnson's letter and his enclosure will also be found in Nichols's *Literary Anecdotes*, ix. 35–6. (The originals were bought by Mr. Ernest Maggs at one of Sotheby's sales, 6 Nov. 1951.) A letter of Rev. Dr. Michael Lort to Percy (31 Oct. 1785), reproduced in Nichols's *Illustrations*, vii. 472–4, says: 'Sir John Hawkins tells me that his Life and edition of Johnson's Works is in great forwardness. His son is labouring hard at an edition of *Ignoramus*, with explanatory notes; he has been fortunate enough to be in possession of the Italian play of Baptista Porta, whence Ruggles is said to have borrowed his design from, and which was Ruggles' own copy, having his name on it. Farmer [Dr. Richard Farmer, Master of Emmanuel College, Cambridge] hunted this out amongst some literary lumber thrown aside in Clare Hall Library.'

preparing which he calls 'one of the most anxious and unfortunate of my life'. The reason he spoke of it in such terms
has been summarized as follows by Wilfrid Whitten in his
edition of the Nollekens book:[1]

Smith's 'unfortunate task', *The Antiquities of Westminster, The Old
Palace, St. Stephen's Chapel, etc., etc.*, was published on June 9th, 1807.
It originated in the discovery in 1800 of some important mural
paintings behind the wainscoting of the Chamber. These were brought
to Smith's notice by his friend Dr. Charles Gower, of Middlesex
Hospital.

Little official interest seems to have been taken in these paintings,
but Smith resolved to copy them. He matched his pencil against the
crow-bars to accomplish the task, beginning his work at daylight each
morning, giving way at nine o'clock to the workmen, who often
removed in the course of the day the painting he had just copied. His
method was to draw the subjects and make careful memoranda of their
colouring.

Smith then began the preparation of his volume in collaboration
with John Sidney Hawkins, the antiquary, eldest son of Sir John
Hawkins; but this gentleman, whose 'talents were overshadowed by a
sour and jealous temper' (*Gentleman's Magazine*), proved a difficult
partner. The progress of the work was delayed, and Hawkins, who
had written the preface and the first 144 pages of the work, required
Smith to remove his name from the title page. Smith's explanation
to the subscribers, embodied in the work, led to a controversy with
Hawkins which is now without interest.

The matter J. S. Hawkins had provided for Smith's book
and then withdrawn was published independently in 1813,
with considerable additions, as *An History of the Origin and
Establishment of Gothic Architecture.* This was strongly attacked
in the *Gentleman's Magazine* by the prominent draughtsman
and author on architectural history, John Carter, who inserted some beautiful plates of his own drawing to illustrate
his points. Hawkins vigorously defended himself and the
attack and defence, carried on rather sporadically, occupied
the attention of the magazine's readers (if they did give it
attention) from October 1813 to October 1815.

[1] ii. 183.

A publication of 'Supplemental Prints' to Smith's book has inserted in it a page with the heading 'Mr. John Thomas Smith's Vindication in Answer to a Pamphlet written and published by John Sidney Hawkins Esq., F.S.A., concerning Mr. Smith's conduct to Mr. Hawkins in relation to "The Antiquities of Westminster". N.B. to be bound up with the work, immediately after the "Advertisement".' A small item in the 'vindication' is an allusion to Hawkins's complaint that Smith had charged him with obscenity. Smith denies that he ever used any words that could be so interpreted:

On the contrary, I am bound to observe that I ever found him particular on this head, and scrupulously attentive to religious ceremonies, by having heard him read prayers to the family and servants every morning and evening during my stay in Twickenham.

To this 'vindication' Hawkins replied with a pamphlet 'A correct Statement and Vindication'. In this he includes an insulting warning to Smith that he cannot hope to suppress the pamphlet by buying up copies, 'for a numerous impression has been printed and such effectual measures have been taken for a very extensive circulation before any for sale were delivered out, as no exertion of his can counter'.

During this same period J. S. Hawkins was engaged in another controversy in the same Magazine—this one with Isaac D'Israeli. A reviewer of D'Israeli's Quarrels of Authors had quoted him as saying:

The personal motives of an Author have often influenced his literary conduct to practise meannesses, which no author can be allowed. One remarkable instance of this nature, is that of Sir John Hawkins, who indeed had been so hardly used by the caustic pleasantries of George Steevens.

Sir John, in his edition of Johnson, with ingenious malice, contrived to suppress the acknowledgment made by Johnson to Steevens, of his diligence and sagacity, at the close of his Preface to Shakespeare. To preserve the panegyrick of Steevens, mortified Hawkins beyond endurance; yet to suppress it openly, his character as an Editor did not permit. In this dilemma, he pretended he reprinted the Preface from the Edition of 1765; which, as it appeared before Johnson's acquaintance with Steevens, could not contain the tender passage. However, this was unluckily discovered to be only a subterfuge, to get rid of the offensive panegyrick. On examination it proved not true: Hawkins did not reprint from this early edition, but from the latest, for all the corrections are inserted in his own. 'If Sir John were to be tried at Hicks's Hall (long the seat of that Justice's glory), he would be found guilty of *Clipping*', archly remarkes the Periodical Critic.[1]

To this J. S. Hawkins replies in the June issue, giving us, by the way, an impression of a rather irresponsible attitude on the part of the Editor of Johnson's Works, with consequent slipshod methods. It is stated that the intention had been to reproduce the earlier edition of Johnson's Shakespeare (why?) with its own preface. But—

With three different Printers employed, and consequently three different presses constantly at work, as was the case, it was impossible that any one man could have corrected all the proof-sheets; not to mention the delay which must necessarily have taken place in sending the sheets backwards and forwards for my father's inspection. It was, therefore, on the first arrangement of the plan, determined that, except where any new and original matter was introduced by way of note, the proof-sheets, to save time and trouble, should not be sent to my father, but be corrected by the foreman at each printing-house; and this method was accordingly pursued.

A list of the pieces, which each volume was to contain, was therefore delivered out by my father for the Printers; and, as in many instances they had before been printed, it was the bookseller's business to borrow, as he did, from such persons as happened to possess them, the original works in which the different compositions had at first appeared. For the reasons above mentioned, I am fully convinced, that my father expressly directed the edition of Johnson's Shakespeare of the year 1765 to be borrowed. But probably the bookseller could not readily procure that; and, conceiving that there had been no alteration in the subsequent editions, except the addition of what related to Mr. S.'s share in the revision, he sent one of the later editions to be printed from. Of this circumstance, I am confident, my father was never informed; because, living with him as I constantly did, it is

---

[1] *Gentleman's Magazine*, Apr. 1814, 360. For Steevens see in the present book, pp. 131 et seq.

scarcely likely that, if he had known it, I should not have heard of it, which I never did.[1]

In July D'Israeli comes swaggering back into the field and quickly drives his antagonist out of it—dismissing him, however, with a limited compliment which in the end finds itself transformed into a graceful one to the novelist daughter:

> Yet let it not be imagined that I wrote from any personal motive against the late Sir John Hawkins. With me it was mere matter of History. Of Hawkins's literary character I am inclined to think far better than the Criticks have hitherto allowed; the confused statements of objects which had passed under his eye, his feeble taste, his imperfect views, originate in the contraction of his intellect, and will for ever exclude him from the order of genius; but his fervent researches, his literary habits, and that passion for Literature he inspired through his family, excite our respect, and rank him among the esteemable men of letters. The redeeming genius of that family, the genius which, like the figure of the antients, bears wings on its shoulders and a flame on its head—must be a Female!

Another literary quarrel of J. S. Hawkins is discussed by him in the *Gentleman's Magazine* of January 1809. It appears that 'A Bookseller in the Strand of the name of Bagster' (a name still well remembered in connexion with students' editions of Bibles—a line of activity he had introduced and which the firm bearing his name continues) had planned a reprint of Sir John Hawkins's edition of Walton's *Compleat Angler*, and this without the consent of this son, who had been responsible for some of the later editions and who maintained that the copyright was held by the firm of Rivington (who, however, Bagster stated, had refused to publish the work further). J. S. Hawkins discusses the incident in a way that supports

---

[1] Dr. L. F. Powell writes: 'I have made a full collation of the editions of Johnson's Preface to Shakespeare and have no hesitation in saying that Hawkins, or rather his publishers, reprinted the text of the 1785 edition, the third edition of the Johnson-Steevens edition, and omitted the final paragraph containing the panegyric of Steevens. This edition re-punctuates, often justifiably, and introduces some errors (e.g. "He is not soft" *for* "He is not long soft").'

'All editions of Johnson's *Works* have, following Hawkins, omitted the last paragraph, which was added by Johnson in the third edition, the first Johnson-Steevens edition, in 1773.'

the statement on a previous page that his talents were 'overshadowed by a sour and jealous temper'. The impression left on one's mind is that Bagster was probably an honourable man, that J. S. Hawkins played fast and loose with him, and, moreover, has probably not left us anything like an impartial account of the affair.

Amongst the publications of J. S. Hawkins was an *Inquiry into the Nature and Principles of Thorough Bass* (1817). This was compassionately intended for the 'young female' but must have been totally useless to her, for it consists of purely theoretical and arithmetical discussion, with many dry tables. The preface shows the author as musically a true 'chip of the old block', for it pleads for the teacher's use of 'the old masters, Handel, Corelli, Geminiani, etc.', in preference to 'the modern fashionable compositions of the day'. Regret is expressed at the introduction in concerts of selections from Haydn and Mozart, so lessening proportionably the number of those taken from the works of Handel.

The obituary of J. S. Hawkins in the *Gentleman's Magazine* of December 1842 ends as follows (a phrase of this has already been quoted):

Mr. Hawkins was an antiquary of much learning, research, and industry, but his talents were overshadowed by a sour and jealous temper; and he had long lived in such retirement that his existence was scarcely known to the present generation at Somerset House.

The following year there was sold by auction '*the Valuable and Extensive Library of the late John Sidney Hawkins, F.S.A., consisting of books in every department of Literature, together with some historic and interesting Manuscripts*'. The catalogue consists of one hundred and fourteen pages, and the sale was to occupy nine days. At the end of the catalogue is an announcement of three further sales—one of the deceased's musical library, another of his engravings, and still another of his musical instruments, including 'violins and violoncellos by Stradivari, Guarneri, Amati, Stainer, etc.'

Evidently, then, this son of Sir John was a considerable collector.

Sir John's younger son was named HENRY. In the *Dictionary of National Biography* Leslie Stephen says that Sir John Hawkins left 'a son', and to that son, John Sidney, he accords the dignity of an independent article. But this other son Henry is also authentic enough as we have seen from his father's will.[1] Laetitia frequently mentions and quotes her younger brother in her *Anecdotes* and *Memoirs*, and in an appendix to the former supplies us with a neat collection of English, Latin, and Greek poetry by him, describing this as fulfilling a wish to 'rescue from oblivion the various trifles which a near relative, an indolent, thinking brother, tost over to me, without even preserving a copy'. De Quincey, in the essay mentioned on p. 230, finds some grammatical and metrical slips in these productions, and concludes: 'On the whole our opinion of Mr. Hawkins as a Greek poet is that in seven hundred, or say seven hundred and fifty years, he may become a pretty—yes, we will say, a *very* pretty poet: as he cannot be more than one-tenth of that age at present we look upon his performances as singularly promising.'

To the second volume of *Memoirs* Laetitia appends, at an expense of eighty-five pages, this brother's *Reform of Parliament the Ruin of Parliament*, which had appeared in *The Pamphleteer* in 1813. This latter is of the nature that its title suggests: the following brief extract will show that Henry Hawkins stood firmly in the ranks of those who, by their sturdy opposition to the almost annual efforts to secure a fairer representation of the people, deferred that dangerous innovation until 1832:

> Let us then depict a *pure* House of Commons, purified from all its dross, under the new arrangement; and in order to do this, we must consider, what description of persons would then be the voters to choose; for I have before stated that part of this new arrangement was to extend the right of voting so as to include those of a lower rank in society than are now admitted: the voters would then be not merely

---

[1] A paper on Sir John Hawkins read before the Johnson Society of London in May 1946 shows ignorance of the existence of this son of Sir John and actually transfers the nickname title of 'Classic Harry' to John Sidney Hawkins.

the opulent, or those who have what we frequently hear denominated, 'a stake in the hedge', but amongst them would be found the lowest of the rabble; the purchasers of half-crown freeholds; men who, by means of perjury, procured an admission of votes for freeholds thus purchased; the mechanic, the handicraftsman, and these of the lowest description; who not choosing to attend to his occupation at the time of an election, preferred the idleness and drunkenness inseparable from it to the honest industry by which his wife and family were to be kept from want; the rabble, perhaps not sober at the moment of giving their suffrage, and exhibiting, in their general deportment, the most disgusting scenes of profligacy and wickedness; the rabble, the sturdy beggar; the VAGA-BOND! doubtless, competent judges of the merits of a candidate to represent a county or borough in the senate of the nation!

On the question of 'Rotten Boroughs' this sound old Tory is equally strong:

It would not be merely the borough of Old Sarum that would be attacked and consequently it is not the borough of Old Sarum that we defend. It is the *principle* that we contend for; the borough alluded to may, perhaps, not have above half-a-dozen inhabitants left in it; the right is binding; great and little, many and few, are relative terms.

And as to electoral corruption, the writer also boldly defends even that:

It is asserted by some, that seats are subjects of bargain and sale; and that this traffic is so openly carried on that no one can doubt it. . . . From the experience we have had, the members who have come into Parliament by this method, have been in general as independent and as well informed, and have been as zealous in the discharge of their Parliamentary duties as any other description of members: the public, therefore, have been no *sufferers* by the practice.[1]

Henry Hawkins, as his father's will shows, was a Chancery lawyer. He died on 18 April 1841, 'in the 80th year of his age'.[2]

We come now to Hawkins's literary daughter. The date of birth of LAETITIA MATILDA HAWKINS was somewhere between the dates of birth of her two brothers.

Many of her early memories were of Johnson's friendship

---

[1] *Memoirs*, ii. 346. [2] R. S. Cobbett, *Memorials of Twickenham*.

with her father and his visits to the house. She becomes vividly descriptive as to his general appearance:

When first I remember him, I used to see him sometimes at a little distance from the house, coming to call on my father; his look directed downwards, or rather in such apparent distraction as to have *no* direction. His walk was heavy, but he got on at a great rate, his left arm always fixed across his breast, so as to bring the hand under his chin, and he walked wide, as if to support his weight. . . .

His clothes hung loose, and the pocket on the right hand swung violently, the lining of his coat being always visible. I can now call to mind his brown hand, his metal sleeve-buttons, and my surprise at seeing him with plain wristbands, when all gentlemen wore ruffles; his coat-sleeve being very wide, showed his linen almost to his elbow. His wig in common was cut and bushy; if by chance he had one that had been drest in separate curls, it gave him a disagreeable look, not suited to his years or character.

I certainly had no idea that this same Dr. Johnson, whom I thought rather a disgraceful visitor at our house, and who was never mentioned by ladies but with a smile, was to be one day an honour, not only to us but to his country.[1]

And as to the smiles of the ladies she footnotes the passage as follows:

I remember a tailor's bringing his pattern-book to my brothers, and pointing out a purple, such as no one else wore, as the doctor's usual choice. We all shouted with astonishment, at hearing that Polypheme, as, shame to say! we had nicknamed him, ever *had* a new coat; but the tailor assured us he was a good customer. After this I took notice, and *ex pede Herculem*, concluded from what remained visible, that the coat had been originally of this fugitive colour.

The impression the great man made on Laetitia (or probably on any child he met) was not one to be recollected in after life with unmingled delight. She says he 'was slow, and kind in his way to children, detaining me standing first on one foot and then on the other till I was weary', and this, she

[1] *Memoirs*, i. 86. D. Nichol Smith, in the *Cambridge History of English Literature* (x. 189), has paid Laetitia a compliment which such a passage as this goes far to justify: 'There is no work of the same size as her *Anecdotes* that gives a better portrait of Johnson' (and by '*Anecdotes*' the writer assuredly includes the *Memoirs* which are a mere continuation of them).

remarks, her father 'seldom observed without recollecting "the lion dandling the kid" '.[1]
Another passage of Laetitia's is of similar purport:

> Dr. Johnson *fondled* me *in his way*; that is to say, he kept me standing before a good fire, unconscious that he had not dismissed me from his *urbanities*, while to my terror, from the displeasure of my nurse-maid, he leant his wig on my shoulder. When he recollected me, he would ask me if I would be his little housekeeper. It was happily not necessary to reply.[2]

She recalls that Johnson supported her father in his 'depressing system' of bringing up his daughter. It is not very pleasant', she complains, 'to fancy one's self, for perhaps nearly half one's life, utterly good for nothing', but she admits that the criticism their friend, Mrs. Welch, expressed that she would suffer for it in after life proved to be wrong and Johnson to be right—to this extent, that such a system 'is greatly conducive to the security and satisfaction of the later half [of one's life], by fencing us against many vexations, by giving a zest to every rational pleasure, and making every kindness doubly felt'.[3]

To be taken to Johnson's house was, it seems, a heavy punishment. Her father would say 'Miss' (which was my designation of disgrace), 'I intend to take you to Dr. Johnson's this evening':

> It came to my ear in the same form as a threat some years before, when we were all three *under a cloud* for some exertion of *fidelity* in what Sir J. used to call, at such times, 'the triple alliance:'—the threat was that we should all be taken to see King Lear! . . . I made a friend of my mother, and represented that if I was incapacitated from labour, by the effect on my nerves, nothing would be got. . . . From the visit to Dr. Johnson, I could not, however, get off: but here I behaved worse; for I revenged myself by the wretched expedient of listening and replying, exclusively, to the inanities of one of his inmates, Mrs. Desmoulins. I am sure Johnson neither saw me nor heard me; but I stayed

---

[1] *Anecdotes*, 23. Possibly this last phrase was a favourite quotation with Hawkins. We find it in his *Life of Johnson*, apropos of Johnson's treatment of a certain controversial adversary:

> 'Sporting the lion ramp'd, and in his paw
> Dandled the kid. (*Paradise Lost*, Bk. iv, line 343).'

[2] *Anecdotes*, 8.   [3] *Memoirs*, i. 219.

my time out, and as there was nothing said 'in the bond' about being agreeable, or making up to the Doctor, I was acquitted. Even my father had nothing to say; for I was *en règle*.[1]

The way in which Mrs. Desmoulins is spoken of above shows us that the child felt no attraction to one of the female 'inmates' of Johnson's house. Of another, the blind Mrs. Williams, she speaks very differently:

'Mrs. Anna Williams I remember as long as I can remember any one. While residing in Johnson's house, her only home, she gave a sort of creditable consistency to the *ménage*, and, being herself a gentlewoman, conferred on her protector the character of a gentleman. Together with him, before he was ingulfed at Streatham, she often, in the course of the winter, dined with my father and mother, and frequently without other company. I see her now, a pale shrunken old lady, dressed in scarlet made in the handsome French fashion of the time, with a lace cap, with two stiffened projecting wings on the temples, and a black lace hood over it; her grey or powdered hair appearing. Her temper has been recorded as marked with the Welsh fire, and this might be excited by some of the meaner inmates of the upper floors; but her gentle kindness to *me* I never shall forget, or think consistent with a *bad* temper.[2]

Laetitia, in later life, imbibed her father's dislike of Johnson's negro attendant and was ready to believe the worst of him:

The immortalised Frank, the *faithful* black servant of Dr. Johnson, could scarcely, I think, less deserve the credit given him. What he would have done by or with his master in case of extremity, I do not wish to surmise, but I know certainly that he took bribes for denying him to others, when Mr. Steevens wanted his assistance in his Shakespeare, and, I believe, it is incontestable that, *vice versa*, he sold intelligence to Boswell.[3]

The list of distinguished visitors to Laetitia's home during her childhood is a very long one. Two of them are mentioned in the following passage. She is lamenting that she was not

[1] *Memoirs*, i. 141–2.   [2] Ibid. 151.
[3] Ibid. 153. It is true that Boswell induced Frank to obtain for him, from Sir John Hawkins, some of Johnson's letters, but as Frank was Johnson's residuary legatee they were his property and he was within his rights in disposing of them.

born older, so that she could have remembered the conversations she heard:

The politics of the time, indeed, could not have interested me, even had I been much beyond childhood. The subject had not then the character it has now. 'The King of Prussia' and 'the balance of power' were sounds that wearied my ear;—the latter, then and long after, wholly unintelligible to me. But there were small dinner-parties at my father's, in which common things were brought forward; and though my brothers and myself came into the dining-parlour only with the almonds and raisins, the then existing custom of permitting children to sit upon the carpet in the drawing-room till dinner was announced, gave me opportunities of seeing persons whom I did not know to be, and have since wondered to find, eminent. We were well-disciplined children, and taught to be very respectful; but I little thought what I should have to boast when Goldsmith taught me to play Jack and Gill by two bits of paper on his fingers. . . . Of any notice bestowed on me by Sir Joshua Reynolds I cannot brag.[1]

The admirable editor of *The Early Diary of Frances Burney*, Mrs. Annie Raine Ellis, has in her preface drawn attention to the curious parallel between the occupations and circumstances of the daughters of the two British historians of music —culling her information as to Hawkins's daughter from various scattered passages in her *Anecdotes* and *Memoirs*:

The whole book of Sir John Hawkins, and part of that of Dr. Burney, were published the same year, 1776. Each father employed his daughter as his amanuensis. Each daughter was secretly occupied in writing a novel, which the youngest brother of each aided her in getting published without her name. In Fanny's case, Dr. Burney's consent was asked, but so far as we see, Sir John Hawkins died in ignorance that his '*girl*' had published several novels anonymously. 'I was,' (wrote Miss Hawkins) 'I will not say *educated*, but *broke*, to the drudgery of my father's pursuits. I had no time but what I could *purloin* from my incessant task of copying, or writing from dictation— writing six hours a day for my father, and reading nearly as long to my mother.' Fanny nowhere mentions how much time *she* spent daily in copying for her father, until at last she feared that her handwriting had become so well known among compositors that she was fain to disguise

[1] *Anecdotes*, 6–8.

it when transcribing her own 'Evelina' for the press. *She* never complains; once only she speaks of 'stealing time to write'; but the letters of Mr. Crisp and Mrs. Rishton show how seldom she was spared to visit her friends.

These two clever girls knew more or less the same people of note;—from Johnson, Hawkesworth, Garrick, and Horace Walpole, down to Nollekens and Jenny Barsanti; but there is no sign that they were ever acquainted with each other.

A decorous reserve prevails in Fanny's early diaries towards the works and deeds of the rival historian of Music, Peter Pindar's 'fiddling knight', Sir John Hawkins. His book is merely named, without praise or blame. Each of these girls followed her father in his opinions; but what a difference there was between the fathers! To borrow Mr. Crisp's phrase, Laetitia had been 'planted against a north wall', Fanny against a southern. Sir John was a pragmatical person, 'stiff in opinions', often 'in the wrong'; a Puritan by birth and in grain, notwithstanding his love of music:[1] Lady Hawkins, a severe disciplinarian towards her children and servants. All about Laetitia was what Peter Pindar calls *'magistratial'*;—all was intended to awe the vicious, and encourage the deserving. Laetitia's 'Reminiscences', and her novels bristle with moral opinions, magisterially given forth. They leave on the mind how much better it was to have been born a Burney than a daughter of Sir John Hawkins.

The way in which Fanny Burney became a novelist she has related in her *Memoirs* of her father,[2] and Laetitia Hawkins, in her *Memoirs*, has likewise left us a record of her becoming one:

Being in want of a sum of money for a whim of girlish patronage, and having no *honest* means of raising it, I wrote a downright novel. It could do nobody any harm—indeed *I* thought it a marvellous moral performance, as it punished the culprits and rewarded the virtuous of my *dramatis personae*—but it was a temerarious undertaking, as descriptive of manners and situations of which I knew little but by hearsay. It was done in the secrecy of a coiner, my only confidential

---

[1] This old idea that the Puritans objected to music has, of course, nothing whatever in it beyond the fact that they shared the Calvinist objection to the use of organs and choirs *in church* (see the present author's *The Puritans and Music in England and New England*, 1934). Cf. p. 129.

[2] See also the present author's *The Great Doctor Burney*, i. 349 et seq.

friend being my younger brother. Not at all foreseeing the open contact into which I might be called with any bookseller, I had written to Cadell on the subject of publishing my manuscript—he had declined it unless he might know the writer. I was not ignorant of the sagacious scent of these agents between authors and the public; and when called on to write what Mr. Cadell was to see, I dreaded his recognition of my handwriting, and his incautiously betraying me; but the matter, I suppose, had slipped out of his mind, and I escaped harmless.

On this subject, may I be allowed to say a few words more? The manuscript was published for me by Hookham, who, as I have elsewhere stated, was content to remain in ignorance, and who most honourably sent me for it twice as much as I needed, and most kindly encouraged me to proceed.[1]

'I scarcely know why I acted thus clandestinely', she continues. And how she found time and energy for novel writing is not very clear, for, as we have seen, a great part of every day was, for many years, occupied in work as her father's amanuensis (cf. p. 187), and what time her father spared her was, apparently, earmarked for her mother:

I had no time but what I could *purloin*, and was writing six hours in the day for my father, and reading aloud to my mother nearly as long. But two thousand pages never daunted me. I learnt Italian, and extracted from every book that came in my way; I made as large a part of my clothes as could be made at home; I worked muslin; I learnt botany; and I was my mother's storekeeper. Air and exercise were little thought on. I aired indeed with Lady H. in the carriage, but I read or worked.[2]

A list of Laetitia's writings is included in the Bibliography at the end of the present book. One would have supposed that her activity in this direction would have been felt to entitle her novels to mention in works of reference such as the *Dictionary of National Biography*, the *Cambridge Bibliography of English Literature*, and the *Oxford Companion to English Literature*, but it has not been so. As a novelist she is today, apparently,

---

[1] *Memoirs*, i. 156. It might have been pointed out by Mrs. Raine Ellis as another parallel of detail that just as Cadell refused publication 'unless he might know the writer' so did Lowndes, to whom Fanny Burney first applied.

[2] Ibid. 157.

completely forgotten. Yet 'George Paston', in her *Side-lights on the Georgian Period* (1902), tells us:

> *The Countess and Gertrude* made an instant success, and retained its popularity for many years. In the feminine correspondence of that period it is frequently mentioned with enthusiasm, and is sometimes bracketed with Mrs. Brunton's *Self-Control*.[1] It is a didactic tale in four volumes, wherein are set forth the various modes of discipline to which Gertrude, the heroine, is subjected by her foolish patroness, the Countess, and by her various teachers and pastors. It was highly appreciated by those persons, apparently a numerous class, who rapturously accepted advice and assistance from unmarried ladies on the subject of the education of children. Miss Hawkins tells us in a preface to the second edition that she had received innumerable letters from parents and guardians thanking her for the help she had given them in their task of training the young.

Laetitia's three volumes of *Anecdotes* and *Memoirs* are dedicated to three friends—'Richard Clark Esq., Chamberlain of London, etc., etc., etc.'; 'Dr. Fergusson of Windsor'; and 'Samuel Tolfrey, Esq., etc., etc., etc.'

For Clark see p. 44. As for Fergusson, he was, no doubt, that 'kind physician whose care and conversation has done more for me than all medicine' and who, in her convalescence after a long illness, encouraged her 'to return moderately' to her 'usual habits and pursuits'—whence her embarking on the *Anecdotes*. After a career as Inspector-General of Military Hospitals he had retired to Windsor, where Laetitia also was spending some of her later years. To Tolfrey she expressed herself as greatly indebted for his 'memory and conversation' and also his example. Who he was the present writer does not know.

In the present work it has been necessary to draw heavily upon those *Anecdotes* and *Memoirs* and it is hoped that no

---

[1] Mrs. Mary Brunton (1778–1818). Wife of a Scottish parson who was later Professor of Oriental Languages at Edinburgh University. *Self-Control*, a novel published in 1818, continued to be republished up to 1852, and a French translation appeared in 1872. Another of her novels was *Self-Discipline*. Her object was to 'procure admission for the religion of a sound mind and the Bible where it cannot find access in any other form'.

passage quoted has been seriously erroneous. But those works are too full of details recollected after many years to be entirely free from slips. J. T. Smith, in his *Nollekens and his Times*, complains of one or two such. Speaking of the eminent engraver, J. K. Sherwin, he remarks:

As Miss Hawkins did not think proper to exempt me from Mr. Sherwin's 'pupils in punch', and as I have no wish to leave the world and my family with the slander of drunkenness attached to my memory, when at no period of my life have I merited that stigma, I shall endeavour to show how little this lady, who is so fond of running a tilt at others, is to be believed in some of her assertions.

At page 32, in the second volume of her Memoirs, she states, when speaking of Sherwin's eccentricities and follies (and well knowing that I was his pupil at that time), that, 'He fired pistols out of his window half the night, and half drowned his pupils; for, sad to say, he had pupils in punch.'

Miss Hawkins states on the same page, that 'Sherwin expired, forlorn and comfortless, in a poor apartment of a public-inn, in Oxford-street': whereas the fact is, that Sherwin died in the house of the late Mr. Robert Wilkinson, the printseller, in Cornhill, who kindly attended him, afforded him every comfort, and paid respect to his remains; his body having been conveyed to Hampstead, and buried in a respectable manner in the church-yard, near the north-east corner of the front entrance, in the very grave where his brother George had been interred.

He then gives two other examples of error:

Miss Hawkins states that her mother's portrait was painted 'by Prince Hoare of Bath'; she should have said *William* Hoare Esq., R.A., Prince Hoare's father.

Miss Hawkins, who so often considers herself obliged to her brother for a *good* thing, allowed the following to be printed in page 218 of the first volume of her Memoirs.

Speaking of Doctor Johnson, H.H. says, 'Calling upon him shortly after the death of Lord Mansfield, and mentioning the event, he answered, "Ah, Sir, there was little learning and less virtue!"'

Now, unfortunately for Miss Hawkins and her brother, H.H., this fabricated invective can never stand, for that highly respected and learned judge, Lord Mansfield, died on Wednesday, March 20th,

1794, ten years after the death of Dr. Johnson, with whom H.H. so roundly declares he conversed upon his Lordship's death.[1]

De Quincey, soon after the *Anecdotes* appeared, poked fun at them in an amusing essay. He began, 'This orange we mean to squeeze for the public use', and then reproduced many of Laetitia's stories, bringing out the authoress's naïvety, or inaccuracy, or slipshod use of English or of Latin.[2] In another essay, eight years later, he alludes regretfully to the rumour that 'the fair authoress was offended at one jest'.[3]

Laetitia Hawkins died on 22 November 1835, aged seventy-six.[4] She and her brother Henry had lived for some time in the house at Twickenham which was at one time the residence of John Sydenham, the physician. With her was a companion, a Miss Mary Mitchell, and the three of them formed 'as grotesque a trio as can well be imagined'.[5]

In closing our little account of Laetitia (and it really did seem time that someone should undertake the task of drafting some slight record of her activities and thoughts) let us not forget one really great thing about her—*her hat*! At a certain period of her life, she tells us, ladies carried on their heads immense coverings:

Mrs. Hastings, O happy woman! had one thirty-three inches in *diameter*. Father and mother, cruel as they were, kept *me* to twenty-seven.

Well, Mrs. Hastings and Laetitia did not have to travel in a London bus or tube at the evening rush hour!

[1] As to that date of 1794 Smith himself is not quite right. Books of reference are somewhat strangely at variance about the date of Lord Mansfield's death. The correct date (as established by the obituary article in the *Gentleman's Magazine*) is 20 Mar. 1793.
    As for Laetitia's mistake, compare Boswell, who, in mentioning a remark of Johnson on Mansfield, very similar to that quoted by Henry Hawkins, alludes to him as a 'late eminent judge'. The meaning here is evidently 'late' *as a judge*, for at the date at which Boswell was writing Mansfield though alive was in retirement. And probably Laetitia's slip is the simple one of writing 'after the death' instead of 'after the retirement'. She had forgotten exactly what her brother had said.
[2] *London Magazine*, Mar. 1823; De Quincey's collected writings, 1859 (with slight changes); Masson's edn. of De Quincey's Works, 1890, v. 146.
[3] *Story of a Libel*, in *Tait's Magazine*, Feb. 1841. Masson's edn. of De Quincey's Works, iii. 160.   [4] *Gentleman's Magazine*, Jan. 1836.
[5] R. S. Cobbett, *Memorials of Twickenham.*

Books and Articles by Hawkins and his family

BOOKS AND PAMPHLETS, ETC., BY SIR JOHN HAWKINS

(OR EDITED BY HIM)

1740(?) *Memoirs of the late Sig. Agostino Steffani, some time Master of the Electoral Chapel at Hanover, etc.* (8 pp. oblong folio, 'the better to adapt them to the Size and Form of the Books in which Manuscript Copies of Duets, Cantatas, and Songs are usually made'. The copy in the British Museum is so placed before a manuscript collection. Hawkins's name does not appear anywhere on it, but the catalogue gives it as 'attributed' to him.[1]

1760 Walton and Cotton's *Compleat Angler*, with lives of the authors and extensive notes. Other editions in 1775–84–92–97–1802–8–11–26–36–93. (In the first edition the life of Cotton is by William Oldys.)

1763 *Observations on the State of the Highways and on the Laws for amending and keeping them in repair. With a Draught of a Bill for a reducing into one Act the most essential parts of all the Statutes in force relating to the Highways, etc.* (Largely reproduced in the *Gentleman's Magazine* of the same year, p. 234.)

1770 *A Charge to the Grand Jury of the County of Middlesex.* (Delivered . . . the eighth of January.)

1770 *An Account of the Institution and Progress of the Academy of Ancient Music.* (Pub. anonymously; reprinted in Laetitia Hawkins's *Memoirs*, 1824.) See Appendix 3.

c. 1775 *The Case of the County of Middlesex with respect to the Gaol of Newgate.* (Reprinted in Laetitia Hawkins's *Memoirs*, 1824.)

1776 *A General History of Music*, 5 vols. Also in 2 vols. and album of plates

[1] See Hawkins, *Johnson*, 319, footnote:
'I have sometimes thought that music was positive pain to him. . . . As a science of which he was ignorant he condemned it. In the early part of my life I had collected some memoirs of Abbate Steffani, Mr. Handel's predecessor at the court of Hanover, and the composer of those fine duets that go under his name, with a view to print them, as presents to some musical friends: I submitted the manuscript to Johnson's perusal, and he returned it with corrections that turned to ridicule all I had said of him and his works.'

1853 and 1875—these with the Author's emendations from his personal copy in the British Museum.

The British Museum also has *Remarks on Hawkins's History of Music by* W. Cole (as to whom see Nichols's *Literary Anecdotes*, i, and *D.N.B.*); they are as follows—Add. MSS. 580, ff. 626, 636, 646.

1779 *On the Practice of Bidding Prayers, with an Ancient Form of such Bidding, as also a Form of Cursing.*

This has its beginning in a communication made to the Society of Antiquaries, 6 Nov. 1777, in the form of a letter to the Secretary by the Hon. Daines Barrington on behalf of Hawkins (he not being a Fellow of the Society). The Society's records state:

'Sir John Hawkins's Letter informs Mr. Barrington that among the Ancient Music Books in his Collection, he has lately met with a Set of Madrigals, published about the year 1600, and sewed (as many such are) in Covers of Vellum, which appear to have been the Leaves of one of these Rituals, or Service Books. . . . They contain a very ancient Formula, of what the Liturgical Writers call Bidding of Prayers; as also a very singular Form of Malediction; both, as he conceives, intended for the Use of York Cathedral. These curious Relicks of Antiquity have led Sir John to an Enquiry into the Practice of Bidding Prayers . . .'

There follow several pages of discussion.

(See also letter by J. C. Brooke in Nichols's *Illustrations*, vi, 367).

1780 *A Charge to the Grand Jury of Middlesex.* (The second such Charge: 'delivered . . . the eleventh of September.')

1780 *A Dissertation on the Armorial Ensigns of the County of Middlesex and of the Abbey and City of Westminster by Sir John Hawkins, Knt., Chairman of the Quarter and General Sessions of the Peace and of Oyer and Terminer for the same County* (8 pp. 4to).

1782 *An Account of the Lamb's Conduit.*

1787 *The Works of Samuel Johnson, LL.D., together with his Life and Notes on his Lives of the Poets,* 11 vols., the first volume being the Life—of which a revised edition and a (pirated) Dublin edition appeared the same year. The 11 vols. were augmented to 15 by other editors (*Debates* and *Miscellaneous Pieces*, and the *Voyage to Abyssinia*), 1787–9.

The Principles and Powers of Harmony (1771), sometimes attributed to Hawkins, is really by Benjamin Stillingfleet. (As a matter of fact Hawkins, in his *History of Music*, ch. 195, condemns it as 'diffuse' and 'obscure'.)

OTHER WRITINGS

1739   *Essay on Honesty.* In *Gentleman's Magazine*, Mar., p. 117 (attacks and replies appear in May, pp. 176, 232; June, p. 297).

1741   Poem: *To Mr. John Stanley, occasioned by looking over some Compositions of his lately published.* (This is dated 19 Feb. 1740 but was published in the *Daily Advertiser*, 21 Feb. 1741.)

1742-3   Poems for Cantatas by Stanley (see p. 10). These are alternate Recitatives and Airs on well-worn themes of love. The name of the poet is unmentioned. They all appeared, at various times, in the *Gentleman's Magazine*.

c. 1777   *Lines on the Death of Gostling.* (Set by Boyce and performed in Westminster Abbey. Possibly unpublished.)

1777   *The General History of Arcangelo Corelli.* (In *Universal Magazine of Knowledge and Pleasure*, Apr., p. 418. Adler, in his *Handbuch der Musikgeschichte*, ii, p. 1236, speaks of this as though it were a separate publication.)

1788   Memoir of Boyce (11 pp. prefixed to 2nd edn. of Boyce's collection of Cathedral Music).

Hawkins is said to have contributed in early life not only to the *Gentleman's Magazine*, but also to the *Universal Spectator* ('by Henry Stonecastle, of Northumberland, Esquire'; 3 vols. 1747; republished, 5 vols., 1756) and the *Westminster Journal* ('In some of the essays he contributed the author favoured the public with specimens of his poetical abilities'—Allibone's *Critical Dictionary of English Literature*, Philadelphia, 1858). It is also sometimes stated that he was a contributor to the *Monthly Review*, but this statement is probably incorrect, as Nangle's Index of Contributors does not include his name. He contributed notes to Hanmer's edition of Shakespeare of 1770-1 (see p. 67) and to Johnson and Steevens's edition of 1773, and further notes to the edition of 1778. In 1819 appeared *Annotations of the Plays of Shakespeare by Johnson, Steevens, Malone, Theobald, Warburton, Farmer, Heath, Pope, Hawkins, Percy, etc., etc.* (2 vols., assembling the notes by all these writers, play by play and act by act).

BOOKS BY JOHN SIDNEY HAWKINS

1787   *Ignoramus, Comoedia; scriptore Georgio Ruggle, A.M., Aulae Clarensis, apud Cantabrigienses, olim Socio; nunc denuo in Lucem edita cum Notis*

Historicis et Criticis: quibus insuper praeponitur Vita Auctoris, et sub-
jicitur Glossarium Vocabula Forensia dilucide exponens; accurante
Johanna Sidneio Hawkins, Arm.

1789 *Emblems of Mortality representing, in upwards of fifty cuts, Death seizing*
      all ranks and degrees of people . . . with an Apostrophe to each translated
      from the Latin and French. The preface states: 'The work here presented
      to the Reader is a Copy, with a small variation as to the Cuts, and a
      Translation as to the Letter Press, of one well known to the curious by
      the Title of *Imagines Mortis.*'[1]

1802 *Leonardo da Vinci. A Treatise on Painting . . . translated by J. F. Rigaud.*
      To which is prefixed a new Life of the Author, drawn up from materials
      till now inaccessible, by J. S. Hawkins.

1807 *A correct statement and Vindication of the Conduct of John Sidney*
      Hawkins, Esq., F.A.S., towards Mr. John Thomas Smith, against the
      misrepresentation contained in the Advertisement prefixed to Mr. Smith's
      Antiquities of Westminster, and in such of the Notes, Alterations, Inser-
      tions, Additions, and other parts of that Work, as have been introduced by
      Mr. Smith without Mr. Hawkins's Knowledge, since the Letter-press was
      written by Mr. Hawkins and approved by Mr. Smith, and since the Proof-
      Sheets were corrected by Mr. Hawkins. (89 pp.)

1808 *A Reply to Mr. John Thomas Smith's dedication prefixed to the first*
      Number of his Supplemental Plates to his Antiquities of Westminster,
      containing also some Remarks on the Review of the Antiquities of West-
      minster inserted in the European Magazine for the Months of August,
      September, and October. (79 pp.)

1813 *An History of the Origin and Establishment of Gothic Architecture; com-*
      prehending also an Account, from his own Writings, of Caesar Caesareanus,
      the first professed Commentator on Vitruvius, and of his Translation of that
      Author: an Investigation of the Principles and Proportions of that Style of
      Architecture called the Gothic; and an Inquiry into the Mode of Painting
      upon and Staining Glass, as practised in the ecclesiastical Structures of the
      Middle Ages (250 pp., with many large plates. This includes the
      material originally provided for Smith's book.)

---

[1] This work appeared anonymously but a copy presented by J. S. Hawkins to
Francis Douce is now in the Bodleian and in it Douce has written, 'I supplied
Hawkins with most of the material in the preface; but for the numerous errors in
it he is solely responsible. The Sternhold and Hopkins [type of] verses are entirely
his own. The cuts were done by a brother of Bewick of Newcastle, the apprentice of
old Hodgson the publisher [Clerkenwell] and who would have executed them in a
better manner if the editor had had a better taste or the master more liberality.'

Another edition (undated; *c.* 1815), with different cuts and 'apostrophes', was
published by Whittingham and Arliss, from their 'Juvenile Library' in Paternoster
Row.

1817 *An Inquiry into the Nature and History of Greek and Latin Poetry; more particularly of the Dramatic Species tending to ascertain the Laws of Comic Metre in both those Languages; to show*

> I. *That POETICAL LICENCES have no real Existence but are mere Corruptions:*
>
> II. *That the Verses of PLAUTUS, TERENCE, PINDAR, and HORACE, are in many Instances erroneously regulated; and to suggest a more rational and musical Division of the Verses.*

(This lays down 'that the Principles of Music must be considered as the Laws of Poetry. That those principles allow an exchange of any measure for all equivalent quantities, in whatever order the long and short quantities occur'. And so on ! 480 pp.).

1817 *An Inquiry into the Nature and Principles of Thorough Bass, on a new Plan; calculated to explain and reconcile its Rules and Precepts; and to elucidate and justify its Regulations; intended as an elementary Introduction to the Knowledge of Thorough Bass, by clearly developing the Principles and Rules of that hitherto obscure Branch of Musical Science; and affording a definite and rational Guide towards its Attainment.* (87 pp.)

In addition to the above there are J. S. Hawkins's reprints (1802, &c.) of his father's edition of Walton's *Compleat Angler*.

OTHER WRITINGS

1791 *An Account of the Paintings on the south side over the Monument of Sebert, King of the East Saxons, in Westminster Abbey.* (In Jacob Schnebbelie's *Antiquaries' Museum*, 1791.)

1807 Reply in *Gentleman's Magazine*, July (p. 626), to a letter in the June issue (p. 410) referring to the edition of *Ignoramus*.

1828 *Plan and Account of the Powder Plot Cellar in Westminster* (In *Gentleman's Magazine*, p. 209).
For his attack on Bagster in the *Gentleman's Magazine* (1809) see p. 218 of the present book. For his dispute with Isaac D'Israeli in the same magazine (1814) see pp. 219 et seq.

J. S. Hawkins, in 1796, projected a Life of Erasmus, as the following interesting letter to Messrs. Cadell and Davies shows (Bodleian; MS. Montagu d. 13):

'Gentlemen,
Having a strong inclination for literary composition, and being able to command a good deal of leisure, I am induced to entertain thoughts

of writing a new life of Erasmus, and should be glad to know whether you are disposed to engage in the publication of such a work.

This period of history is, undoubtedly, a most interesting one to all lovers of learning, and has not been illustrated in a manner equal to its importance. The two lives by Dr. Knight and Dr. Jortin, the only ones that have appeared in our language, are now both become very scarce; and are, besides, such heavy uninteresting performances, and so ill written as to be obsolete and not worth reprinting.[1] Ample materials for a new one are in existence and accessible, and I know that, for these and other reasons, Dr. Johnson strongly recommended the subject to one of his friends, as a work that was much wanted, but, from indolence and want of application, he declined it.

With respect to myself, I must inform you, that I am of a literary family, my father Sir John Hawkins being well known as an author, and that this is not the first work in which I have been engaged; for that, not to mention others, I some years since published an edition of the Latin comedy of Ignoramus, with notes, a Life of the Author and a glossary, and consequently know pretty well what materials are wanting on such an occasion, and how to make use of them. Indeed I have always had a propensity to collecting literary intelligence, and have by me at this time abundant materials for a new edition of Ben Jonson's three celebrated comedies with a complete commentary if I thought such a work would be acceptable.

In so early a stage it is impossible for me to say what would be the precise extent of this Life of Erasmus. From the materials I have already in my mind I could venture to promise, that, if comprised in one volume octavo, it would not be a small one, and possibly it might reach to two handsome volumes; but this must depend on the manner in which it is printed.

My plan would be to dispose of the copyright to you for such a consideration as shall be equitable between us; and I wish to know by a line, as soon as suits your convenience, whether you are willing to accept my offer, and on what terms. If you are, on being so informed, I will call when I come your way, as I often do, to talk to you further on the subject, and am Gentlemen,

Broad Sanctuary,   Your humble Servant
Westminster,   John Sidney Hawkins.
18 May 1796.

The manuscript here quoted has a note to the effect that Messrs. C. & D. after 'availing themselves of the opinion of a judicious and confidential friend' gracefully declined engaging in such a work.

[1] Johnson thought Jortin's book a dull one (Hill, *Johnsonian Miscellanies*, ii. 12); Coleridge said that it was seriously defective (*The Friend*, i. 226).

BOOKS BY LAETITIA MATILDA HAWKINS

1806 *Siegwart*, 3 vols. (A translation from J. M. Miller the younger. The original appeared in 1775 and had much celebrity and many editions: there is a long account of it in the *Allgemeine Deutsche Biographie*, 1885.)

The Countess and Gertrude, or Modes of Discipline (4 vols. of religious and moral instruction through which trickles a tiny rill of fiction: much of the instruction is supplied by copious footnotes. 2nd edn. 1812).

1814 *Rosanne, or a Father's Labour Lost*, 3 vols. (On similar lines to *The Countess and Gertrude*, with footnotes of one to five full pages.)

Sermonets. See under 'Writings by Henry Hawkins', below.

1821 *Heraline; or Opposite Proceedings* (4 vols., 1821; a very long novel, dedicated to H.R.H. the Duchess of Gloucester).

Annaline; or Motive Hunting, 3 vols. (Anonymous but attributed to L.M.H. by B.M. Catalogue.)

1823–4 *Anecdotes, Biographical Sketches and Memoirs*, vol. i (all published), and *Memoirs, Anecdotes, Facts, and Opinions*, 2 vols. These really form one book. An abridgement exists, as *Gossip about Dr. Johnson and others*, ed. F. H. Skrine, 1926. See also a chapter in *Side-lights on the Georgian Period* by 'George Paston' (Miss E. M. Symonds).

1823 *Devotional Exercises, extracted from Bishop Patrick's 'Christian Sacrifice' and adapted to the Present Time and to General Use.*

———————

A book descriptive of the author's travels in England exists in manuscript. In the 1930's it was in the possession of Mr. Webster, Bookseller (of Tunbridge Wells), who lent it to Dr. L. F. Powell.

There seems to have been also a quite early novel, published but now apparently untraceable.

WRITINGS BY HENRY HAWKINS

1813 *Reform of Parliament the Ruin of Parliament.* (In *The Pamphleteer.* Reprinted at the end of vol. ii of Laetitia Hawkins's *Memoirs*, 1824.)

1814 *Sermonets.* (Part author: see under 'Books by Laetitia Matilda Hawkins'.)

There are passages and poems by Henry Hawkins in his sister's *Memoirs*.

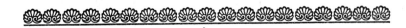

APPENDICES

APPENDIX I

Two Letters of Burney Concerning Hawkins's coming 'History'[1]

Queen's Square
28th Apr. 1773.

Without further Preface, I shall send you a rough sketch of my Plan, such as I carried with me into Germany, & wch. I had once a design to print, but the Hatton-Garden Knight prevented me by the slowness of his Motions. I heartily wished him to come out first; but finding how Voluminous he would be, & that there was little likelihood of his being out soon, I did not Chuse to let him know my Ideas & resources for the work I had undertaken. I have therefore only offered to the Public proposals in a Common form, without endeavouring to raise Expectation by magnificent promises. After the two Journeys I have taken I hope I shall have credit for persevering Diligence; & after mentioning the opportunities I have had for accumulating materials, I hope a display of them will be unnecessary.

With respect to Brother H. I must own to you that when I first heard of his having Embarked in the same Business, my Courage was somewhat abated; I doubted of my competence for entering the Lists with such a Champion, till I fortunately met with his Edition of Walton's Angler, & the Notes to this revived my ardor for Action, & I have ever since regarded him in the Light of a Rival by no means formidable. The passage you mention I have for some Time had in soak for him, in Case we shd. ever be obliged to *Compare notes, whereof* I hope there will be no occasion. I thank you heartily for what you tell me relative to his progress—Modern Music & Musicians are likely to have little Quarter from such a writer, who besides his little knowledge in practice, delights so much in old musty Conundrums that he will not give a hearing to anything better. He confessed to me that he had not been

---

[1] British Museum Add. MS. 39929, fol. 54 and 59. The letters are to Burney's friend, the Rev. Thomas Twining.

at an opera these 20 years—that he *never* was at the annual Concert
for the Benefit of decayed musicians—that he neither liked Tartini's
Compositions nor his Book. (I'm sure he understands neither)—he
made up to me two or three Times by way of acquaintance, & I
naturally gave way to it & was as open & Frank as if he had been my
Brother, till I heard several stories abt. him well authenticated which
made me shy—when I came from Italy & Called upon him, he conversed with me pen in Hand, in the *Deposition* way.—This I did not
much like—however I sent him my Book as soon as printed, & before
publication—I did the same by my Edition of the Miserere of Allegri
& the rest of the Music performed in the Pope's Chapel during Passion
Week—& wished heartily to forget that we were in each other's way.
however I have been advised by several who know him better than
myself not to be too intimate with him nor too Communicative. My
feelings are ever repugnant to reserve, Mystery & suspicion, however
they must in the present Case, I believe, take place

If Sr. John had ever had any Taste, the reading of such a pack of
old rubbish as he seems most to delight in wd. have spoilt it.

Augst. 30. 1773.

If I could know when the Knight's last sheet was in the press, I
would perhaps re-touch & publish my plan —— I like you for
disliking my medling with the *old stuff*. However, I wish you could
see what I *have* done, before it is too late to change my manner, &
with what Humility I begin & end every thing I hazard on the subject. . . .

Your *scale* of admiration at Blainville's Histy. though I cannot
compose my Muscles in it, has *worked* 'em *soundly*. He seems just the
reverse of the Knight—the one tells you *Nothing*, & the other *every
thing*. . . .

Having now dispatched Corelli & Geminiani, I must bestow a few
words on the Knight, who, par parenthèse, has borrowed of Worgan
the Book of Books, *El porqué della Musica*; but declared to me
that he found nothing extraordinary in it; he shd. have added, *except
the difficulty of reading it.*—What a pity it is that his Majesty, wth.
his Title cd. not bestow on him the Gift of Tongues! . . .

I like your Acct. of the Knight's Erudition much—& his own
Specimens of English, as well as the importance of his Conjectures &
discoveries, in the notes upon Walton do not repress my scribling ardor
perhaps as much as they ought.

The First Time I saw him, I was such a Fool, in the course of our Conversation, as to *bolt out* that *Fontanini* wth, Apostolo Zeno's notes, was a useful Book for Lovers of Italian Literature.—& likewise that the Italians & French had quarrelled abt. music so long since as in the Time of Charlemagne.—The next Time I saw him he told me, as *News*, that Apostolo Zeno's notes on Fontanini (neither of whose Names he seemed to have heard of when I first saw him) had supplied him with much knowledge of Ital. Musical authors & that he had found an acct. of the Quarrel between the Roman and Gallic Singers I suppose in Rousseau. You will find that he'll make a huge pother abt. a MS. which the late Mr. West lent him, at the request of Mr. Daines Barrington, after he had put it in my Hands, just before I set out for Italy. He told me at my return that this MS. not a word of wch. he could read, had been, 'of singular service to him respecting English Music'—I cd. not give much Time to the Book while it was in my Hands; but I took a list of its Contents—among other things there was a Tract which he took for the Micrologus of Guido, & which was only by somebody else upon his principles. Another by John de Muris (?), because somebody helped him to make out his name in it.—The MS was written, I mean transcribed, but a little while before the Invention of printing, in the 15th Centy.—I have seen in Italy much older Copies of Guido's Micrologus in Padre Martini's Collection & in the Lorenzinian Library at Florence than Sr. Jno. can have met wth., and of John de Muris besides the Copy in the King's Library at Paris, I saw a very good one the other Day in the Bodleian at Oxford. All these matters must perhaps be mentioned; but to dwell upon them in my Histy., as an antiquarian wd. be but adding one volume more to the long list of *unread* Books, already written on the subject of Music. The Knight's reasoning abt. Musical Expression is curious. For my part I think good music well executed wants *no words* to explain its meaning to me—it says everything that the Musician pleases.—and Addison & others who make such a Fuss abt. not understanding Words, when People sing, say, perhaps, only that they Love Poetry better than Music. Handel's Air, 'Return O God of Hosts,' is a fine supplication, & whether it was first made to a mistress or to the Divinity proves nothing against Music being capable of expressing the passions.

Three Letters from Sir John Hawkins to Bishop Percy[1]

Great Sanctuary, Westminster,
8th December, 1786.

MY LORD,

Your letter, though dated 14th November, came not to hand till the 27th, and, as I learned, too late for me to send the books by the ship therein mentioned; but of this hereafter.

I am extremely glad to find that you and your family are settled so much to your liking, and that you are far removed from those mischiefs of which we receive almost daily accounts in the public papers. I am more particularly pleased to be informed that you are in a country that gives you encouragement in the discharge of your pastoral office, and that you have been able to erect such monuments of your zeal as churches are.

In such a situation, you are capable of enjoying pleasures that, in this country, every thinking man is a stranger to—religion, operating on the minds of men, and manifesting its influence in their general behaviour and intercourse with each other, in an orderly submission to law and government, in the exercises of industry, and an abstinence from criminal gratifications.

The reverse of this is the case in England. The spirit of luxury rages here with greater violence than ever. The bands of society are dissolved; laws are infringed as soon as enacted; the coin of the realm is counterfeited and adulterated to a degree never known; places of public diversion are daily increasing; the great articles of trade in the metropolis are superfluities, mock-plate, toys, perfumery, millinery, prints, and music; so that were you to be here, and pass from Charing Cross to the Exchange, you would be astonished at the different appearance London makes from what it did ten years ago.

Besides this, the sense of religion seems to be nearly extinct among us; few, except the Methodists, pretend to it; and the middle rank of the people, formerly esteemed the most virtuous, have contracted the habits of the upper. Tradesmen keep mistresses, and avow it; and the

---

[1] These letters have been reproduced here as illustrating Hawkins's clear epistolary style (so superior to his general literary style as found in his books) and also the gloomy views that oppressed him towards the end of his life. They are to be found in Nichols's *Illustrations of the Literary History of the Eighteenth Century*, viii. 249 et seq. Percy had become Bishop of Dromore, Ireland, in 1782.

new buildings in the suburbs are harbours for women, who are visited by people from the city: to all which I add, that rapine and plunder have made almost every kind of property insecure, and that those who live by it acquire wealth, and become proprietors in the funds. The judges are tired of pronouncing sentence on capital offenders; executions yearly increase in numbers; and, at this time, upwards of a thousand felons are consigned to banishment.

I mention these particulars, that you may be able to estimate the felicity you enjoy in a situation that conceals from your view the degeneracy of our manners, and gives no occasion for those painful reflections and sad presages that here disturb the minds of all who are concerned for the good of posterity.

You express a wish for literary communications: I have little to send you. I have finished Dr. Johnson's Life. It is printed, and makes upwards of six hundred octavo pages; that and his Works make eleven volumes; they will be out early in the spring.

By the newspaper I shall send you in a parcel of books, you will see that a new edition of Shakespeare is proposed to be published. I think the undertaking an extravagant one, and doubt of its success.

I am now retired from my public station, and am occupied in such studies as become a man who has passed his grand climacteric nearly five years; your commission respecting Bishop Taylor's Works I have therefore executed with great pleasure and very little trouble, and shall commit to Mr. Dodsley's care such books of his as I think most valuable; these are, his 'Sermons', his 'Polemical Discourses,' and his 'Ductor Dubitantium,' in the latter whereof, page 89, you will find the story on which Mr. Walpole's tragedy, 'The Mysterious Mother', is founded. His notion of it is, that it was a case of conscience propounded to Archbishop Tillotson, but you will see he is mistaken. Neither is the relation in the 'Ductor Dubitantium' to be credited; for I find the same in Luther's 'Colloquia Mensalia,' who says, that he knew the parties, and that they dwelt at Erfurth.

Among the 'Polemical Discourses' you will find a Preface to an Apology for Set Forms of Liturgy; a most admirable discourse indeed; it is also prefixed to a Collection of Divine Offices composed by the Bishop to supply the want of the Liturgy during the Usurpation. In a visit which the Bishop of Worcester made me, I read to him some passages from it, and he begged the book of me and gave it to the King.

The above are the chief of Bishop Taylor's Works. His 'Holy Living and Dying' I must suppose you have.

I have presumed to exceed my commission, and to the above books have added three folio volumes containing the Works of Dr. Thomas Jackson, a divine of the last age, now forgotten, but of the first eminence in his time. They are a treasure of curious and valuable learning and sound theology, and for strength of argument, and the style of writing, which is nervous and eloquent in a high degree, are, in my judgment, admirable. Mr. Merrick, the translator of Tryphiodorus, and who has finely paraphrased the Psalms, was so zealous in recommending this book in Oxford, that he raised the price to nearly three times what you will see I paid for it.

Francis Barber is an exceedingly worthless fellow. He is gone to reside at Lichfield, and I have settled my account with him. He has your bond, indorsed whereon is a receipt for the interest, which I made him sign, referring to the receipt that you inquire about, and have put it into the 'Ductor Dubitantium.'

I must retract what I have above said concerning the proposed edition of Shakespeare, having just heard that two hundred subscriptions have been received, and as many more are expected in the space of a week.

It was mentioned to me at Northumberland House, some time ago, that there was a chance of your visiting England. I should be glad to hear that expectation confirmed; till then, believe that every information I can receive from you touching the welfare and happiness of yourself and your family will afford me singular pleasure.

My wife and daughter present their best respects to Mrs. Percy and the young ladies. My sons do the same to you and them. My eldest, though in great business, has been employed nearly ten years on an edition of the old comedy of 'Ignoramus', with copious and very learned notes, a life of an hundred pages of the author, and a glossary. It will be out early in the spring. I have the honour to be, with the truest esteem,

> Your Lordship's obedient humble servant,
> JOHN HAWKINS.

> Great Sanctuary, Westminster,
> 10th May, 1787.

My Lord,

I have made it my business to seek after the books you want, but to complete your list would take me up many years. I have, however, found for you, at a very cheap rate, the two Liturgies of Edward VI.

one of them perfected by writing, the other wanting only a leaf, which you may easily supply. Think yourself lucky, for they both come at less than twenty shillings, and either, in good condition, would fetch from a guinea and a half to two guineas. Two Liturgical Tracts I have also picked up for a trifle. I have given a copy of your list to Dr. Lort.

I have compared Ritson's 'Remarks' with the 'Reliques,' and think so ill of them and the author, that I cannot suggest a wish that your Lordship would alter anything in the next edition. All that can be supposed he has done is, that he had made use of copies of old ballads, different from, and, probably, less authentic than yours; therefore, to follow his corrections, would, in my opinion, be a very futile labour.

I know somewhat of the man; he is a conceited and very impudent fellow, totally ignorant of good manners, regardless of decorum, as appears in the tenth page of his Preface, and of no account among men of literature. I shall therefore return the 'Reliques' to Dodsley, with this censure of him and his work.

I have given to the world Dr. Johnson's Works in eleven volumes, including one of his Life, which is also printed separately. The Life alone is out of print, I am preparing another edition for the press, with some additions. My son has just published his 'Ignoramus,' and made it a fine book.

I delivered your bond to Francis Barber in August last, the time I settled with him. His residence is at Lichfield.

Your Lordship has doubtless heard of the late attempt of the Dissenters at a repeal of the Test Act, and that it failed, but failed by such a number of votes against the repeal as has encouraged Dr. Priestley, in terms more impudent than can be conceived, to declare in print that they will never cease their endeavours till, in effect, our national church is level with the ground. May God avert their designs! But I fear much from the indolence and ignorance of those whose duty it is to protect our religious and civil establishment—our representatives, few of whom seem to understand or appear to have studied the controversy between us and the enemies of both; a subject in which our adversaries are expert.

The few books I have been able to collect for you, I have committed to the care of Mr. Dodsley. The prices I paid for them are as follows:

First Liturgy	7s.	6d.
Second	10	6
Liturgy of the Ancients considered	1	6
Liturgy on the Universal Principles, &c.	0	6

As our newspapers have for some time ceased to give accounts of those horrid transactions that have long disturbed the peace of the country, I hope the exertions mentioned in your last letter have put a stop to them, and shall be well pleased to hear that public tranquillity is restored.

If any call of business should induce your Lordship to cross the sea, it will be a great happiness to me and my whole family to see you and as many of yours as shall accompany you. Our respects and best wishes attend you all.

I have the honour to be, with great truth and esteem, your Lordship's sincere friend and humble servant,

JOHN HAWKINS.

Great Sanctuary, Westminster,
9th November, 1787.

MY LORD,

I had sent the parcel containing the Liturgies of Edward VI. &c. to Mr. Dodsley's, and upon the receipt of your letter of 6th Oct. gave him the directions for forwarding it therein contained; since which, he informs me that Mr. Taylor refuses to take charge of it, having, as he says, no correspondence with Mr. Sleater of Dublin.

In the last edition of your Reliques, vol. I. 305, I find a passage that must by no means stand in any future one: it is a reference to what you term Birde's *Bassus*. This is an indefinite designation: most music books of old were printed in separate books, that is to say, in parts and not in score; these were for performance, and not for study, and were entitled Cantus, Altus, Discantus, Tenor, Bassus, &c. to direct the distribution of them among the several voices. Your reference must therefore be to the title of the book, which you will, no doubt, find in my History of Music, vol. I. 286; it may possibly be either the first or the third article there mentioned. I must remark to you that Dr. Ward, in his Lives of the Gresham Professors, page 200, in note, has made a mistake of the like nature in the use of the word *Discantus*, which, had he known it, he would have regretted to the end of his days.[1]

In the former edition of your book, vol. III. at the end of the Essay, you did me the honour to mention my work as not then completed.

---

[1] In Percy's fourth edition he corrects the error to which Hawkins had called his attention.

If your Lordship shall in the next think proper to notice it, you will please to do it in such terms as the actual publication of it makes necessary. Voluminous as it is, it is growing scarce,[1] and has found its way into many of the best libraries in this kingdom.

The 'Ignoramus' has been published near six months, and has met with a reception that exceeds my son's most sanguine hopes.

The distance of our situations and the consequent suspension of personal intercourse does not lessen the interest myself and my family take in whatever concerns yours. My wife, my sons, and my daughter beg to join in respectful compliments to your Lordship, Mrs. Percy, and the young ladies, with

Your Lordship's very humble servant,

JOHN HAWKINS.

[1] But compare the statements on pp. 132 ff. suggesting that the book had very poor sales.

APPENDIX 3

An Account of the Academy of Antient Music

By Sir John Hawkins[1]

The Academy of Antient Music, at the Crown and Anchor Tavern, in the Strand, was instituted about the year 1710,[2] by a number of gentlemen, performers on different instruments, in conjunction with some of the most eminent masters of the time. The design of this establishment was to promote the study and practice of vocal and instrumental harmony; in which, the foundation of a library was laid, consisting of the most celebrated compositions, as well in manuscript as in print, that could be procured, either at home or abroad.

Under the direction of the late Dr. John Christopher Pepusch, whose memory will be ever revered by all lovers of music, and with the assistance of Mr. Galliard, Dr. Maurice Greene, Mr. Bernard Gates, and the gentlemen and boys of St. Paul's Cathedral, and the Chapel Royal, the academy continued in a very flourishing state, till about the year 1728, when Dr. Greene thought proper to leave it, and set up an academy at the Devil Tavern, Temple Bar, which subsisted but a few years.[3]

The secession of Dr. Greene and his dependents, was not such an injury to the Academy, as it was feared it would prove: they left it, it is true, but they left it in peace; and the members of which it was composed, in consequence of the loss they had sustained, became emulous

---

[1] This appeared in 1770. His daughter reproduced it in her *Memoirs*. She says, 'To prevent the dissolution of this primitive establishment Sir J. H. printed and liberally distributed what he entitled An Account of the Academy of Ancient Music'.

[2] As to this date, which is certainly incorrect, see p. 23 of the present book.

[3] For PEPUSCH see p. 119.

JOHN ERNEST GAILLARD (*c.* 1687–1749) was a Hanoverian oboist and composer who settled in England about 1706 and took an active part in theatrical performance and composition, also producing some successful church music. He published *Observations on the Florid Song*—a translation of Tosi's famous little work of 1723.

For Dr. MAURICE GREENE see p. 8. His secession from the Academy, with his choir boys, was due to his unsuccessful championship of his friend (and Handel's chief competitor) Bononcini, who was accused of passing off as his own a madrigal alleged to be really one of Lotti.

BERNARD GATES (1685–1773) was a Gentleman of the Chapel Royal (afterwards Master of the Choristers there) and a member of the choir of Westminster Abbey. Handel's masque *Esther* (composed 1720 for the Duke of Chandos) had a performance (with action) at his house in 1732 and was then repeated at a concert of this Academy.

to excel each other in their endeavours to promote its interests, and to disseminate the love of harmony throughout the kingdom.

With these assistances, and that which the academy derived from the performance of the amiable Henry Needler, Esq., who for many years led the orchestra, the late Earl of Abercorn, Mr. Mulso, Mr. Millan, Mr. Dobson, and many other gentlemen, who were excellent performers, it continued to flourish until the year 1734, when Mr. Gates retired, and drew off with him the children of the Chapel Royal.[1]

In the interval between the secession of Dr. Greene, and Mr. Gates, viz. in the month of February 1731–2, the academy had given a signal proof of the advantages arising from its institution. The oratorio of Esther, originally composed for the Duke of Chandos, was performed in character by the members of the academy, and the children of the Chapel Royal; and the applause with which it was received, suggested to Mr. Handel, the thought of exhibiting that species of composition at Covent Garden theatre; and to this event it may be said to be owing, that the public have not only been delighted with the hearing, but are now in possession of some of the most valuable works of that great master.

The loss which the academy sustained by the secession of some members, the death of others, and above all, by the want of boys, laid them under great difficulties, and drove them to the necessity of trying what could be done without the assistance of treble voices; but the experience of one season drove them to the alternative of an increased expence, or annihilation. In this predicament, they resolved upon an expedient that should not only make good the loss they had sustained, but convey a benefit to posterity. In short, they determined upon such an establishment, and such a subscription, as would render the academy at once a society for the entertainment of its members, and a seminary for the instruction of youth in the principles of music, and the laws of harmony. Invitations to parents, and offers of such an education to their

---

[1] HENRY NEEDLER (1685–1760), Accountant-General of the Excise, was a good amateur violinist, and the leader at the first English performance of Corelli's Concertos. He transcribed much old music (now in the British Museum). He was a friend of Handel (see Hawkins's *History*, ch. clxx).

The EARL OF ABERCORN (James Hamilton, 7th Earl, but at the date in question Viscount Paisley; *c.* 1686–1744) was an F.R.S. and author of a work on *The Attractive Power of Loadstone*. He was also a musician and a pupil of Pepusch and is thought to have been responsible for the first (unauthorized) publication of the master's *Treatise of Harmony*.

Mr. MULSO was possibly the father (d. 1763) of the famous bluestocking authoress Mrs. Chapone—or possibly some other member of her family.

Mr. MILLAN and Mr. DOBSON are untraced.

children, as would fit them as well for trades and businesses, as the profession of music, were given by advertisements in the public papers: these brought in a great number of children, and such of them as were likely to be made capable of performing the soprano parts in vocal compositions, were retained. Dr. Pepusch generously undertook the care of their instruction for a stipend, the largest the academy could afford, though greatly disproportionate to his merit, and succeeded so well in his endeavours to improve them, that some of the most eminent professors of the science owe their skill and reputation to his masterly method of tuition.

A subscription of two guineas, and a resolution to admit auditors as members, enabled the managers to carry this their benevolent design into execution; they enriched their collection with such a variety of compositions, as rendered it, even then, perhaps, the most valuable repository of musical treasure in Europe. Abbate Steffani transmitted to them from Hanover, the most valuable of his works from time to time, as they were composed. Mr. Handel and Signor Geminiani lent the academy their countenance, the latter frequently honouring it with his own exquisite performance, and it continued to flourish till the year 1752, when it sustained a loss which will long be deplored, in the death of Pepusch, and which was far from being repaired by his generous benefaction to it, of the most valuable part of his library.[1]

Soon after this melancholy event, some of the members of the academy, reflecting on the great encouragement given to concerts, thought it might tend to the interests of the society, to give it a new form, and by engaging some of the most excellent performers on particular instruments, derive assistance to it as a concert, from persons who might be apt to disregard it as an academy. But here they were involved in a new difficulty: the great increase of late years in the number of places of public diversion, and the consequent increase in the demands of eminent performers, made it impossible, even with a subscription

[1] Although the Academy existed primarily for the revival of fine compositions of the past it also performed some contemporary work, confining itself to such as was felt to maintain the old standard of excellence and to be free from offensive modern innovations.

As for STEFFANI Hawkins in his *History* (ch. cxli) says—'About the year 1724 the Academy was become so famous as to attract the notice of foreigners and Steffani, as a testimony of his regard for so estimable an institution, having presented the society with many of his own valuable compositions, the Academy, in return for so great a favour, unanimously elected him their President, and received from him a very polite acknowledgement of the honour done him.'

of two guineas and a half, to continue a competition against greater resources than private contribution, and they now find, that these latter are not adequate to the expence of the plan which they last adopted.

The members of the academy therefore find themselves reduced to the necessity of recurring to the principles of its first institution; and they desire, if possible, to perpetuate the existence of a society, calculated for the improvement of one of the noblest sciences, and the communication of rational and social delight; to which end they wish for the assistance of those, who profess to love and admire music, such as are susceptible of its powers, such in short as are capable of distinguishing between the feeble efforts of simple melody, and the irresistible charms of elegant modulation and well-studied harmony.

The friends of this institution are sensible of the prejudices which its very name, 'The Academy of Antient Music,' may excite; and that those persons, who think no music can be good which is not new, will hardly be induced to join in the support of an establishment, professedly intended for the study and practice of that which is old.

To obviate prejudices of this kind, little more is necessary than barely to state them: those now under consideration are reducible to the following two positions:

Nothing in music is estimable, that is not new. No music tolerable which has been heard before.

In answer to which, it may be said, that this kind of reasoning is never applied to other intellectual gratifications; for no man was ever yet so weak as to object to the works of Virgil or Raffaëlle, that the one wrote seventeen hundred, or that the other painted two hundred and fifty years ago.

But, perhaps, nothing more is meant by the objection, than that the efficacy of music is abated by repetition.

Not to enquire what kind of music that must be, the merit whereof evaporates in the performance, let it be asked, does any man forbear the perusal of an Epic Poem, merely because he has read it before? or does any admirer of painting or sculpture, withdraw his eye from a fine picture or statue because it has once surveyed them? Nay, rather, does he not employ all his attention to explore their several beauties, and, in the exercise of a learned curiosity, find continual delight?

Again, let it be asked, are these objections to the best music of the best times, founded in truth and experience? or are they the result of a vicious taste, and a depraved judgment? Much of the music now in the possession of the academy, is as new to us as it was to our fathers; and will any one in his sober senses assert, that they had not ears and rational souls as well as ourselves? or that those sweet interchanges of melody, those artful combinations of concordant sounds, which inspired such men as Shakespeare and Milton with the praises of this divine science, can at any time be heard with indifference by a nice and unprejudiced ear? If this be the case, music, the principles whereof seem interwoven in the very constitution of the universe, is mere delusion, and the pleasure arising from it, resolvable into caprice, fashion, into any thing but reason and philosophy.

Farther, let it be enquired, how far the love of novelty has contributed to the variety of music, and it will be found to have excluded some of the most valuable kinds of composition, and thereby produced uniformity instead of variety.

Every judge of music is aware of the effects of compositions in the minor third of the several keys,[1] and that by the hearing of such, the sweetest sensations are excited; and the artful contexture of fugue and canon are the admiration of all who are skilled in the science: these two kinds of music are in danger of being lost; for the compositions of this day are almost solely in the major third, and their structure little better than divided counterpoint, and what is still worse, on a monotonic bass; nor are the compositions, which some affect to admire, less liable to the objection of uniformity in respect to their several divisions or strains. For reasons, which no one is willing to avow, *adagio* music is exploded, and we are content to forego the majesty and dignity of the *largo* and *andante* movements, with all the variety arising from the interchange of different airs and measures, for the noise and rattle of an unisonous *allegro*, to which no name can be given, or the intoxicating softness of that too-often iterated air, the minuet.[2]

He that reflects on such instances of modern levity as these, and that the effect of new productions is such, as that no one pretends, or even wishes, to remember the music that pleased him a month ago, may very reasonably demand who are the competitors with the composers of the

[1] That is, simply, in minor keys.
[2] The expression 'monotonic bass' does not seem to have any precise meaning. It is difficult to see why Hawkins, writing in 1770, should allege that all the slower types of composition were abandoned; as for the 'unisonous *allegro*' he probably means by that pieces such as had the treble alone in rapid notes, the bass merely accompanying in slower ones. Anyhow, if he could only have known it, in that very year was born a great composer who was to endow the world abundantly with *adagios, largos,* and *andantes* of 'majesty' and 'dignity'.

last century, and the former half of the present; or of which of them can it be said, that his crudities are less evanescent than the form of a cloud, or that his most laboured studies have survived the fate of an almanac.

But lest it should be imagined, that an unwarrantable fondness for antiquity is the motive with the academy for the cultivation of antient music, they desire it may be understood, that they apply the epithet *antient* to the compositions of the sixteenth century,[1] and that they carry their researches no farther back than the time when Palestrina and his contemporaries, those glorious luminaries of the musical world, attracted the admiration of the ablest judges, and that they have ever paid a sedulous attention to such productions as their intrinsic merit has, at any period, rendered worthy of regard.

After so much care and pains to enrich it, it will hardly be objected to the Academy's collection of music, that it is deficient in variety; and when it is known that the countries of Italy, Germany, France, Spain, the Netherlands, and England, have severally contributed, and that very largely, to the forming it, very little dread will remain of that satiety or indifference which attends the hearing of music calculated for the present hour, and not intended for posterity. For, not to mention the great number of compositions which the academy are possessed of, even so great as that the youngest person now living might hope in vain to hear them all, nor that variety of style observable in them, which is the characteristic of different masters, every species of vocal

[1] Here Hawkins inserts as footnote the following not very well-informed slice of musical history. (To Gaforius, Gafori, or Gafurius, whom he mentions, his *History of Music* devotes some pages):

'In order to understand the reason of this restriction, it is necessary to advert to the history of music, which, so far as is material to the present purpose, is this. About the year 1500, Gafurius, or as he is otherwise called, Franchinus, a native of Lodi in Italy, having with great pains and expence procured copies and translations of Aristides Quintilianus, Bacchius Senioris, Manuel Bryennius, Ptolemy, and others of the Greek musicians, and having thoroughly studied Boetius and Guido Aretinus, read lectures on music in the public schools of Mantua, Verona, Milan, and other provinces and cities in Italy. The Provençal *violars* and *musars* were almost the only composers and musicians of the preceding ages; but the knowledge of the science which Gafurius diffused throughout Italy, gave rise to a new species of composition, of which, under the patronage of the Roman pontiffs, Palestrina is supposed to have been the improver, if not the inventor, the nature whereof is best to be judged by his motet, "*Exaltabo te Domine*", and his no less excellent madrigal, "*Veramente in amore*". He was organist and chapel-master of St. Peter's at Rome, and flourished about the year 1580. The improvements in music since his time, consist in the associating instruments with voices, and the invention of new combinations, which, without transgressing the laws of harmony, are supposed to be capable of an almost infinite variety.'

and instrumental music is in its turn exhibited by the academy for the entertainment of its members: the general arrangement of these is into compositions for the church, the theatre, and the chamber; the first head includes masses, motets, anthems, hymns, and psalms; the second, oratorios, masques, serenatas, overtures, and concertos; the third, madrigals, trios, duettos, and cantatas; to the true and just performance whereof, the academy have hitherto been, and with the assistance which they now solicit, trust they shall yet be, equal.

The hopes of success in these endeavours, arise from that propensity which they observe in people of this country, to the cultivation of the politer arts, and the general encouragement it affords to laudable pursuits. They behold, with pleasure, persons of the first rank in this kingdom associated for the improvement of a particular species of vocal harmony, and with exemplary munificence, dispensing rewards proportioned to the merits of such as are emulous to excel in it.[1] Farther, they repose great confidence in the good sense of this nation, of which they have a convincing proof, in the respect which, for a succession of ages, has been paid to the works of our great dramatic poet of Elizabeth's days, whose best compositions, by the way, are as liable to reproach on the score of their antiquity, as any of those which the academy have long laboured to recommend. In short, they flatter themselves that the studies of such men as Palestrina, Tallis, Bird, Carissimi, Colonna, Stradella, Purcell, Bassani, Gasparini, Latti [Lotti], Steffani, Marcello, Buononcini, Pergolesi, Handel, Perez, and many others, abounding in evidences of the deepest skill and finest invention, when duly attended to, will be thought worthy the admiration of every musical ear, and afford a manly and rational delight to all the votaries of this noble science.

A society founded on principles like these, can hardly fail of proving an inexhaustible fund of benefit and entertainment. Here the student in the musical faculty will find the means of forming his style after the most perfect models. Here the timid and modest performer may acquire that degree of firmness and confidence which is necessary for displaying his excellencies in public. Here the ingenuous youth, who prefers the innocent pleasures of music, to riot and intemperance, may taste of that mirth which draws no repentance after it; and hither may

---

[1] This allusion is probably to the Noblemen and Gentlemen's Catch Club (founded 1761). It offered prizes annually for the best catches, canons, and glees— as it is still doing, or was until recently (see Viscount Gladstone's *The Story of the Noblemen and Gentlemen's Catch Club*; privately printed 1931).

those repair, to whom the studies or labours of a day must necessarily endear the elegant delights of a musical evening.

Padre Paolo Sarpi resigned his breath with a prayer for the republic of Venice, which, it is to be hoped, every friend of the muses, applying it to the academy of antient music, will adopt; and in the words of that excellent man, cry out

ESTO PERPETUA![1]

---

[1] This was the motto of the Literary Club.

APPENDIX 4

Errors Concerning Hawkins

A NUMBER of errors concerning Hawkins are current in works of reference. For the benefit of compilers of such books the chief of these are here mentioned:

1. Many foreign books say that he became (in French) 'un avocat', or (in German) 'ein Advokat'. Such terms generally designate the higher branch of the legal profession, to which Hawkins did not belong. He was not even a 'solicitor' but merely an 'attorney' (see p. 4 for the distinction at that time made in the use of these terms).

2. It is frequently stated that he was a 'founder' of the Madrigal Society. This is not so.

3. Two publications have been ascribed to him with which he had nothing to do—*The Principles and Power of Harmony*, 1771 (really by B. Stillingfleet; see p. 232), and *A new Set of Psalm and Hymn Tunes* (*c.* 1810), which was the work of another John Hawkins, being much too late in date to have been by the subject of the present book (see Eitner, *Quellenlexikon*).

4. Books previous to the present one, if they mention the occasion of the knighthood, fall in error about this (see pp. 107 ff.).

5. Many books, in English, French, Italian, etc., give the place of his death as 'Spa', in Belgium. The fact is that he was taken ill at *Islington* Spa, London, and died in his house in Westminster (see p. 211).

6. The date of his birth has sometimes been given as 1720 (instead of 1719) and the date of death, variously, as 1790, 1791, and 1798 (instead of 1789).

APPENDIX 5

The Popular Hawkins–Burney Catch

HAVE YOU SIR JOHN HAWKINS' HIST'RY?

N.B.—Leave out the Bars between + + till the 3rd voice comes in, then go on.

J. W. CALLCOTT (1766–1821).

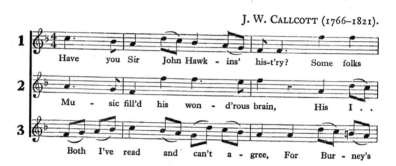

1. Have you Sir John Hawk - ins' his-t'ry? Some folks
2. Mu - sic fill'd his won - d'rous brain, His I . .
3. Both I've read and can't a - gree, For Bur - ney's

think it quite a . . mys - t'ry, Sir John Hawk - ins',
like best, 'tis so plain, his I like best, his I
his - t'ry pleas - es . . me, Bur - ney's

Sir John Hawk-ins', Sir John
like best, his I like best, his I like best, his I
his - t'ry, Bur - ney's his - t'ry, Bur - ney's his - t'ry, Bur - ney's

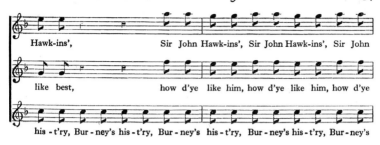

The above setting forth of this once popular catch is that which still appears in Messrs. Novello's catalogue. If it be studied it will be seen that the effect in performance is:

'Sir John Hawkins
Burn 'is History!
How d'ye like him?
Burn 'is History!'

PROFESSOR J. L. CLIFFORD of Columbia University has kindly drawn my attention to a manuscript in the Bodleian, MS. Eng. poet. c. 9, which adds considerably to our knowledge of Sir John Hawkins's early literary friendships and activities; it, in particular, reveals him as the author of several pieces in prose and verse contributed during the period 1740–4 to various periodicals and newspapers and gives further details of his collaboration with the blind organist John Stanley in the publication of the first set of *Six Cantatas for a Voice and Instruments.*

The manuscript is entitled 'Miscellanies' and consists of some 270 poems, essays, letters, &c., copied from printed or manuscript sources. The period of compilation appears to have been 1740–57. The compiler is stated to be Thos. Phillibrown and all the pieces, save some dozen, are in his hand. Mr. Phillibrown was the compiler of another manuscript in the Bodleian, MS. Eng. hist. c. 50, which is entirely holograph. The precise nature of this later manuscript is described by its title, 'A Chronological and Historical Account of Material Transactions and Occurences in my Time; and all of Them Particularly in My Memory, Excepting those Markt Thus *. Begining with Mar^h ye 26. 1720. . . . But not begun to be wrote by me, Tho. Phillibrown, untill May the 9th 1748.'[1] The last entry in the manuscript, which is called 'Vol. 1', is dated 5 December 1758. Mr. Phillibrown acknowledges his indebtedness to Salmon's *Chronological Historian* (3rd edition, 1747) for 'many of the remarks', presumably those marked with an asterisk, which are fairly numerous, especially in the first half of the volume.

Mr. Phillibrown was the son, probably the elder son, of Thomas Phillibrown and his wife Anne, who were married in February 1711. His father was a wine-cooper, whose place of business, in which he resided, was in Devonshire Street, a small street leading from Bishopsgate

---

[1] Referred to in this Appendix as *Account.*

Street to Devonshire Square, the same street, it is interesting to note, in which John Scott, the attorney to whom the young Hawkins was articled, lived.[1] I do not know when he was born; perhaps it was on 26 March 1720, the *terminus a quo* of his *Chronological Account*. He was taken by his grandfather in 1724 to see the lying-in-state of Thomas Guy, the founder of Guy's hospital, obviously when he was very young.[2] He attended at least four schools: a boarding-school kept by a Mrs. Waters, two unnamed schools at St. Albans (where he was in 1728, 1729, and 1730) and Uxbridge, and Samuel Watkins's academy in Spittal Square, which was a nursery of contributors to the *Gentleman's Magazine*.[3] He never mentions his occupation or business, but

[1] Thomas Phillibrown or Phillibrowne, Sen., was, according to his son's MS. *Account* (fol. 338), born on 26 June 1682. He was a parishioner of St. Botolph's, Bishopsgate, and married firstly Anne King, daughter of Thomas King, of the parish of St. Dionis Backchurch, on 21 Feb. 1711. She died on 1 Feb. 1727 in her 43rd year and he, over eighteen years later, married Elizabeth Shepherd, a widow, on 11 Oct. 1745. See *Register of St. Dionis Backchurch*, 1878, pp. 55, 295 and *Parish Register of St. Antholin*, 1883, p. 153. Daniel Neal, the historian of the Puritans and Pastor of an Independent congregation, whose meeting house was in Jewin Street, Aldersgate Street, preached a sermon at the first Mrs. Phillibrown's funeral, in which he records that she had been a member of the congregation for above nineteen years and that she had 'filled up the marriage relation for the space of sixteen years.' See *A Sermon occasion'd by the Death of Mrs. Anne Phillibrowne* (1727). Phillibrown's name, address, and occupation are given in Kent's London Directory, 26th edition, 1759, p. 88: 'Phillibrown, Thomas, wine-cooper, Devonshire Street, Bishopsgate Street.' His son speaks of 'our Door in Devonshire Street' under date 9 Aug. 1735 and 'our compting house on the ground floor' in 1750. He was apparently still living in 1758 when his son's MS. *Account* ends. Mr. Raymond Smith, Librarian of Guildhall, to whom I am greatly indebted, tells me that 'the records of the Coopers' Company are full of Phillibrownes'.
[2] His record under date 27 Dec. 1724 is the first entry in his MS. *Account* that is not marked with an asterisk: 'Tho. Guy, esq. formerly a bookseller of London, afterwards Member of Parliament for Tamworth, died in ye 80th year of his age.... He was buried from Mercers Chapel in Cheapside and I went with my Grandfather King to see him lay in state, but I being terrified by the great concourse of People could not be prevailed on to go in to see him' (fol. 31).
[3] Under date 15 June 1727 he records: 'This day I being to return in the afternoon to my Boarding School at Mrs. Waters's had not an opportunity to see the Proclamation [of the Accession of George II]: *Account*, fol. 39. Under date 5 July 1748 he describes Nathan and William James as his particular intimates when at school 'both at Uxbridge and St. Albans', ibid. fol. 179; and on 30 Nov. 1751 he reports: 'Mr. Canton is Master of the Academy in Spittal Square which was Mr. Sam'l Watkins's and at which I was a Scholar when Mr. Watkins was Master.' Ibid. fol. 263. John Canton, F.R.S., had been Watkins's 'apprentice'. Notable pupils of this academy were Foster Webb, Hawkins's intimate friend, John Smith who, like Webb, died prematurely, William Rider, chaplain and surmaster at St. Paul's School, and Adam Calamy, son of Dr. Edmund Calamy (1671–1732) and Hawkins's fellow clerk and friendly opponent in 1739 (*ante*, p. 5). Hawkins's *Life of Johnson*, 1787, p. 48.

he presumably assisted his father, with whom he certainly lived.[1] Mr. Phillibrown's interests were chiefly in the city: he regularly records the election and death of the Lord Mayor, Aldermen, and other civic officials, and he was a frequent attender of public ceremonies and executions, which latter he describes in great detail; he never seems to have gone to the theatre or to concerts and his attendance at a place of worship was rare.[2] His grammar is very far from impeccable, and his spelling frequently distressing; his handwriting, while not scholarly, is fairly good and uniform throughout both manuscripts.

The pieces assigned by Phillibrown to Hawkins in his *Miscellanies*, apart from his contributions to Stanley's *Six Cantatas*, which are otherwise known, are ten in number, four in verse and six in prose. The first of the poems is the second piece in the manuscript, in which it occurs on fol. 2; it is described as 'A Song by Mr. John Hawkins set to Musick by Mr. Boyce, organist to the King's Chappell at St. James's, 1741.'[3] The song is in three stanzas:

> In vain Philander at my Feet
>   You urge your guilty Flame;
> With well dissembled Tears intreat,
> New oaths and impious vows repeat,
>   And wrong Love's sacred Name

[1] He was a member of a City Company, no doubt the Coopers' Company. 'Dined at my Hall and went in the Eve[ning] to my Lord Mayor's Ball at Guildhall' is his record on 9 Nov. 1758 in his MS. *Account* (fol. 370). In this he mentions a brother John, a sister Phillibrown, various cousins, including one of his '2d. mother', and a number of friends, especially one Thurgood, with whom he walked and went fishing: he knew intimately Capt. Coram of the Foundling Hospital and Capt. Richard Girlington of the Navy. He never mentions Hawkins or his writings in this manuscript.

[2] On Good Friday, 11 Feb. 1757, he records in his MS. *Account* (fol. 341): 'This Day was observ'd as a General Fast. The Bishop of Bangor Preach'd before ye Lords at ye Abbey-Church, and Dr. Taylor before ye House of Commons at St. Margaret's-Church at Westminster. I was at both ye Churches; the House of Lords consisted of only their Speaker, . . 7 Temporal Lords, and 10 Bishops; the House of Commons consisted of their Speaker and 200 Members.' The preacher at St. Margaret's was not, as the Rev. Canon Smyth, Rector of St. Margaret's, points out to me, Johnson's friend, but Dr. John Taylor, 1704–66, Rector of Lawford, Essex, and Canon of St. Paul's: the sermon was published. According to the *Gentleman's Magazine* the London and Westminster churches were on this day 'everywhere crowded and in many parishes large sums were collected for the poor'.

[3] The song was printed in a single, undated, sheet, with the title 'Song set by Mr. Boyce' (Mus. 9 c. 6 in the Bodleian). The words of the song are not in this print ascribed to Hawkins. Boyce was appointed organist of the Chapel Royal in 1758. He assisted Hawkins with his *History of Music*. Scholes, *The Great Dr. Burney*, 1948, i. 296.

Ah ! cease to call that Passion Love
   Whose end is to betray;
Too soon should I comply you'd prove
What sensual views your Ardour move
   And your Affection sway

And when to all my fondness blind,
   You'd chase me from your Breast;
Deluded wretch! when could I find
That calm content, that peace of mind,
   Which I before possest.

Copies of two letters from Boyce follow. The first clearly refers to this song. It is headed by Phillibrown 'A Letter from Mr. Boyce to Mr. Hawkins', and is dated 'Friday Even. Nov. 6th'.

Sir. I am much oblig'd to You for the Song you was so kind to favour me with on Tuesday last. I have already set it, and have endeavour'd to render the Musick agreable to the Words, which I confess in my opinion are as pretty as any thing of the kind I've yet met with. If the Musick shou'd have the good luck to please you, as the words have done me, I shall be highly satisfied. If not, I desire you'll attribute the cause to my Incapacity, and not want of Inclination. I'm now in close waiting at St. James's, which will deprive me of an opportunity of seeing You, till the latter part of next week, when I shall take care to have a Copy of the Musick transcrib'd for You, and in the mean time, shall be much oblig'd for an Information from You what Day, Time, and place will be ye most agreable to You, after Thursday next, for a meeting to compare Notes: which I desire you'd inform me of, by a Line directed for William Boyce (my Father's Name being John) at Joyners' Hall in Thames Street, near Dowgate. I am S^r (tho' without knowing who I'm obligated to) your much Oblig'd humble Serv't   Wm. Boyce.

A week later Boyce wrote—the letter is dated 'Friday Even. Nov. 13th.'

S^r. I'm exceedingly sorry I can't have ye pleasure of waiting on You personally this Ev'ning, by reason of an engagement which has been fix'd on this fortnight, therefore can no ways wave it. However I've sent you the Notes to your very agreeable words, and shall be always ready and willing to adapt Musick to any thing you'll please to favour me with,[1] and am,
        S^r your most obed^t
         humble Servt
          Wm. BOYCE.

---

[1] At a much later date (c. 1777), Boyce set Hawkins's Lines on the Death of the Rev. William Gostling: see *ante*, pp. 117, 233.

About the same time Hawkins, in friendly competition with Foster Webb, tried his hand at imitating Donne, as the following letter shows. It is briefly introduced by Phillibrown (*Miscellanies*, fol. 12), 'Mr. Hawkins sent the 2 foregoing Sonnets, No. 1 and 2, to Mr. Moses Browne (a very ingenious Author of several Poems, and who won most of ye prices in ye Gent. Mag. and some time stiles him self under ye Name of Astrophil)[1] desireing his Judgement upon them, and receiv'd the following Ans^r'—the letter is dated 'Nov. 23^d 1741'.

S^r. I have considerately read over the enclosed Peices and compared them with Dr. Donne's Cannonization from whence they appear to be imitated. In my Opinion they have both their Merit and are each of them Improvements of the D^rs. The Peice I have taken the Liberty to mark No. 1 abounds with very musical Numbers, but if I may be allow'd my Observation discovers some Redundancies and Puerilities which the Author of No. 2 has avoided. . . . The Author of No. 2 has fallen more into the Laconic stile and betrays a more ripen'd Judgement, yet I must condemn his two last lines of the 3rd Stanza as wholy darkning the Sentiment, and there is too great a sameness of Thought in the two first Lines of the 4th. The 3rd Line of the first also is rough and rather prosaic, the rest is very masterly. To be plain there are great Marks of Genius in both and I could single out distinguishing Beauties. I am at a loss where to give my Approbation, but upon the whole I believe No 2 to be the most finished peice, which I hope as I know neither of the Gentlemen will not give Offence when I give it, if the mistaken, yet as the unprejudiced Judgment of S^r y^r very humble Servt.

Moses Browne.

The judge's preference of his poem to that of Foster Webb (No. 1) and the high praise he gave it, no doubt pleased Hawkins, but he does not appear to have succeeded in getting it published. Phillibrown gives no printed source for it, or the rival piece, and I have not found either in the *Gentleman's Magazine*, which would be the most likely place. The 'Sonnet, imitated from Dr. Donne by Mr. J. Hawkins, 1741' is, like 'The Canonization', in four stanzas. The first and fourth are:

I

I Prithee cease to chide my harmless Love,
    Nor tire my Patience with thy loath'd Advice;

---

[1] Moses Browne, 1704–87, was 'so far as concerned the poetical part of it, the chief support of the Magazine' (Hawkins, *Life of Johnson*, p. 46). For his separately published poems see the *Cambridge Bibliography of English Literature*, ii. 312. He, like Hawkins, was a fisherman and he edited, 'at the instigation' of Johnson, Walton's *Compleat Angler*. See *ante*, p. 64 and Boswell, *Life of Johnson*, ed. Hill-Powell, ii, 520. He became the vicar of Olney.

[1]The Sordid Pleasures which thoud'st have me prove,
    May suit the aged Sons of Avarice
But the mean Wisdom of acquiring Gold
As ill becomes the Young as Love the Old.

4

Let him whose hireling Sword promiscuous slays,
    Or those whom Blood and Massacre delight,
Or him whose venal Eloquence betrays,
In Courts how feeble a Pretence is Right.
Rather let these thy Indignation move,
Than the calm Joys of inoffensive Love.

A poem that Hawkins did succeed in getting into print was the ode 'To Mr. John Stanley, occasion'd by looking over some compositions[2] of his lately published'. Phillibrown notes (*Miscellanies*, fol. 69) that this was 'made by Mr. Jn° Hawkins' and printed in the *Daily Advertiser* of 21 February 1741. The ode occurs on the front page of the newspaper for that date and is initialed 'J. H.' As no copy of this issue is in the British Museum or in the Bodleian it is here reprinted.[3]

To Mr. John Stanley
Occasion'd by looking over some Compositions of his lately publish'd.

No more let *Italy*, with scornful Pride,
Our want of Taste in Arts polite, deride;
No more *Corelli* lead the ravish'd Throng,
Nor famed Scarlatti charm us with his Song;
Since thou, O Stanley, has convinc'd Mankind,
Musick to foreign Realms is not confin'd.
Purcell at first their Empire did controul;
With Airs unknown to them he mov'd the Soul:
Thine was the Vict'ry to complete;
He made Them humble, Thou has made Us great.

---

[1] Phillibrown records in a footnote the variants 'as improvements since [made] ye author': 'Canst thou expect a soul like mine to move
        Or tempt my Youth to sordid Avarice
    In vain! The selfish Act of heaping Gold
        As ill, etc.'
[2] *Eight Solos for a German Flute*, published 1741.
[3] Dr. A. T. Hazen kindly confirms Phillibrown's attribution from a copy of the *Daily Advertiser* in the New York Public Library. The author of the inaccurate Life of Hawkins prefixed to the 1853 edition of his *History of Music* mentions the poem, but does not print it.

Long may'st thou live, thus kindly to impart,
In moving Sounds, the Influence of thy Art;
With melting Airs our Passions to command,
And spread thy Lustre o'er thy native Land.

19 Feb. 1740   J. H.

The last of the poetical pieces ascribed by Phillibrown to Hawkins occurs on fol. 100 of *Miscellanies*. It is entitled 'A Rebus—by Mr. John Hawkins, 1743'. No source is given and I have not found it in print. Here it is:

The word of a Thief when he comes for your purse,
And the fault of a Child never whipt by his Nurse,
Make the Name of the Man who in Musick excells:
If you're curious to know in what place he dwells
What Environs a City, what thro' a Mead glides
Is enough to direct you to where he resides.

The prose pieces newly ascribed to Hawkins in the *Miscellanies* consist of four essays, a character or appreciation of Foster Webb, and a controversial letter of some length: they are all copied out in Phillibrown's hand. The essays are: (1) 'On Politeness. To the Author of the Westminster Journal, or the New Weekly Miscellany. By Thomas Touchit, of Spring-Gardens, Esq.' Initialed 'J. H.' (*Miscellanies*, foll. 14–22). (2) 'On Business. From ye Westminster Journal, Saturday March 6 1741–2.' Initialed 'J. H.' (*Miscellanies*, foll. 24–32). The original numbers of the *Westminster Journal* are not available to me, but I find both these essays in *Letters from the Westminster Journal* (1747), pp. 19–25, 90–95, where they are dated 19 December 1741 and 6 March 1742 respectively: both are initialed at the end 'J. H.' No other essays in the volume are similarly signed. (3) 'On Love by Mr. Jnº Hawkins' (*Miscellanies*, foll. 34–40). This essay is slightly incomplete at the end. No source is given and I have not found it in print. The opening sentence is, 'There is none of all the Passions, yᵗ has so much employ'd the Thoughts of Moralists and Philosophers, and perhaps of almost every other Species of Writers, as yᵗ of Love.' (4) 'An Essay on Conversation. Pub. in Universal Spectator about Dec. 1740 by Mr. J. H.' (*Miscellanies*, foll. 253–262). This essay, like those contributed by Hawkins to the *Westminster Journal*, was thought worthy of being reprinted. It will be found in a collection of essays, from the original periodical, entitled *The Universal Spectator*, first published in four volumes in 1747. The essay, which is undated, occurs in vol. iv, pp.

152–6 and issigned 'Pharamond', as it is in Phillibrown's copy. It is the only essay with this signature. There remain (1) 'The character of Mr. Foster Webb by Mr. John Hawkins' and (2) a 'Letter by Mr. John Hawkins on the Ellection of Ld. Mayor, 1739'. The first occurs in the *Gentleman's Magazine* for March 1744, as Phillibrown says (*Miscellanies*, fol. 144) it does. It is an unrestrained panegyric of his bosom friend and collaborator who died prematurely in the twenty-second year of his age. Hawkins gave a much more sober account of him in his *Life of Johnson* (p. 47). The earlier 'character', which is unsigned, states that 'the excellence of his genius in Poetry will here appear by his inimitable translations of Horace . . . and several other Pieces with which he has obliged the world under the names of Vedastus, Lycidas, and Phylander': the later that 'his signature was sometimes Telarius, at others Vedastus'. The second piece, and probably one of the earliest of the products of Hawkins's pen, was sent to the *Daily Post*, 'but not inserted'. It took the form of an open letter (*Miscellanies*, foll. 249, 253) 'To the worthy Liverymen of the City of London' and was written before September 1739, when, according to the *Gentleman's Magazine* (vol. ix, p. 495), 'many Advertisements were inserted in the Daily Papers to animate the livery to assert their antient Right of a free choice and drop the modern absurd Practice of Rotation'. The youthful Hawkins's contention was that Members of Parliament should 'upon very important Occasions apply to their respective Corporations for Instructions for their Behaviour' and that as Sir George Champion, who as senior alderman was a candidate for the Lord Mayoralty, had not done this in the important question of the Spanish Convention, he was not fit to be entrusted with the government of the City.

Phillibrown knew of Hawkins's collaboration with the blind musician John Stanley (see *ante*, pp. 10, 158) in the first set of *Six Cantatas for a Voice and Instrument*, published in 1742 or 1743[1], and copied into

---

[1] He does not appear to have known of Hawkins's provision of the songs of the second set, with the same title, published some years later. Miss Hawkins was better informed. She writes: 'At Mr. Stanley's request he had written eleven of the Cantatas, which he had set to music; his bosom-friend Foster Webb furnished the twelfth, that beginning "the God Vertumnus loved Pomona fair". "Who'll buy a heart?" became the most popular.' *Anecdotes*, p. 130. Foster Webb's song is the sixth of the first set; Hawkins's 'Who'll buy a heart? Myrtilla cries' is the first of the second set. Mr. Gerald Finzi kindly informs me that Stanley published a third set of cantatas in 1751, the first of which, 'As in pensive Form Myrtilla sate', appeared also in the *Muses Delight* (1754) as a sequel to 'Who'll buy a heart?'. It is probable therefore, as Mr. Finzi suggests, that the songs of the third set, or some of them, may also be by Hawkins.

his *Miscellanies* (foll. 94, 96) the fourth of these by Hawkins and the sixth by Foster Webb. He also copied the Preface (fol. 92), which I think is more likely to have been written by Hawkins than by Foster Webb or Stanley. It will be seen that the opening paragraph repeats in prose the nationalism in matters musical that Hawkins had expressed in his verses to Stanley, previously quoted; it runs: 'The slender Regard that is usually paid to Works of this Nature where they have not the Sanction of a foreign Name will, we hope, be a sufficient Excuse for our introducing the following Cantatas into the world with the Ceremony of a Preface, the Design of which is not so much to bespeak its Approbation as to shew how little the performances of other Countries are entitled to the Preeminence so generally allowed them.' The Preface concludes with the statement that 'The writer's Avocations from Business are too few to permit his being an Author otherwise than by Accident, and that he desires the Reputation of a Poet as little as he merits it.' The frequency with which Foster Webb indulged 'his Genius for Poetry' indicates that he at any rate did aspire to some reputation as a poet[1].

Phillibrown copied into his *Miscellanies*, in addition to those already given, two other letters addressed to Hawkins, one by Cave, the owner-editor of the *Gentleman's Magazine*, the other by Foster Webb. That by Cave is headed 'To Mr. John Hawkins on his having sent several Dissertations to the Gent. Magazine' (fol. 249). It is dated from 'St. John's Gate, Decr. 16: 1740' and is as follows:

'S^r. I am obliged to you for ye Dissertations wch you have favoured me with, and as I prefer'd them to several wch I have yet by me in MS from other Hands, it is as good a Testimony as I can give that what you shall please to send will be acceptable. There is then little room to fear, that your Time will be thrown away wch you think proper to employ for ye Intertainment of ye Publick.

I am, Sir
Your much obliged humble serv^t
Edwd Cave.'

The 'dissertations' mentioned are almost certainly Hawkins's letters to the editor on honesty, published in the *Gentleman's Magazine* for March, May, and July of the previous year (see *ante*, pp. 5, 6). I do not find that Hawkins made any contributions to the magazine in the succeeding years. The most interesting point about Foster Webb's

---

[1] There are in Phillibrown's MS. *Miscellanies* more poems by Foster Webb than by any other author.

letter (fol. 265),[1] which is dated from 'Westgate near Dorking. April 29th 1743' and subscribed 'your affectionate Friend and Servant', is the address: this is 'To Mr. John Hawkins Jun[r]. in Sweet Apple Court, Bishopsgate Street Without'. This tells us that Hawkins had the same Christian name as his father, that his father was living in 1743, and that Hawkins was probably living with him. 'Sweet Apple Court', now occupied by railway lines, is not otherwise known in connexion with Hawkins.[2]

I do not know how Phillibrown came to have access to Hawkins's papers relating to his early writings, but I suspect that he obtained it through the friends of Foster Webb, whose writings he so freely copied and with the details of whose life he was so familiar. It is significant that he had no knowledge of any piece by Hawkins subsequent to the obituary notice of Webb.[3] However this may be, Phillibrown's attributions are I think to be trusted. Some, e.g. the essays on Politeness, Business, and Conversation, are, as I have shown, confirmed by other evidence, and others, e.g. the song set by Boyce and the imitation of Donne, are amply authenticated by the letters accompanying them.

L. F. POWELL.

[1] The letter did not pass through the post and is, I am confident, a copy. It is not in Phillibrown's hand.

[2] See Harben, *Dictionary of London*, 1918, p. 365.

[3] Phillibrown copied into his *Miscellanies* a letter from Foster Webb to a Mr. Harford (6 May 1743) and added some fairly long passages in shorthand, a subject of which I am completely ignorant, to Foster Webb's verses on his last sickness, and to Hawkins's essay on Business.

INDEX AND 'WHO'S WHO'[1]

[1] Not including Appendix 6 (see Acknowledgements, p. v.)

PRINTED IN
GREAT BRITAIN
AT THE
UNIVERSITY PRESS
OXFORD
BY
CHARLES BATEY
PRINTER
TO THE
UNIVERSITY